OVER NINE WAVES

Marie Heaney was born in County Tyrone and began her teaching career in schools in Northern Ireland. She and her family moved to Dublin in 1972 where she still lives.

She has also written *The Names Upon the Harp*, a book of Irish legends for children (Faber, illustrated by PJ Lynch) and as an editor with Townhouse Publishing in Dublin has produced several anthologies, including *Heart Mysteries*, a personal selection of Irish Poetry.

Marie Heaney has contributed to newspapers and journals and has written for radio and television.

OVER NINE WAVES
A Book of
IRISH LEGENDS

————

Marie Heaney

FARRAR, STRAUS AND GIROUX

NEW YORK

Farrar, Straus and Giroux
18 West 18th Street, New York 10011

Copyright © 1994 by Marie Heaney
All rights reserved
Printed in the United States of America
Originally published in 1994 by Faber and Faber Limited,
Great Britain
Published in the United States by Farrar, Straus and Giroux
This paperback edition, 1995

ISBN: 978-0-571-17518-5

Our books may be purchased in bulk for promotional, educational,
or business use. Please contact your local bookseller or the
Macmillan Corporate and Premium Sales Department
at 1-800-221-7945, extension 5442, or by e-mail at
MacmillanSpecialMarkets@macmillan.com.

www.fsgbooks.com
www.twitter.com/fsgbooks • www.facebook.com/fsgbooks

29 30

For
Seamus, Michael, Christopher and Catherine
with love

Contents

THE MUSIC OF WHAT HAPPENED
The Finn Cycle

THREE SAINTS ONE GRAVE DO FILL
The Patron Saints of Ireland

Foreword

Some of the stories retold in this book are among the oldest in Europe. They belong to a culture and language with a long, unbroken, and highly elaborated oral tradition, one of the most venerable in Western Europe.

There are two main reasons why these legends have survived from such an early time. The first is that the Romans did not invade Ireland. Because of this the spoken language was largely unaffected by the Latin which, in countries under Roman rule, replaced or marginalized the indigenous language. The second is that the Irish were among the first peoples outside the Roman Empire to develop the art of writing. But even before they learnt the Roman alphabet and evolved their own script, they were already in possession of a rich store of native learning which had been preserved by the strong oral tradition in Irish society. This body of knowledge had been maintained by the druidic schools and when the technique of writing came to Ireland with Christianity the scribes in the early monastic settlements wrote down not only sacred texts in Latin, but the stories they were familiar with in their Irish vernacular.

In the ensuing centuries many of these vellum compendiums were lost or destroyed through wars and Viking raids. A few survived and the oldest of the stories gathered here are to be found in manuscripts that were copied in the eleventh and twelfth centuries from previous manuscripts prepared perhaps three or four centuries earlier. These original manuscripts contained the first written versions of stories and poems that had been part of the oral tradition for centuries. It is a measure of the worth of this ancient material that it has continued to be transcribed and translated, retold and published in different versions down to our own times.

Scholars have divided early Irish literature into four main cycles: the Mythological Cycle, the Ulster Cycle, the Fenian Cycle and the

Historical Cycle (also known as the Cycle of the Kings). The chief characters in the Mythological Cycle are the Tuatha De Danaan, the semi-divine people who inhabited Ireland until they were banished by the Milesians, the ancestors of the present-day inhabitants. The struggle of the Tuatha De Danaan against the Fomorians, a semi-demonic race who lived on the islands scattered around Ireland, constitutes one of the central stories of this cycle. After their final defeat by the Milesians, the Tuatha De Dannan went underground to live in the *sidhes*, those earthworks and raths that are scattered all over Ireland. They become variously known in folklore and legend as the People of the Sidhe, the Faery, the Little Folk or the Good People. From time to time these mysterious beings would enter the mortal world, especially at Hallowe'en and on May Day, to mingle with the humans and come and go in their affairs in much the same way as they wander in and out of the other cycles of early Irish literature.

The Ulster Cycle tells of the heroic exploits of Conor Mac Nessa and the Red Branch Knights, who are supposed to have lived around the time of the birth of Christ. Cuchulainn is the best-known character in this cycle and most of the action is located in the north of Ireland in the great hill fort of Emain Macha and along the borders of the province of Ulster. The Fenian Cycle revolves around Finn Mac Cumhaill and his band of followers, the Fianna, who roamed all over Ireland about three hundred years after Conor and Cuchulainn had gone from Emain Macha. The Cycle of the Kings contains legends about the High Kings of Ireland, mostly historical figures, and is centred mainly in Tara.

I have included stories from the first three cycles in this collection but have replaced the tales of the medieval kings with stories about the three patron saints of Ireland, Patrick, Brigid and Columcille. The legends surrounding these saints belong more intimately to the folk tradition; yet they are as old as many of the earliest secular stories and are found in the same manuscripts.

It was extremely difficult to decide what to include or exclude from the book. In the end I opted for the better-known stories, the ones that I felt should be available to anyone who wants to have a general knowledge of the scope and variety of Irish legend.

I worked at all times from translations, usually from a single text, but here and there inserting a detail from another source if I thought it would benefit the story. In some of the stories I had to lose certain incidents and details because of considerations of length. In others, notably the legends of the saints, I had to stitch together a narrative from several sources. My aim has been to make the material accessible to the general reader while remaining as faithful as possible to the texts I used.

I have already mentioned the antiquity of these stories but it is not their historical or mythological value that gives them their significance and interest. Indeed it is almost the reverse. What ensures their place in world literature is their agelessness, their value as expressions of the perennial art of the storyteller. The societies and traditions that these stories reflect have long gone, but the characters from them, the heroes, the tyrants, the troublemakers, the passionate headstrong women and men have survived.

Marie Heaney
August 1993
Dublin

Acknowledgements

My first acknowledgement is to the scholars of the nineteenth and twentieth centuries whose work on the old manuscripts made this modest effort possible.

I would like to pay tribute to the estates of the National Library of Ireland, the Royal Irish Academy and the Widener Library at Harvard and thank the staff of these institutions for their help.

I am very grateful to Christopher Reid, my editor at Faber and Faber, for the encouragement he gave me when it was most needed and for all his help and advice, and to Gillian Bate for her timely suggestions and assistance.

Lastly I would like to thank my family for all their loving support.

OVER NINE WAVES

———

The Mythological Cycle

The Tuatha De Danaan

L ONG AGO the Tuatha De Danaan came to Ireland in a great fleet of ships to take the land from the Fir Bolgs who lived there. These newcomers were the People of the Goddess Danu and their men of learning possessed great powers and were revered as if they were gods. They were accomplished in the various arts of druidry, namely magic, prophecy and occult lore. They had learnt their druidic skills in Falias, Gorias, Findias and Murias, the four cities of the northern islands.

When they reached Ireland and landed on the western shore, they set fire to their boats so that there would be no turning back. The smoke from the burning boats darkened the sun and filled the land for three days, and the Fir Bolgs thought the Tuatha De Danaan had arrived in a magic mist.

The invaders brought with them the four great treasures of their tribe. From Falias they brought Lia Fail, the Stone of Destiny. They brought it to Tara and it screamed when a rightful king of Ireland sat on it. From Gorias they brought Lugh's spear. Anyone who held it was invincible in battle. From Findias they brought Nuada's irresistible sword. No one could escape it once it was unsheathed. From Murias they brought the Dagda's cauldron. No one ever left it hungry.

Nuada was the king of the Tuatha De Danaan and he led them against the Fir Bolgs. They fought a fierce battle on the Plain of Moytura, the first one the Tuatha De Danaan fought in a place of that name. Thousands of the Fir Bolgs were killed, a hundred thousand in all, and among them their king, Eochai Mac Erc. Many of the Tuatha De Danaan died too, and their king, Nuada, had his arm severed from his body in the fight.

In the end the Tuatha De Danaan overcame the Fir Bolgs and routed them until only a handful of them survived. These survivors boarded their ships and set sail to the far-scattered islands around Ireland.

When the Fir Bolgs had fled, the Tuatha De Danaan took over the country and went with their treasures to Tara to establish themselves as masters of the island. But another struggle lay ahead. Though they had defeated the Fir Bolgs, a more powerful enemy awaited them. These were the Fomorians, a demon-like race who lived in the islands to which the Fir Bolgs had fled.

Balor of the Evil Eye

Balor was the most powerful Fomorian king. Some of his followers were so ugly and rough they were frightful to look at, and some of them had only one hand and one foot. Balor built a shining tower on his island. It was made of glass, but shone like gold in the sun and from this tower Balor could watch out for ships and send his fierce pirates out to seize them if they came close. Not only did the Fomorians capture ships, but they sailed to Ireland and made raids there, seizing lands and slaves and levying taxes. Their druids had powerful magic spells, and it was through one of these spells that Balor got his power and his name.

One day when the young Balor was passing a house he heard chanting inside. He knew this place was out of bounds, for it was there the magicians gathered to work new spells, but curiosity overcame him. Seeing a window that was open high in the wall, he scrambled up and looked furtively through it, but he could see nothing for the room was filled with fumes and gases. Just as he peered through the window the chants grew louder and a strong plume of smoke rose in the air straight into Balor's face. He was blinded by the poisonous fumes and could not open his eye. He struggled to the ground, writhing with pain, and before he could escape one of the magicians came out of the house.

When the druid saw what had happened he said to Balor, 'That spell we were making was a spell of death and the fumes from it have brought the power of death to your eye. If you look on anyone with that evil eye it means they will die!' And so Balor got his name.

4

Among his own people his eye remained shut, but if he opened it against his enemies they dropped dead when he turned its deadly power on them. As he grew older his eyelid grew heavier and heavier until in the end he could not open it without help. An ivory ring was driven through the lid and through this ring ropes were threaded to make a pulley. It took ten men to raise the great heavy lid, but ten times that number were slain at a single glance. His evil eye made him of great importance to the Fomorians and he became the most powerful of them all. His ships raided Ireland again and again and Balor's pirates made slaves of the learned people of De Danaan.

But Balor had a secret fear. One of his druids had foretold that he would die at the hand of his own grandson. Balor had only one child, a daughter called Eithlinn, so he built another tower and shut the girl up in it with twelve women to guard her. He warned the women that not only should Eithlinn never see a man, but a man's name must never be mentioned in her presence. When this was done, Balor felt safe, for without a husband Eithlinn could not have a child and so he would not die.

He harried the Tuatha De Danaan more and more. He levied heavy taxes on them. They had to send him one-third of their grain, one-third of their milk, and, worst of all, one child in every three. So the Fomorians were feared and hated for their greed and cruelty and Balor was feared most of all.

Eithlinn grew up into a beautiful woman, a prisoner in the tower. Her companions were kind to her, entertained her and taught her skills, but Eithlinn felt lonely. As she looked out to sea from the high window of her tower, she would see long curraghs in the distance skimming over the waves and in these boats people unlike any she had seen before. In a dream, too, the same face would appear again and again and she felt a longing to meet this person. She asked the women who guarded her what they were called, these people that she had watched from a distance and seen in her dreams, but her companions remained silent. They remembered Balor's command that a man's name could not be mentioned in his daughter's presence.

The Birth of Lugh

Though he had cattle enough, Balor particularly coveted one wonderful cow, the Glas Gaibhleann, which never ran dry and belonged to a man of the Tuatha De Danaan called Cian. Balor would disguise himself in different ways and follow Cian and his marvellous cow around, waiting for a chance to seize it and bring it back to his island.

One day Balor saw Cian and his brother go to the forge of another brother, Goibniu, to get some weapons made by him. Cian had his cow with him on a halter because so many people had tried to steal her that she could not go loose, but had to be guarded night and day. Cian went into the forge to speak to Goibniu, while the other brother stayed outside with the Glas Gaibhleann. Balor saw his chance. Turning himself into a red-headed boy, he came up to the man who stood by the cow and began to talk to him.

'Are you getting a sword made as well?' he asked.

'I am,' said the brother, 'in my turn. When Cian comes out of the forge he'll guard the cow and I'll go into Goibniu and get my weapon made.'

'That's what you think,' said the boy. 'But there'll be no steel left for your sword. Your brothers have tricked you. They are using all the steel to make heavier weapons for themselves and you'll have none!'

When the third brother heard this he was furious. He stuffed the cow's halter into the boy's hand and ran into the forge to confront his brothers. Instantly Balor cast off his disguise and, dragging the cow behind him by the tail, he hurried to the strand and into the sea and headed back to the safety of his own island.

When his brother came storming into the forge yelling abuse at him, Cian realized he had been tricked. He raced outside just in time to see Balor pulling the Glas Gaibhleann behind him through the water, and as he watched cow and man became a speck on the horizon. It was Cian's turn to be angry now and he ranted at his brother for falling for such a trick, but it was too late. The cow was gone.

Cian went to a druid to ask for his help but the magician reminded him that no one could go near Balor without risking death, because of his evil eye. Cian was still determined to retrieve his cow, so he went to a woman druid called Birog, who had even greater powers. She disguised Cian as a woman and then she conjured up a wind so strong that Cian and she were carried off in a blast, high in the air, until they reached Balor's island.

The wind dropped and they landed safely at the foot of the tower where Eithlinn was imprisoned. Birog called out to the Eithlinn's guardians in the tower, 'Help us! Please help us! My companion is a queen of the Tuatha De Danaan. She is escaping from enemies who want to kill her. It's getting dark! Take pity on us and let us in!'

The women did not like to refuse another woman in distress and they let Cian and Birog in.

As soon as they were inside, Birog cast another spell and all the women fell fast asleep. All the women, that is, except Eithlinn herself. Cian, who had thrown off his woman's robes, ran up the stairs and in a small room at the top of the tower found Eithlinn staring sadly out to sea. He thought she was the most beautiful woman he had ever seen. As he stared at her, Eithlinn turned round and there, in the room with her, was the figure she thought about all day long and dreamt about each night. Declaring their love for each other, they embraced with delight.

Because he and Eithlinn loved each other, it was Cian's wish to take his beloved from her prison and bring her home with him. He went to find Birog to persuade her to use her powers to help them to escape together. But Birog was afraid of Balor. She was terrified that the Fomorian king would discover them and kill them with his evil eye, so, in spite of Cian's protests, she swept him away from Eithlinn on another enchanted wind and took him back with her to Ireland.

Eithlinn was brokenhearted when Cian left her, but she was comforted when she discovered that she would give birth to his child. In due course the boy was born and she called him Lugh.

When Balor heard the news of his grandson's birth he made up his mind to kill the infant straight away so that the druid's prophecy could not come true. He gave orders that the baby be thrown into the sea. Despite the desperate pleading of Eithlinn, the child was snatched from her and carried to the shore. Wrapped in a blanket held in place by a pin, Lugh was cast into a current by Eithlinn's guardians. As the weeping women watched, the pin opened and the baby rolled into the sea, leaving the empty blanket spread over the waves. Balor was relieved to hear that Lugh had been drowned. Once more he felt safe. Now he had no grandson to bring about his end.

But Lugh had been saved. Birog, who had been riding the winds, saw what happened and lifted the baby out of the water and carried him with her through the air, away from the island and back to Ireland. Just as she had carried Cian to Eithlinn, so she carried Lugh safely back to his father. Cian was overjoyed that his son had been saved and fostered him out with a king's daughter who loved Lugh as if he were her own child.

In his foster mother's house Lugh learnt many skills. The craftsmen taught him to work in wood and metal, the champions and athletes performed amazing feats for him and invited him to join them in their training. From the poets and musicians he heard the stories of the heroes and learnt to play on the harp and timpan. The court physician taught him the use of herbs and elixirs to cure illness and the magicians revealed to him their secret powers. He got the name Lugh of the Long Arm and grew up as skilful as he was handsome. Moreover, though he did not know it, he had within him the power to slay his grandfather, Balor of the Evil Eye.

The Reign of Bres

While Lugh was growing up in the house of his foster mother and learning all the arts and crafts that were practised there, another half-Fomorian was king of the Tuatha De Danaan and sat on the throne at Tara. He too was handsome, so handsome that he was called Bres the Beautiful. But he was greedy and cowardly as well.

Before Bres had been made ruler, Nuada had been the king of the De Danaan tribe. Nuada it was who had gained Ireland for his people by leading them in battle against the Fir Bolgs. His powerful army had driven the Fir Bolgs out of Ireland, then taken over the island and established the king's stronghold at Tara. In that battle Nuada lost an arm. It was severed from his body by the sword of Sreng and though he won the battle this accident cost Nuada his kingship. The Tuatha De Danaan had a law that only a man in perfect shape could rule them, and without his arm Nuada could no longer be king.

The people then chose Bres the Beautiful to be king of his place. Bres's father was a Fomorian and because of this the Tuatha De Danaan hoped that their new leader would form an alliance with Balor and put an end at last to the fierce Fomorian raids up the rivers and seas of Ireland. As it turned out the reign of Bres was disastrous for the Tuatha De Danaan. The Fomorians *did* form an alliance but their treaty was with Bres alone. Playing on his weakness and greed, they loaded heavier and heavier taxes on the Tuatha De Danaan and Bres added to his subjects' burden by imposing taxes of his own. He stripped the leaders of their wealth and power and made them do menial tasks. Ogma was set to chop wood and the Dagda to build fortifications around the king's stronghold.

As Bres grew greedier and more miserly the court at Tara became a cold and cheerless place. The poets and musicians were silent and the champions and heroes reduced to slavery. The chiefs who came to visit the king were given neither food nor drink and no entertainment was provided for them.

One day the poet Cairbre arrived at Bres's fort expecting the hospitality that poets were accustomed to receiving from their patrons. Instead he was shown into a narrow, mean, dark little house without a bed or a stick of furniture and no fire in the hearth. He was given three small dry cakes on a little plate and that was all. Cairbre was furious at Bres for this insulting treatment and the next morning as he crossed the enclosure on his way out of Tara, he composed a satirical poem against the king. This was the first satire ever made in Ireland, and through it the poet cursed Bres. 'Bres's prosperity is no more!' he cried, and his words came true. From that moment on, Bres's fortunes failed, his wealth dwindled and

9

his people became poorer and more oppressed.

But Cairbre's satire had another effect as well; it gave the Tuatha De Danaan leaders the courage to rebel against their king. They made up their minds to depose Bres but their problem was they had no one suitable to put in his place. They would have loved to restore Nuada to the throne but while he had only one arm they could not.

Then something happened to help them. Nuada's arm was restored to him through the skill of two men, Dian Cecht, the chief physician of the Tuatha De Danaan, and his son Miach.

First of all Dian Cecht fashioned an arm out of silver for Nuada. It worked as well as a real arm, the elbow bent, the fingers moved, the wrist was flexible and Nuada was pleased to have the use of his limb again. He became known as Nuada of the Silver Arm.

But he was still not perfect and therefore not fit to be king. So Miach, the physician's son, who had been taught the secrets of medicine by his father, decided to try to replace the silver arm with Nuada's real arm. He got Nuada's severed arm, which had been embalmed, and brought it to him. He removed the silver arm and set the severed arm into the socket. Then he said incantations over it:

> 'Joint to joint and sinew to sinew!
> Sinew to sinew and joint to joint!'

The operation took nine days and during that time Miach never left the king's side. For the first three days he bound Nuada's arm straight down along his side until it had rejoined the body at the armpit. For the second three days he bent the elbow and bound the arm across the king's breast and movement was restored. For the last three days he put a powder made of charred bulrushes on it and the arm was completely healed. It was as strong and flexible as it had ever been. Now Nuada could be king again and the De Danaan rejoiced.

But Miach paid a terrible price for his kindness and skill. His father became mad with jealousy that his student and his son, moreover, was now more powerful and skilled in medicine than he was himself. In a frenzy of rage and envy, he slashed at Miach's head with his sword. The first stroke cut into the skin and Miach healed himself on the instant. The second stroke reached the bone but Miach healed himself again. Though the third stroke went through the bone to the membrane of the brain still Miach was able to heal himself. With the fourth stroke, Dian Cecht cut out his son's brain and Miach fell dead.

Dian Cecht buried Miach on the plain outside Tara. By the next day a miraculous growth of herbs had sprung up, outlining Miach's body, every organ and bone and sinew. Each herb had special powers relating to the part of the body from which it had sprung. Airmed, Miach's sister, came to mourn for her brother and she saw the herbs, three hundred and sixty-five in all, growing out of his grave. She spread her cloak on the ground and started gathering the herbs to dry them, sorting them out according to their healing properties. But the jealous Dian Cecht came upon her as she was completing the task. He grabbed the cloak and scattered the herbs, mixing them all up together so that it was impossible to sort them out again, and to this day no one person really knows all the healing properties of herbs.

Lugh Comes to Tara

Nuada was perfect again and deemed fit to be king. The Tuatha De Danaan made up their minds to banish Bres and put Nuada back on the throne.

They went to Bres and, complaining bitterly to him about his cruel and miserly treatment of them, they told him to abdicate and restore the kingship to Nuada who was now whole again. Bres was very angry to be deposed, but he was too cowardly to resist so he agreed, and once more Nuada was king of the Tuatha De Danaan.

Bres was determined to take revenge for his humiliation. He left Ireland for the remote island where his Fomorian father lived to seek help from him.

'Why have you come here?' his father said. 'You were king in

Ireland and had great power. What happened to bring you down?'

'It was my own fault. My injustice, arrogance and greed brought about my downfall!' Bres confessed. 'I put taxes on the people that they had never paid before, and I reduced them to poverty and hunger. I have only myself to blame for what has happened.'

'That is bad,' his father told him sadly. 'The prosperity of your people should have been more important to you than your own position. Their blessing would have been better than their curses. What do you want from me?'

'I have come to gather an army to take back the land by force,' said Bres.

'What you lost through injustice you shouldn't regain through injustice!' said his father, and though he would not help Bres himself, he sent him on to Balor's island to raise an army there.

When Balor heard Bres's story he rallied to his aid for he knew that without Bres on the throne of Ireland, his own tyranny and extortion would be threatened. He assembled a fleet so big it could form an unbroken bridge from his farthest island across to Ireland. He gathered a great army and started to prepare for war.

Nuada, reigning justly now in Tara, knew nothing of this. With Bres gone, he had restored the kingship to its full glory. The poets and musicians who had been silent in Bres's day now entertained the household. There was plenty to eat and drink, and once more Tara resounded to the noise of feasting and entertainments of all kinds. But Nuada was uneasy, nevertheless, for he knew that Balor's raiders would return.

One day, when a feast was in progress, a young warrior in the clothing of a prince appeared at the gate of the king's fort. He was as beautiful as Bres had been, but was nobler in bearing and he had with him a band of warriors.

As he rode up to the gates of Tara, his troops behind him, the two doorkeepers, Gamal and Camall, challenged him.

'Who are you?' they asked, and 'Why have you come here?'

'I am Lugh of the Long Arm,' the warrior said, 'son of Cian and Eithlinn and grandson of Balor. Tell the king I am at the gates and want to join his household!'

'No one finds a place in Nuada's household unless he has a special skill,' said Camall. 'So I must ask what skill you have.'

'Question me,' said Lugh. 'I am a carpenter.'

'We have a carpenter already named Luchta and we do not need you,' replied Camall.

'Question me. I am a smith.'

'We have a smith as well. Colum is his name and so we do not need another.'

'Question me. I am a champion, stronger than any other,' said Lugh.

'The king's own brother, Ogma, is a champion and one champion is enough. We do not need you.'

'Question me. I am a harper.'

'We have a harper of our own. He is called Abcan. You are of no use to us.'

'Question me, doorkeeper. I am a warrior.'

Camall answered, 'We do not need you. We have a warrior already. Bresal is his name.'

'Question me. I am a poet who can tell many stories.'

'We have a bard already. We do not need another.'

'Question me. I am a magician.'

'We have many druids and magicians. We need no more.'

'Question me. I am a physician.'

'Still we do not need you. Dian Cecht, our physician, is the best in the land.'

'I will bear the king's cup at table if you will let me in!'

'We have nine cupbearers and that is enough. We do not need you.'

'Question me for the last time! I am a skilled worker in brass and enamelling.'

'Credne is our metalsmith, famous for his skill. We do not need you.'

'Then,' said Lugh, 'go and ask the king if he has in his household any single person who can do all these things. If he has, I will leave these gates and will no longer try to enter Tara.'

Camall left Gamal at the gate and went with Lugh's message to the king.

'A young man is at the gate asking to be let in. His name is Lugh, but by his own account he is so gifted that he should go by the name Samildanach, that is, master of all the arts. He says he can do by himself all the arts, crafts and skilled work of this entire household.'

'Let us see if he is as talented as he claims,' the king ordered. 'Bring the chessboard out to him and let him compete against our best players.'

Camall ran off and did as he had been commanded. Lugh played against the best chess players in the land and won every game until there was no one left unbeaten.

When Nuada heard this he said to the doorkeeper, 'Let this young hero in! Samildanach is a fitting name for him. He *is* a master of all arts. His like has never been seen in Tara before.'

Gamal and Camall opened the gates and Lugh entered Tara. He went straight to the hall where Nuada sat, surrounded by chiefs and bards and champions. The four great leaders of the Tuatha De Danaan were there too, the Dagda, the chief druid, Dian Cecht, the physician, Ogma, the champion, and Goibniu, the smith. Lugh passed by them all and sat down on the Seat of Wisdom next to the king.

Ogma, the champion, was proud of his own great strength and annoyed by the young man's arrogance, so he decided to test Lugh and discover if he really had all the powers he had boasted about. He lifted a huge flagstone, one that had taken several yokes of oxen to put there, and hurled it through the thick wall of the fort and out on to the plain. Lugh walked out to where the flagstone lay, lifted it and cast it back through the gaping hole it had made. It landed in the hall and settled in the exact spot where it had been before. He lifted the piece of wall that the flagstone had carried with it and set it back in place so that Nuada's hall was sound again.

Then taking up the harp that was slung over his shoulder Lugh began to play. As he plucked the strings gently and soothingly Nuada and his company fell into a peaceful sleep. When they woke, Lugh played for them slow airs that made them weep. Then the music got faster and happier and, drying their tears, the whole

14

company began to smile and laugh. Their laughter got louder and louder until the rafters rang with the sound.

Seeing that Lugh did indeed possess the mastery he claimed, Nuada decided to enlist his aid against Balor and his followers. He told Lugh about the evil of the Fomorians, about the tyranny of their taxes, their piracy round his shores and their cruelty to the captured sailors. He asked the young warrior to help him and Lugh agreed to be an ally. Then Nuada gave him the authority to rule by stepping off the throne while Lugh ascended it in his place.

Lugh was king of the Tuatha De Danaan for thirteen days and then, with Nuada and the four other leaders, he left Tara and went into a quiet place to plan the battle. They were in conference for a full year discussing their tactics and they kept their whereabouts and their plans secret so that the Fomorians would not suspect anything. Then, promising to meet again in three years, they left their hiding place. Nuada and the other leaders returned to Tara and Lugh went to seek the help of Manannan Mac Lir, the powerful ruler of the sea.

One day, nearly three years later, Nuada was looking out across the ramparts of his fort when he saw a troop of warriors coming towards him. His eyes were dazzled by a bright light as if he had looked full into the sun, but then he saw that the brilliant rays shone from the face of the leader of the troop and from his long golden hair. Darts of light came off the young man's armour and off his weapons and the gold-embossed harness of his horse. A great jewel blazed from the front of the golden helmet he wore on his shining hair, and Nuada knew that Lugh had come back to Tara.

This time Lugh was riding Manannan Mac Lir's magic horse that could gallop on the sea as if it were dry land and from whose back no one ever fell. He was wearing Manannan's breastplate that no weapon could penetrate, and in his hand he held Manannan's sword that was so deadly no one survived a blow from it.

Nuada, the king, and the De Danaan chiefs welcomed Lugh and brought him into Tara and they all sat down together. They had barely taken their places when another troop of men appeared on the horizon approaching Tara, but they were as different from Lugh and his noble followers as night is from day. Unkempt and surly, they slouched towards Nuada's fort as if they owned it. The doorkeepers who had questioned Lugh so closely when he had first arrived in Tara rushed to open the door for them, and without ceremony the slovenly crew shambled into the room where the king and Lugh were seated. Nuada and his household rose to their feet as soon as they entered while Lugh looked on in amazement and vexation.

'Why are you rising to your feet for this miserable, hostile rabble when you didn't stand for me?' he cried.

'We must rise,' Nuada replied, 'or they will kill us all, down to the youngest child! These are the Fomorians who have come back again to harry us as they did during Bres's rule. They have come to claim their taxes, a third of our crops and our cattle and a third of our children as slaves!'

Lugh was so furious when he heard these words that he drew Manannan's deadly sword and rushed at the Fomorian crowd and killed all but nine of them. 'You should be killed as well,' he told the cringing survivors, 'but I'll spare your lives so that you can return to Balor empty-handed and tell him what happened here!' The terrified messengers fled from Tara like hunted animals and made for the islands of the Fomorians as quickly as they could.

When they arrived at Balor's tower and told him about the fate of their companions, his rage was as great as Lugh's and he was determined to invade Ireland and regain his hold over the country and its inhabitants. He called a council of war and the most powerful Fomorians came to his tower, among them his wife, Queen Ceithlinn of the Crooked Teeth, his twelve sons, and his warriors and wise men. Bres, who had just arrived at Balor's tower to seek allies to regain his throne from Nuada, was there as well.

'Who is this upstart,' Balor roared, 'who dares to kill my men and send an insulting message back to me?'

Ceithlinn answered him. 'I know well who he is from the description these men give of him, and it is bad news for us. He is our own grandson, the son of our daughter Eithlinn, and he is known as Lugh of the Long Arm. It has been foretold that he will banish the Fomorians from Ireland for all time and that it will be at his hand, the hand of your grandson, that you, Balor, will meet your end.'

When Bres heard this he said to Balor, 'I came to you here to ask you to help me recover my throne. Now we can help each other. Get ready ships and men and arms for me and pack our boats with provisions and I'll go to Ireland and meet Lugh in battle myself. I'll cut off his head and bring it back to you.'

'Do that if you can,' said Balor, 'but I will come too, and for all his skills I'll overcome my insolent grandson. When that's done, I'll tie that rebellious island to the stern of my ship and tow it back here where none of the De Danaan will dare to follow. And where Ireland once lay there will be empty ocean.'

Then marshalling his fearsome army and accompanied by Ceithlinn and his warriors, he made for the harbour. Every ship in the huge fleet raised a bright sail and, catching the wind, set out for Ireland.

The Battle of Moytura

As soon as the Fomorian messengers had fled from Tara, Lugh and Nuada began to make plans for battle too, for they knew that Balor would seek revenge for the men who had been killed, and would try to gain control over the Tuatha De Danaan and impose the same taxes as before. They called together the magician and cupbearers, the druid and craftsmen, the poet and physicians, all the people who possessed special skills, and Lugh asked each one of them what contribution he would make to the struggle.

The magician told him he would topple the mountains of Ireland and cause them to roll along the ground towards the Fomorian army, but these same mountains would shelter the Tuatha De Danaan during the fight.

The cupbearers promised to bring a great thirst on the Fomorians and then drain the lakes and rivers of Ireland so that there was no water for them to drink. But there would be water for Nuada's army even if the war lasted seven years.

The druid said he would send a shower of fire to fall on the heads of the Fomorians and rob them of their strength, but every breath the Tuatha De Danaan drew would make them stronger.

Then Lugh questioned the craftsmen and the wise men in the same way as to what special powers they would bring to battle.

Goibniu, the smith, promised to make swords and spearheads that would never miss their mark and to supply them to the Tuatha De Danaan for as long as the battle raged.

Credne, the worker in brass, said he would provide rivets and sockets for spears and swords and rims for shields as long as they were needed, and Luchta, the carpenter, swore he would make the strongest spearshafts and shields and would do so until Lugh's army was victorious.

Then Lugh questioned Cairbre, the poet who had cursed Bres, about his contribution to the struggle.

'The weapons I use are invisible,' Cairbre, replied, 'but no less strong for that. I attack the mind. At daybreak I will compose a satirical poem about the Fomorians and because of this poem they will be full of shame and will lose heart and their will to win.

Lugh addressed Dian Cecht last of all and the physician answered, 'My daughter Airmed and I will go to the battlefield each evening and bring back the injured. We will treat their wounds with herbs and bathe them in our miraculous well and unless they have been mortally wounded they will be cured. In the morning they will join the ranks more eager than ever for battle and fight more fiercely than before.'

As he finished speaking, the Morrigu, the fierce goddess of battle-fields, appeared in the shape of a crow. She spoke to the leaders of the Tuatha De Danaan and promised them that she would help them when they most needed her, at the hour of their greatest danger, and she foretold a victory for them.

'But you must prepare yourselves immediately,' she said, 'for I have seen the warriors of Balor's mighty army stream off the ships at Scetne. They have already started marching across Ireland towards Tara!'

Lugh marshalled his troops and told them everything he had heard. He spoke to every man in turn, encouraging them and exhorting them to fight and he filled them full of battle fury.

But Lugh himself was so precious to the Tuatha De Danaan that the king and his advisers imprisoned him behind the lines and left nine champions with him to keep him there. Nuada and the other leaders stayed with Lugh while the battle lines were drawn and the ordinary soldiers made ready to fight. Then the two armies marched towards each other and met on the Plain of Moytura. Though they had been fired for battle by Lugh's encouragement and fought fiercely and bravely, Nuada's army could not overcome the countless men the Fomorians sent out to meet them. Day after day the battle raged and each morning the De Danaan soldiers who had been injured in the action the day before were back in battle file, their wounds healed and their weapons intact. The Fomorians noticed this and were angry at the tactics the Tuatha De Danaan were using against them, but they fought all the more fiercely and held fast. The struggle went on for days with heavy losses on both sides and no side gaining the upper hand. As the troops became more and more war-weary the Fomorians decided to make a final assault.

Balor himself, with Bres and Ceithlinn at his side, went to the head of the Fomorian army, and led the horde, vast still in spite of the losses, on to the Plain of Moytura. Helmeted and well-armed, they marched in their thousands in close formation, men and women side by side.

The Tuatha De Danaan closed ranks and moved against them. Lugh could bear it no longer. Using all his strength he escaped from his guards and raced to the front of the line to lead the De Danaan army. Nuada and the Dagda and all the champions joined him, while the Morrigu, the Battle Crow, hovered above them to watch the battle. Lugh stood facing his troops as the plain behind him grew dark with the Fomorian warriors.

'You must fight now and fight to the death,' he shouted, 'for if we lose this battle we will lose everything and live in slavery for all time!'

He turned towards the advancing host and with a great shout the two armies rushed to meet each other. The battle was fierce and bloody. There was no time now for the physicians to heal the wounded or the smiths to repair weapons. The warriors fought hand to hand. Sword clashed against sword, spears whistled through the air and battle-axes thudded against shields.

The warriors roared as they fought and the wounded screamed as they fell. The tumult rolled over the Plain of Moytura like thunder and the ground became slippery with blood. Still the two sides fought on. Face to face they fought and when they slipped and fell to their knees they continued to hack at each other, forehead braced against forehead. The river carried away the dead, friend and enemy side by side. Ceithlinn of the Crooked Teeth hurled a spear at the Dagda, inflicting a terrible wound. Other De Danaan leaders fell, men and women together, and it seemed as if the Fomorians would be victorious. But Nuada rallied his forces and led them afresh into battle. He marched at the head of his troops and at last the two leaders met. Balor raised his sword over his head and felled Nuada with one blow. When the Tuatha De Danaan saw their king dying at Balor's feet a groan of despair arose from them and they faltered. At that instant the black crow shape of the Morrigu appeared above the battle lines screaming the encouragement she had promised them at their darkest hour and fresh courage surged into the De Danaan troops.

Lugh rushed to the side of the dying Nuada and angrily taunted Balor. His abuse drove his grandfather into a rage.

'Lift up my eyelid so I can see this gabbling loudmouth who dares to insult me like this!' he roared. A terrified hush fell over the multitude for everyone knew the dreadful power of the Evil Eye. Ten Fomorian champions pulled on the ropes to raise the heavy lid as those nearest to Balor fell to the ground to escape his deadly stare. Lugh stood his ground, put a stone in his sling, took aim and let fly directly at Balor's eye as it opened. The force of the stone drove the eye back through Balor's head and it landed in the midst of the Fomorian lines. Balor fell dead and hundreds of his followers were killed by the eye's fatal power.

Then Lugh cut off Balor's head and led the Tuatha De Danaan in a fierce assault against the Fomorians. With the Morrigu hovering above them, they broke through their enemy's lines, and what had been a battle became a rout. The Fomorians were beaten back to the sea by Lugh and his army. They fled to their ships, boarded them in great haste and speedily set sail for their islands, never to return to Ireland. Bres survived the battle and was captured by the Tuatha De Danaan but Lugh, who had become king in Nuada's place, spared his life on condition that he would share with him his knowledge of husbandry and farming. So Bres taught the Tuatha De Danaan when to plough and sow and reap and, when they had mastered these crafts, he too left Ireland for good.

The Tuatha De Danaan survivors cleared the battlefield of the dead who were as countless as the stars in the sky or the grass underfoot, as countless as flakes of snow in the air or Manannan's horses, the white-capped waves of the sea.

When this sad task was done the battle goddess, the Morrigu, declared victory to the Tuatha De Danaan. Then, from the mountain summits and riverbanks and estuaries, she proclaimed peace to the land of Ireland:

> 'Peace in this land
> From the earth up to the skies
> And back down to the earth.
> Honey and mead in abundance
> And strength to everyone.'

Midir and Etain

M IDIR THE PROUD, a prince of the Tuatha De Danaan, was famous for his beauty and the magnificence of his clothes. He lived in great splendour with his wife, Fuamnach, in his underground fort called a *sidhe*, at Bri Leith.

Aengus Og, the son of the Dagda, had spent his youth in Midir's underground palace in Bri Leith, and Midir loved him like a son. When Aengus Og grew up, he returned to his own sidhe, Brugh na Boinne, beside the River Boyne, the most important one in the land.

Midir was lonely without his foster son's company so one autumn day, just before the feast of Samhain, Midir set off to visit Aengus Og. He left his wife, Fuamnach, at Bri Leith. On the way he met a king's daughter called Etain. Etain's beauty was legendary. Indeed she was so beautiful that there was a saying: 'Nothing can be called beautiful unless tested against Etain.' Midir had heard of Etain's beauty and as soon as he saw her he fell deeply in love with her and carried her off with him to Aengus Og's house at the Boyne. They lived in Brugh na Boinne for a year and Midir was so enthralled by Etain that he forgot everyone else when he was with her.

In Bri Leith, Fuamnach learnt of Midir's love for Etain through the powers of her foster father, a druid called Bresal. As the months passed and Midir did not return to her, she became more and more jealous and she begged Bresal to help her banish Etain from Midir's mind. The druid consented and taught her some of his magic arts, and Fuamnach plotted to get rid of her rival.

When a year was up, Midir decided to return to his own house at Bri Leith. He brought Etain with him and when they arrived Fuamnach welcomed them warmly.

'It is a great honour for us to have a royal guest in the house,' she said. Then she turned to Midir. 'Show your wealth to the king's daughter!'

Etain and Midir wandered round Bri Leith looking at its fine halls, rooms and playing fields and when they had seen all that was to be seen, they returned to Fuamnach.

'Now let me show you to your room,' Fuamnach said to Etain and went ahead of her into the bedchamber. A big fire was burning there and the room was warm and welcoming. In the middle of the chamber stood a chair and Fuamnach invited Etain to sit on it. As soon as Etain was seated she hissed at her, 'You occupy the chair of a good woman!' and struck her with a wand of scarlet rowan berries.

Instantly Etain disappeared, but on the floor beside the chair there lay a little pool of water. Fuamnach ran out of the room and fled from Bri Leith to seek refuge with Bresal, for she was afraid of Midir's anger.

After a while Midir went to Etain's quarters to find her, for he couldn't bear to be parted from her for long. He went into the bedchamber and found it was empty. He searched the house from top to bottom, becoming more alarmed with each passing minute. He called Etain's name and Fuamnach's name again and again. He hurried to the gates of Bri Leith and out to the playing fields but there was no sign of either woman. In a flash Midir realized that something terrible had happened to Etain and that Fuamnach, and her jealousy, were responsible. He went back to the bedchamber but there was still no sign of Etain. Distracted with grief he left the room without even noticing the pool of water on the floor.

When he had gone the fire grew hotter and the floor began to tremble and the water began to seethe and solidify. Slowly it took on the shape of a worm that lay coiled on the floor where the water had been. But the heat and the agitation in the room grew more and more intense until, in the midst of this turmoil, the worm turned into a crimson fly, a large, beautiful fly with jewelled eyes and enamelled wings. As the creature struggled from the floor and slowly began to beat her wings, a music sweeter than the sound of the harp or horn or pipe filled the room. In the darkness and in daylight the fly shone like a jewel and wherever she went she filled the space with a sweet fragrance. Dew fell from her wings and

23

anyone touched by this moisture was soothed and healed. Though she now had the shape of a fly, Etain still retained the nature of a woman and she flew out of the window to search for her beloved Midir.

She found him asleep and flew round the room where he lay. As Etain's fragrance filled the room, Midir woke up and saw the beautiful creature on the windowsill. He knew at once that it was Etain. As the crimson fly moved round the room the music from her wings and the scattering of dew soothed him. His loneliness faded and peace and happiness took its place. Together Etain and Midir travelled through Ireland visiting feasts and assemblies where Etain's exquisite appearance and fragrance brought joy to all who saw her. Etain watched over Midir, warning him of any danger that came close to him and comforting him with the music of her wings. Once again Midir was happy and thought of no one but Etain, and they returned to live in Bri Leith.

In Bresal's house, where she had taken refuge, Fuamnach became more jealous than ever. She had heard about the beautiful crimson fly that lived in a bower in Bri Leith and she knew it was Etain and that Midir loved her as much as ever. At last she could bear it no longer and she went to Midir's house to see what harm she could do to Etain. When she arrived at Bri Leith Midir upbraided her for her jealous deed. Far from being repentant, Fuamnach told him that what she had done she would do again, and that as long as Etain was alive, in whatever shape, she would try to hurt her. And with that she began to chant a spell so strong that all Midir's love for Etain and all his magic was powerless against it. Fuamnach called up a great wind to blow through Bri Leith. It shrieked through the house carrying Etain helplessly before it. She was tossed up over the ramparts and across the open countryside, battered and terrified.

At last Etain was blown to Brugh na Boinne, the fort of Aengus Og and the same house where she had first joined Midir. Aengus was walking outside his liss and the fly landed on his cloak. At once Aengus knew that the weary wanderer was Etain, so he carried her tenderly into his house and set her down. He built a little glass room for her, full of sunlight and flowers, and there Etain felt safe.

Aengus Og loved her too, and she brought as much happiness to him as she had to Midir. Knowing this, Fuamnach's anger and rage knew no bounds. She knew she would not be able to get close enough to Etain to harm her whilst either Midir or Aengus Og was at her side, so she arranged a meeting between herself and the two men a little distance away from Brugh na Boinne.

When Aengus left home to meet Midir, Fuamnach circled round the mound and crept inside when no one was looking. She found Etain in her crystal sun bower and she conjured up the same druid's wind as she had done before, and Etain was swept out of Aengus's fort.

Aengus and Midir waited for Fuamnach to join them and when a long time passed and she didn't arrive, they became uneasy. Aengus ran back to his underground palace and when he saw Etain's empty room he knew Fuamnach had been at her jealous work. He was filled with anger and sorrow and determined to punish her. He found her hiding in another part of the house with Bresal beside her, and in a rage he cut off her head there and then.

For seven years the wind lashed Etain about the length and breadth of Ireland. She could not rest in any high place, not trees or roofs, or cliffs or mountains. She could find peace only in the crevices of rocks, on the seashore or on the crests of the waves. At last, wretched and exhausted, the fly was blown inland towards a great hall and through an open door. Up, up towards the rafters she was tossed and she landed there half dead. Below her a feast was in progress. Etar, the Ulster champion who lived there, was giving a feast for his household. The table was set with gold and silver and the noise of the feast rose around the weary fly. She clung to the beams with the last of her strength but she was so faint with exhaustion that she could cling no more and she fell from the roof into a golden goblet full of wine that Etar's wife was holding. Not noticing what had happened, the woman brought the cup to her lips and swallowed the fly in a mouthful of wine. Nine months later Etar's wife gave birth to a beautiful baby girl and they called the child Etain.

Etar and his wife loved the girl and showered her with riches of all kinds, everything that a king's daughter could wish for. Sixty chieftain's daughters were brought to Etar's house and he kept them, feeding and clothing them, so that Etain would have company at all times. They attended to her every need and she grew up as beautiful as before.

When Etain was twenty years of age, Eochai Airem became High King of Ireland. In the first year of his reign Eochai sent for the kings of the provinces of Ireland and the chieftains and their people, to come to Tara to celebrate the feast of Samhain, our Hallowe'en, one of the most important feasts of the year.

Word came back to Eochai that the kings and chieftains could not come to Tara to celebrate the feast until the king had a wife. It was the custom, they said, that no man came to Tara without his wife for this feast, and no woman came without her husband. The High King, too, must observe this rule.

In great haste the king sent out messengers to find him a fitting queen. She must be a nobleman's daughter and she must never have been married before. The messenger found Etain suitable in every way and told the king about her. Eochai Airem set out with his followers to visit Etar's house and ask for his daughter's hand in marriage.

As the High King and his retinue approached Etar's house they saw a beautiful girl washing herself beside a well. The basin that held the water was made of gold, with purple gemstones set in the rim. Four golden birds perched on the edge of the bowl as if they were drinking from the water. The woman was dressed in a green tunic of lustrous silk, hooded and embroidered with golden thread. On her breast, catching the light, were two brooches made out of gold and silver in the shape of fabulous animals. Round her shoulders lay a rich purple cloak with a silver fringe. As the sun's rays fell on the golden threads in the green silk and on the rich jewellery and on her golden hair Etain shone as brightly as the sun itself. To Eochai Airem she seemed like a creature from another world. Her hair was bound in long golden plaits decorated with golden threads and with a little golden bauble on the end of each plait. As the king watched, she raised her arms to let down her hair and loosen it so that she could wash it and her sleeves fell back revealing her beautiful slender arms and narrow waist. The king stared, speechless at such beauty. Etain's skin was as white as snow in the morning or the white caps of the waves. Her eyebrows were dark and lustrous as a beetle's shell. Her eyes were as blue as wild hyacinths and her cheeks as pink as foxgloves. As he watched, a happy smile lit up her eyes and dimpled her smooth cheeks. She combed her shining hair with a comb of silver inlaid with gold which she held in her delicate hand. Her gestures were graceful and elegant and she moved with the stately bearing of a queen.

The king gestured to his retinue to stay where they were and then alone and gently he approached the girl. She was not alarmed and when the king asked her what her name was, she answered with assurance.

'I am Etain, daughter of Etar, a chieftain and a champion of Ulster.'

'And I am Eochai Airem, High King of Ireland, and I am looking for a wife,' Eochai said. 'I have fallen in love with you at first sight and will look no further if you'll consent to marry me and come with me to Tara.'

'I know who you are,' Etain replied, 'for I have heard about you and loved you since I was a child. I have been waiting for you, and for your sake I've refused all offers of marriage from the young men at my father's house.'

Eochai Airem could hardly believe his ears, and he was overjoyed by this reply. They got married immediately and Etain returned to Tara with the High King.

Now that Eochai had a wife the kings of Ireland were willing to come to Tara for the feast, and so the great feast of Samhain began. Etain was so happy she looked more beautiful than ever and as she poured out the wine, a special skill of hers, all eyes were on her. But one man, Aillil, brother of Eochai, fell instantly in love with her as the king himself had done, and could not drag his eyes away from her all through the meal. A woman near him noticed this and chided him. Aillil felt ashamed and did not look at Etain again while the rest of the feast was in progress. But his obsession with her grew and he began to waste away with longing. For a year he grew more and more ill without any apparent cause and he could not disclose his secret to anyone.

Eochai Airem came to see his brother to find out what the cause of the mysterious illness might be, but Aillil could not tell *him*, above all others, what ailed him, and the king left none the wiser. He was anxious about Aillil so he sent his own physician, Fachtna, to try to cure him. Fachtna put his hand on Aillil's chest and Aillil sighed.

'One of two things is wrong with you,' Fachtna said. 'You're suffering from the pain of jealousy or the pain of a secret love.'

Aillil knew the physician spoke the truth but he could not confess it to anyone, for he was guilty and ashamed to be in love with his brother's wife. And so he became weaker and weaker each day.

The time came round when the High King had to make his royal circuit of Ireland and Eochai was afraid that his brother would die while he was away, so he asked Etain to attend to him and see that he got a proper burial if this happened. Etain began to nurse Aillil and under her care he improved. She noticed how happy he was when she was near and began to wonder about it. She decided to ask him the cause of his illness, and promised to help him if it lay within her power.

'It is love that has made me sick for a year,' Aillil said. 'And though my love is as deep as the sea and endless as the sky, it is like living with a shadow or listening to an echo, for it can never be fulfilled. Etain, I am in love with my brother's wife!'

Etain stared at him in great dismay; she had loved her husband since she was a child and loved only him, but for her sake his brother lay dying. She left Aillil's bedside in distress, her heart full of pity for his plight.

Aillil grew worse and worse now, wasting away with longing. He begged Etain to become his lover because that was the only thing that could save him. Etain did not want to be unfaithful to her husband by giving her love to Aillil, but she saw that her brother-in-law was dying. In desperation she consented to meet him outside Eochai's house the next morning at daybreak.

All night long Aillil lay awake, waiting for the dawn to break when his longing would be appeased, but just before the appointed hour, he fell into a deep sleep. Etain went to the hill where they were meant to meet and waited sadly for Aillil to come and claim her love. A man suddenly appeared climbing towards her up the hill. He looked like Aillil but as he came closer Etain realized that though he had Aillil's shape, it was not he. She turned away from him and did not speak or look in his direction and the strange man went away.

When Aillil woke from his sleep and realized he had missed the meeting he longed for so much, he was heartbroken and became iller than ever. So Etain sadly agreed to meet him in the same place at the same hour the next morning. Afraid that he would sleep again, Aillil kept himself awake by splashing water over his face all night long. But just when the first streak of light appeared in the sky, in spite of all his efforts to stay awake, he fell fast asleep. Once more Etain waited for him on the hill and once more the man who looked like Aillil, but was not he, approached her. Once more Etain turned away.

For the third time Etain took pity on Aillil and again a meeting was arranged. On the third morning the same thing happened but this time Etain, waiting on the hill, spoke to the man who looked like Aillil. 'Who are you,' she said, 'and why have you come here?'

'I have come to meet you,' said the man, 'as you promised.'

'I did not promise to meet you,' cried Etain. 'I promised to meet Aillil and you are not Aillil, though you have taken on his shape! I came to meet Aillil to save him. It is my husband whom I love.'

'Then it is right that you should come to meet *me* and not Aillil,' said the man, 'for I am your husband.'

Etain stared at him. 'What do you mean? My husband is Eochai Airem, High King of Ireland, whom I have loved since I was a child. Who are you, and how can you say such a thing!'

'I am Midir of Bri Leith, a king of the Tuatha De Danaan whose dwellings are underground, and long, long ago you were once my wife. I have always loved you and it was *my* love for you that Aillil felt. I put that desire in his heart so that through him you

29

would remember my love and return it once more.'

Etain was astonished at these words but she knew in her heart that Midir spoke the truth. 'If this is so,' she said, 'and you loved me, why were we separated?'

'Through the jealousy of Fuamnach and her druid's spells,' said Midir. 'And now I am asking you to leave your human husband and come with me to join your own people. It will not be disloyal for you to leave an earthly king for a king of the Otherworld. I love you, Etain. For your sake I sent that sleep on Aillil to prevent him claiming your love. I have cured him of his illness and he no longer wants you. Come with me to Bri Leith, Etain, where you belong, and we will live happily for ever.'

'My love for Eochai is for ever,' said Etain, 'and I will never leave him!' And with that she went back to the fort where Aillil was. He met her at the door, happy and in good health, and the love-sickness that Midir had put on him was gone. Etain told him about her encounter with the man of the Sidhe, Midir of Bri Leith, and when Eochai returned from his journey round Ireland he heard the whole story too. They rejoiced together that things had turned out as they had and that their difficulties were at an end. Both brothers were grateful to Etain for her kindness to them and Eochai Airem loved her more than ever.

The Return of Midir

Etain now lived happily in Tara with Eochai Airem, her beauty and grace a byword and her hospitality acknowledged to be the most generous and accomplished of all.

One sunny day during a festival she was outside the terraces of the fort watching the chariot races and the games when a beautiful young man came towards her. He was as beautiful as she was, and his dress was just as splendid. His tunic was red silk that glowed like gold and was embroidered with golden thread. Over it he wore a long green cloak held in place with a magnificent golden brooch that crossed from shoulder to shoulder. His curly hair was kept in place by a fillet of gold the same colour as his hair. Slung over his shoulder was a five-pronged silver spear with a golden rim and a golden boss, fretted in gold from butt to point. Etain gasped when she saw him and turned towards her companions but they were looking at the games and Etain realized that she alone could see him. He came closer and closer, past the other women who were cheering on the champions completely unaware of his presence. When he reached Etain, he began to speak to her. No one turned a head at the sound of his voice and Etain knew his message was for her alone.

'Golden-haired Etain, will you come with me to a country that is full of music? A place where everyone is as beautiful as you, with hair as yellow as the wild iris, and skin like snow, cheeks with the foxglove's bloom and eyes like a blackbird's egg. Our people move among mortals, but they cannot see us for we are not mortal. We have no worry or sorrow and we stay young forever. The rivers in our land run full of mead and wine, and the land's abundance is shared freely among us all. Lovely Etain, leave Ireland, beautiful as it is, for a fairer land awaits you. And in that land of the Ever Young you will be a queen.'

Etain said she would not go, but the young man pleaded with her and said, 'If your husband gives you to me, Etain, will you come with me to my kingdom?'

'If my husband gives me to you,' said Etain, for she was sure it would never happen, 'I will go with you.'

The young man smiled and disappeared.

Not long after this, on a beautiful summer's morning, Eochai got up early and climbed on to the ramparts of Tara to look across the Plain of Breg. It stretched out below him, wet with dew, green and fertile and bright with scarlet poppies and ox-eye daisies. The king felt a presence beside him and he turned round quickly to see who it might be. Beside him, on the high ground was the most beautiful man he had ever seen. His purple tunic and golden brooch shone in the sun and he held a silver shield with a golden boss in one hand and a five-pointed gold-mounted spear in the other. Eochai felt a moment's fear for he knew that the gates of the fort had not yet opened and this young man had not been among his company the night before.

'Who are you?' he said at last. 'I don't recognize you?'

31

'I am Midir of Bri Leith,' said the warrior, 'and I know well who you are.'

'Why have you come to Tara?' said the High King.

'To play a game of chess with you,' Midir replied.

'I hope you're a good chess player,' said Eochai, 'if you want to play with me!'

'We won't know that till we play,' said Midir.

Eochai began to feel uneasy. 'Unfortunately the chessboard is in the queen's chamber,' he said, 'and she is still asleep, so we cannot play.'

'I have a chessboard with me,' said Midir, 'as fine as yours!' And with that he took from his shoulder a bag woven of golden thread. Out of it he took a chessboard, inlaid with silver, and precious stones, and the shining jewels that were set in the four corners threw light across the board. The chessmen were made of gold.

Midir set up the chessboard and waited for the king to make the first move, but Eochai was still reluctant to play.

'I will not play where there is no stake,' he said.

'What stake will you accept?' said Midir.

'It's all the same to me!' said Eochai.

So Midir offered a fabulous stake of fifty of the finest dappled horses and fifty enamelled bridles with them.

They played the game of chess and Eochai won. Midir slipped away and the king didn't see how or where he had gone.

The next morning, before the gates were opened, Eochai went to the ramparts and there, beside him, was Midir. Cropping the grass were fifty magnificent horses, their enamelled bridles glowing in the sun.

Eochai was delighted at such a prize and when Midir challenged him to another game he accepted gladly. This time the stake Midir offered was richer again: fifty boars, fifty cattle and fifty sheep. Eochai played with great intensity and again he won. The next morning, on the pastures outside his fort, all the animals that Midir had promised were herded together.

When Midir appeared for the third time, ready for a game, Eochai told the visitor that this time he would set the stakes himself.

He set Midir three stupendous tasks. The first was to clear the land of stones and with them to lay a causeway over the Bog of Tethbae; the second to make fertile the rushy ground around his fort; and the third to clothe the bare hills of the district with trees. Midir agreed to do these things if he lost the game, impossible though they seemed, but on the condition that neither Eochai nor any of his household should look out over the terraces that night.

They played and Midir lost this game as well. Eochai was full of jubilation and Midir slipped away as mysteriously as ever.

That night when the gates were shut and the whole household was in bed, Eochai went to the quarters where his chief steward slept. He woke the man and told him to go to the ramparts and look out over the wall. 'Watch carefully and above all remain hidden. In the morning come and tell me what you saw,' he told him.

The steward crept stealthily to the fortifications and looked over. In the moonlight there was a crowd of men so vast that it looked as if all the men in the world were gathered on the Plain of Breg. Crowds milled around like ants, stooping and rising, lifting stones, digging and building, while Midir directed the work from the top of a hill. Then the steward realized that the hill Midir was standing on was made up of a vast heap of clothes that the labourers had discarded while they worked. Before his amazed eyes the familiar landscape was transformed. As Eochai had directed, a bridge was being built across the bog, using the stones from the cleared pastures, and oak and hazel woods clothed the hills.

Next morning, as the steward was telling the king about the marvellous things he had seen, Midir appeared beside them. His face was white with anger, his eyes were blazing and Eochai knew at once that Midir had discovered that he had been betrayed.

'You have treated me dishonourably, High King,' he said, 'though I treated you fairly!'

Eochai was ashamed that he had been caught in his deception and he was frightened of Midir's anger. He tried to placate him and make amends.

'I will not return anger for anger,' he said. 'Whatever you want, I will do.'

'We will play this game for an open stake,' Midir said. 'Whoever wins will then name his prize.'

Eochai was confounded by these terms. He dreaded what stakes Midir would set and the prize he would claim if he won the game but he had to agree to them for he had given his word. They sat down to play at the beautiful chessboard and Eochai played as if his life depended on it, but this time Midir won.

'What is your stake?' the king asked in a low voice, fearing the worst.

'To take your wife, Etain, in my arms,' said Midir, 'and to give her a kiss!'

When Eochai heard this, fear made him speechless but in a short time he composed himself and said to Midir, 'Come back at the end of a month and your stake will be honoured.'

Throughout the month Eochai sent messages to the kings and chiefs of Ireland to come to Tara with their warriors. When the time was up a great army had assembled there. They surrounded the ramparts outside, row upon row, and inside the walls they made the same formation.

At the hour Midir was due to appear, Eochai and Etain sat in the centre of the house surrounded by chiefs and warriors. The doors were locked and barred and the fort encircled by armed soldiers. As Etain bent forward to pour out the wine for the king a sudden hush fell on the crowd. She looked up and there was the young man who had appeared to her on the playing fields standing in their midst. Midir was always handsome but this time his beauty was such that everyone who looked at him fell silent.

'I have come to claim my reward,' he said.

'I have not considered your request long enough,' said the king, playing for time.

'What is due, is due,' Midir replied. 'You have staked Etain herself to me, and she has promised that if you give her to me she will come back to Bri Leith.'

Remembering the careless promise, Etain blushed.

34

'You don't need to be ashamed, Etain,' Midir told her gently. 'You have not been disloyal to your husband. In spite of my offer of beautiful gifts and riches beyond compare you would not listen to me. So I will take you only if Eochai gives you to me. This was the stake we played for.'

'Then let it be like that!' said Etain. 'If my husband permits it, I will go with you.'

'I will not let you go!' Eochai assured Etain. Then he turned to Midir. 'Your wager will be honoured, so I give you leave to put your arms round Etain and claim your kiss.'

Midir put his shield and spear in one hand and with the other he circled Etain's waist. As he bent his head to kiss her, he rose into the air, clasping Etain closely, and they escaped out of the house through the skylight of the hall. The warriors rushed out along with the king to try to stop Midir and Etain leaving Tara, but there was no sign of them and the guards outside had seen nothing. Then the crowd heard the beating of wings and there, high above them, they saw two swans flying close together. They circled Tara once and then flew off in the direction of Bri Leith.

Eochai was furious at the trick Midir had played on him and was determined to get his wife back again. Calling together the champions of his household and the army he had gathered around Tara, he set off immediately to storm Bri Leith. They arrived at the mound and the warriors began to dig. They dug all day long but the next morning the earth that had been taken away the day before was back in place, and the sidhe was intact again. Day after day, week after week the same thing happened, but Eochai would not give up. For nine years he and his armies circled and attacked every earthwork in Ireland, digging down through the mounds, trying to reach the dwellings at the centre. In the end, having laid waste to most of them, Eochai returned to the tumulus at Bri Leith. Just as he was making his final assault on it, Midir called a truce. From inside his underground dwelling, he shouted out to Eochai, 'You can have Etain back if you can find her and point her out to me!'

At that instant, sixty women appeared outside the broken walls of Bri Leith. Eochai stared at them first in amazement, and then in bewilderment, for each one looked exactly like Etain. 'Let them serve wine!' Eochai called out at last, for he knew that Etain had a special way of doing that.

The women took it in turns to pour wine, until only two were left, and still Eochai had not found Etain. Then the second-last woman took the jug and started to pour. She looked like Etain and poured the wine in Etain's special way, so the king thought it must be his wife. But he was uneasy. 'It looks like Etain, but it is not Etain!' he cried out in puzzlement as he stretched out his hand to her. But since he had chosen her, the woman came to him and together they went back to Tara.

Before long Eochai Airem discovered that it was Etain's daughter, and his own, that he had chosen instead of Etain herself. He returned to Bri Leith to sack the sidhe and punish Midir for his trick, but before he had time to attack the dwelling Etain made herself known to him in unmistakable ways. Eochai seized his wife and carried her away from Bri Leith and back to Tara. And so for the second time Midir lost his beloved Etain.

The Children of Lir

LIR, one of the Tuatha De Danaan, and his wife Eve had two children, Fionnuala and Aed, whom they loved dearly. After a few years twin boys, Conn and Fiacra, were born and their parents were delighted. But their joy was short-lived for shortly after the birth of the twins, Eve fell ill and died. Her husband was racked with grief. With his beautiful wife gone he wanted to die himself but his love for his children kept him alive.

Eve's father, the king of the Tuatha de Danaan at that time was called Bodb Dearg, or Bov the Red. He was a wise man and a beloved king and he too was very sad at his daughter's death. Because he loved Lir and did not want to lose his friendship he called him to his fort and gave him his second foster daughter, Aoife, to be his wife. Aoife was as beautiful as Eve had been and she loved her sister's children, so for a year or two Lir and his family were happy again. Everyone who met the children of Lir loved them and the king himself was so fond of them that he often left his own fort to come to Lir's house to visit them. As for Lir, he was so devoted to his children that they slept in his room so that he could see them first thing in the morning and last thing at night.

After a while Aoife grew jealous of all the attention that the children were getting from both Lir and Bodb. Her jealousy grew as the children grew and eventually it turned into hatred. In the end she could stand their presence no longer and took to her bed. For a year she lay tormented by jealousy. At last she decided to get rid of them so that she alone would have the love of her husband and her foster father.

One morning she called the children to her quarters and told them they were going to visit their grandfather, Bodb Dearg. The younger children were pleased for they loved the excitement of the king's house, but Fionnuala was afraid. The night before she had a

37

disturbing dream and she sensed that Aoife was plotting harm. She tried to talk her stepmother out of going to visit the king but Aoife was determined to carry out her plan and would not listen to Fionnuala's plea. Sadly the girl resigned herself to her fate.

The charioteers were called and they yoked the horses to the chariot. Aoife hurried the children out of the house and into her chariot, for she did not want Lir to see her take them away. The horses were whipped up and they swept out of Lir's fort. Halfway to Bodb's fort Aoife ordered the charioteers to rein in. Leaving the children in the chariot she called the servants aside and ordered them to take the children into the wood and kill them. The charioteers were appalled by this command. They were warriors, hardened in battle, but they could not carry out Aoife's cruel orders. They told Aoife that they would not kill the helpless children and they warned her of the punishment that would surely follow such a crime. In a rage, the queen seized a sword from one of the men so that she could kill the children herself, but her cruel heart failed her and she could not bring herself to murder the children that she had once loved.

Fionnuala, waiting in the chariot, was suspicious and scared, but she did not want to alarm her brothers for they were unaware that anything was wrong and so she said nothing. When Aoife came back to the chariot to rejoin the children she was full of feigned affection and kindness towards them. They drove westward in the direction of Bodb Dearg's court until they came to a lake surrounded by oak trees called Lough Derravaragh, the lake of Oaks, and there they halted.

Aoife asked the children if they would like to bathe in the lake and wash off the dust of the journey. The three boys jumped down out of the chariot and rushed into the water, splashing and shouting, but Fionnuala hung back. When Aoife saw this she ordered the girl to join her brothers and Fionnuala waded into the lough.

As soon as the children were all together Aoife took a druid's wand from the folds of her cloak and, pointing it at each child in turn, she raised her voice and chanted a spell:

'Children of Lir, good fortune has always followed you but now your good fortune is over! From now on flocks of waterfowl will be your only family, and your crying will be mingled with the cries of birds.'

By the time her chant was over, Fionnuala, Conn, Aed and Fiacra had disappeared and swimming on the lake where the children had been were four beautiful white swans.

The four swans turned towards Aoife as she stood on the shore and speaking in the voices of the children of Lir cried out to her, 'Oh, why did you do this to us? We did you no harm. You were our stepmother. You loved us once, so have pity on us now! Give us back our own shape! Oh, please, we implore you do not leave us like this!'

Aoife did not answer them. She turned a deaf ear to their pitiful cries and stared unmoved as the frantic creatures threshed the water. Fionnuala rushed to the edge of the lake and hissed at Aoife, 'You will pay dearly for this, Aoife! Our kinsmen will avenge us and they will punish you for this cruel spell. And they will comfort us as best they can.' Still Aoife did not speak. Fionnuala stretched out her long neck towards her stepmother and pleaded with her for the last time.

'Oh, Aoife, if you won't give us back our shape, at least put some limit on this enchantment! Do not condemn us to be swans for ever!'

Aoife's icy heart melted at last as she listened to Fionnuala's desperate pleas, but her remorse came too late to save the children.

'If I could break the spell now, I would,' she cried, 'but what is done is done, and the spell it is too powerful for me to undo. I cannot revoke it but I have the power to ease it. You will not be swans for ever. But you must keep the shape of swans for nine hundred years and must stay on the water, not on dry land! You will spend three hundred years here on Lough Derravaragh, three hundred years on the Sea of Moyle and the last three hundred years by the Atlantic Ocean. When a king from the North marries a queen from the South, and you hear the sound of a bell pealing out a new faith, you will know that your exile is over. Till then, though you will have the appearance of swans, you will speak with your own voices and reason with your own minds and feel with your own noble hearts! Your cry will not be the strange cry of the swan. Instead you will be given a gift of music so sweet that it will comfort all who hear it. But go away from me now! The very sight of you torments me. I cannot bear the sorrow and hardship I have brought on you and I dread Lir's anger and grief.'

Fionnuala's head dipped in despair as she turned slowly away from Aoife and swam back to rejoin her brothers. Then the four swans paddled slowly away. As the full horror of her deed dawned on her, Aoife ran from the shore to her waiting chariot. The frightened charioteers were as anxious as she to get away from the place, and they whipped up the horses and galloped to Bodb Dearg's fort. There Aoife was welcomed by her father, but when he saw that she was alone, he was surprised and disappointed.

'Where are your stepchildren?' he asked her. 'Why didn't you bring them to see me?'

This was the moment Aoife had been dreading, so she had a story ready.

'I came alone,' she said to Bodb Dearg, 'because Lir is jealous of your love for his children and he would not let me bring them to your house. He is afraid that you will take them and keep them as your own!'

When Bodb Dearg heard this he was very angry at first but then he became suspicious. He felt that Aoife was telling a lie, so he sent a message to Lir inviting him to come and visit him the next day as he wanted to talk to him. He told him to be sure to bring his children with him. When Lir received this message he was horrified. He had been alarmed when he had heard that Aoife and his children had hurried away from his fort and had gone to visit the king without telling him. He knew that his wife had come to hate his children and now he was afraid that she had harmed them.

Early next morning Lir and a company of his household set out for Bodb's fort to learn the fate of the children. They took the same south-westerly route as Aoife had taken and eventually they reached Lough Derravaragh.

From the middle of the lough, the children saw the chariots and troop approaching and joyfully Fionnuala called to her brothers to look towards the shore. Aed, Fiacra and Conn watched the company approaching as their sister cried out, 'I know who this is! It's our father's household and, look, there's Lir himself leading them. They are searching for us. That's why they look so sad! Let us get closer to them so they can hear our voices.'

The four swan-children flew to the lakeside and landed there with a clatter of wings. They called out their father's name and the names of his company. Lir heard his children's voices but he could not understand where the sound came from. He stood puzzled, straining his ears, and the children repeated his name. When Lir realized that it was the four swans that called to him he was heartstricken. He knew then that this enchantment was Aoife's evil work and that these swans were his children.

'Fionnuala, Aed, Fiacra, Conn! My beloved children! How can I help you?' he cried out. 'Is there any power that can restore you to your own shapes?'

'None!' Fionnuala called back. 'It was Aoife's jealousy that brought about this change on us. We are doomed to keep this shape for nine hundred years and no power of any kind can change that.'

When they heard this, the whole company let out a shout of anger and Lir cried, 'Come ashore, my dear children. Oh, my children, you have your own senses and voices and you can come on to dry land and live with us and we'll keep you safe.'

'We can't stop on dry land or live with our own people until nine hundred years have passed,' Fionnuala replied. 'We must stay here on the waters of Lough Derravaragh for three hundred years.' Then, seeing the sorrow on her father's face, she tried to comfort him. 'But we can talk to you and sing to you. Our music is enchanted music and it will comfort you and you will be able to forget what has happened.'

The swans started to sing and the desolation that Lir felt began to fade. His rage left him and he and his household were so soothed by the music that they stayed there listening until nightfall when they fell into a peaceful sleep.

In the morning the swans were far out on the lake, and Lir's grief returned. He cursed the day he had brought Aoife to his house and he called out the names of his children again and again. The swans flew to the lakeside and talked to him. Then he took a sad farewell of his swan-children and set off to tell the king the terrible news.

Bodb Dearg was waiting for him with Aoife at his side and when he heard the clatter of hoofs, he ran outside to meet Lir. When the king heard the story of Aoife's treachery he turned on her in a fury. 'You have brought a cruel fate on the children of Lir, so you deserve a great punishment. I will turn you into a demon of the air, doomed for ever to be driven through the clouds and the upper skies!'

As he pointed his druid's wand at her, a bitter blast swept suddenly through the place and in an instant Aoife was seized and flung aloft like a withered leaf, her screams mingling with the howling of the wind. As the hushed crowd watched, she was blown higher and higher until she disappeared from view, but they could still hear her shrieks and moans echoing in the gale. People say that you can still hear her voice on a stormy night sighing and sobbing above the sound of the wind.

When Aoife's cries had died away, Lir, Bodb and their followers went to Lough Derravaragh. The children were delighted with the company and talked to their friends and comforted them with their singing. People flocked from all over Ireland to listen to the music that brought peace and comfort to the sick at heart. Bodb Dearg and Lir stayed there, and gradually a large settlement grew up around the lake. Every evening the swans would swim to the shore and tell stories to the crowds and hear the news from all over Ireland and then they would sing the gathering to sleep.

Season followed season, and the children of Lir, surrounded by loving families and loyal friends, sometimes forgot what had befallen them and were as happy as it was possible for them to be, given their cruel fate.

Years turned into decades, and decades into centuries, until one morning Fionnuala knew that three hundred years had gone by and the time had come for them to go. Sorrowfully she broke the news to her brothers and to Lir and Bodb Dearg.

'Father, we must leave you very soon,' she told Lir. 'We have only one night more on Lough Derravaragh. The years we were allowed to spend here are over and we have to go north to the Sea of Moyle. Your love and companionship have made these calm waters a home from home for us, and it's a bitter blow that we cannot go back to our real home with you. It is our dreadful fate that, instead, we must now leave this quiet lake for the desolate waters of Moyle. There'll be no one there to talk to us or comfort us as you have done here. There'll be nothing for us there, but loneliness and pain.'

Lir and Bodb were as heartbroken as the children, and together they stayed at the side of the lough all that day telling stories and lamenting the cruel spell that was separating them. Then, as night fell, the swans began to sing their enchanted songs. Their father and friends listened to the music for the last time, and their grief melted away at the sound, as it had done throughout the three centuries of vigil, and they fell asleep.

At the break of day the whole company assembled at the water's edge and after a sad farewell the four swans rose into the air. They circled the wailing crowd below them and then, wheeling to the north with Fionnuala leading them, the four swan-children set off for the Sea of Moyle. They flew in arrow formation, dipping and rising, warbling plaintively to themselves as they went. A long sigh rose from the crowd as they gazed at the empty sky. Bodb Dearg and Lir, old men by now, got ready to return to their forts, for they could no longer bear to stay beside Lough Derravaragh. As soon as Bodb reached home he passed a law forbidding anyone to harm a swan and so it remains to this day.

The swans flew northwards, impelled by Aoife's curse, until they reached the Sea of Moyle. This was a stormy band of water between Ireland and Scotland. It was lashed by gales in spring, by ice and hail in winter. In this desolate place the only company the children had was seals and seabirds. Huge waves buffeted them and they were cold and lonely. There was no one to listen to their stories or appreciate their exquisite music. There was no one to be comforted by their song and it brought no ease to their own sad hearts.

One night a fierce storm rose up. Fionnuala shouted to her brothers above the thunder of the waves that if they were separated they must go to the Rock of Seals, Carraignarone, and wait there for one another.

The storm got worse. Great black thunderclouds piled up in the sky and the wind increased. Waves crashed into waves and rose like walls. Lightning split the sky, and the swans were scattered apart like sea spray. All night long they were flung through the air by the fierce gales and when dawn broke Fionnuala was so exhausted she could hardly fly, but she made her way to the meeting place she had named and landed there. She watched the sun rise out of a calm sea and climb into a clear sky, but there was no sign of Conn, Fiacra or Aed. Scanning the skies, Fionnuala began to weep at her own fate and the fate of her brothers. She sank down on the rock in despair, lamenting her loneliness and loss.

Suddenly she saw Conn flying towards the rock. He was so tired he could scarcely clear the waves. He landed beside her, too exhausted to speak, and Fionnuala put him under her right wing. A while later Fiacra appeared on the horizon, his wings heavy with seawater and his head drooping, and when he landed wearily on the rock his sister put him under her left wing. At last Aed arrived, beaten and spent, and crept beneath the feathers of Fionnuala's breast and there they rested till their strength returned.

One cruel winter there was a frost so hard that the Sea of Moyle turned into a sheet of ice and the children of Lir huddled together on a rock to try to keep warm. Their feathers became as hard and brittle as glass and they knew they must fly or freeze to death. When they tried to rise they discovered that they were frozen to the rock. They struggled to free themselves and when they finally did, they left behind them the skin of their feet and the tips of their wings. When the sea melted, they suffered the agony of the salt water in their wounds.

Winter after winter they suffered cold and every spring they were flung from rock to rock by the gales. They began to think their sufferings would never end.

One day as they were swimming near the mouth of the River

Bann on the northern coast of Ireland, the swan-children saw a troop of horsemen galloping along the riverbank. They swam to the side of the river asking each other in their own voices if they recognized the handsome band of riders. The horsemen heard the swans speak and knew they were the children of Lir. They had heard about Aoife's cruelty, for they were the sons of Bodb Dearg. The children talked eagerly to their friends, enquiring about Lir and Bodb. The horsemen told them that the two old men were together at Sidhe Fionnachaid, Lir's fort, celebrating the Feast of Age. Except for their sorrow at the loss of the children, they were happy and content. Fionnuala remembered her former life and cried out with home sickness:

'Lir and his household are happy tonight drinking and feasting in a warm house while his children live without shelter.

'Once we dressed in royal purple, now white feathers are our only covering.

'We used to drink wine and mead from precious goblets and now our drink is salt water and our food grains of sand.

'Hard rocks are our beds, or the crests of the waves, we, who used to sleep on pillows made from the soft down of birds.

'The sons of kings galloped with us across Bodb's hills, but our only companions now are the white waves of the sea.

'I, who loved to lie on the fragrant grass and feel the sun, must ride, without rest, the cold currents of the Sea of Moyle.'

The horsemen listened sadly to Fionnuala's lament and then said goodbye to her and her brothers and rode off to Lir's fort with the news of his children.

One day Fionnuala called her brothers to her and told them once more that three hundred years had gone by and it was time for them to leave the comfortless Sea of Moyle and go to the western ocean, to Inish Glora where they would spend the last term of their exile.

'And on the way,' she said, 'we will call at Sidhe Fionnachaid and see our father.'

They flew to Carraignarone, the rock where they had sheltered from so many storms and landed there. They took a last look at the desolate stretches of the Sea of Moyle and then rose gratefully into the sky and headed west.

As they flew over the lovely landscape of their childhood they scanned the ground below for their first glimpse of Lir's fort, but there was no sign of it. Bewildered, they flew lower and lower, wondering if they had lost their way, until, at last, they saw the familiar hill. They circled the place where Sidhe Fionnachaid had stood, their alarm growing with every turn. There was no sign of the rath or its walls, ramparts or green playing fields. There was no sign of life at all, only a rough grassy mound covered with weeds. Sadly they came to land in the centre of it and there they huddled together staring in disbelief at the scattered heaps of stones and the broken earthworks, the terraces overgrown with nettles and the ragwort and stunted gorse bushes that grew thickly on the slopes.

As they cowered there, their feathers ruffled by the wind that shivered across the drumlins, they remembered Sidhe Fionnachaid as they had left it with Aoife on that fateful morning, and their hearts nearly cracked with grief. They recalled the royal feasts, the chieftains and ladies listening to music, the harpists and the bards reciting their heroic tales. They remembered their comrades, the young men and beautiful girls who laughed together as they watched the hunts and chariot races, the chess games in the halls, and the hurling outside on the green. They remembered the druids with their wisdom, and the champions with their feats of strength. Now there were no doors, no fires, no feasts, not another living thing in sight.

The children of Lir raised their voices and keened a lament for all that had been lost, and the sound re-echoed round the deserted mound with only themselves to hear. Sadly they rose into the air and circled the ruins for the last time. Then they flew on to the western ocean to spend the last three hundred years of their exile.

The Atlantic Ocean was stormy but not as cold and deserted as the Sea of Moyle. When storms swept in from the west, the swan-children could shelter in the inlets and bays that indented the coastline. In one of these bays sat a small island called Inish Glora and on this island was a little lake where the swans would fly for shelter. There they would sing their matchless songs and birds would flock to Inish Glora from Achill and Aran and the other islands around the west of Ireland. They settled in the trees and listened in silence to music far sweeter than any they could ever make and the lough became known as the Lake of Birds. The music of the swans, full of longing for another age, would float across the water on a calm day and people who heard it would recall the old story of the children of Lir.

A new age had dawned in Ireland and the Tuatha De Danaan had been displaced by another race. A new religion had spread across the country, brought by Saint Patrick and his monks, and the people now worshipped the Christian God. The old Gods had gone underground. Mannanan, Lugh, Nuada, the children of Lir themselves, had become legends.

On a tiny island on the Lake of Birds a holy man had come to live. He had heard about the swans of Inish Glora who spoke with human voices and, like many others, he had heard the legend of the fate of the children of Lir. He felt that the time for their release must be close at hand and he wanted to be there to help them. He built a little church on the island and every morning and evening he rang a bronze bell as he began to pray.

One night the swans flew back to Inish Glora from the south. At dawn Conn and Fiacra and Aed woke in alarm as a sound they had never heard before rang out across the water. They moaned with fear and Fionnuala awoke. She too heard the sound, but her cry was one of happiness. She knew that the ringing of this bell announced the freedom that Aoife had promised nearly a thousand years before.

The four swans looked towards the wood on the little island and there they saw a small hut. Through the door they could see the hermit on his knees and beside him shone the bell that had awakened them. They listened to the monk chanting matins and answered with their own sweet music, but now the loneliness and longing of a thousand years was replaced by a note of hope.

Hearing the sound, the hermit hurried down to the lake. There in the morning light he saw four swans. He called to them across the water: 'Are you the children of Lir? Are you Fionnuala and Aed and Fiacra and Conn?'

The four swans crowded together on the lake but they didn't answer his question and they would not come close to land. Then Fionnuala dipped her head in assent.

'Don't be afraid! I won't hurt you,' said the saint. 'It is for your sake I have come to this lake. For hundreds of years people have heard echoes of your beautiful singing and have told the story of your exile. Your ordeal is nearly over now. A new religion, a religion of love has come to Ireland. Through it you will be freed.'

The swans listened to the hermit's comforting words and trusted him, so they followed him ashore. He made a silver chain and tied it round their necks and linked them together, so that they would never be parted again. The children of Lir lived in the saint's hut, talking and praying with him. He fed them and protected them, and they sang for him in return. Although the last part of Aoife's spell had still to come to pass before they could regain their own shapes, they were happy there and peaceful at last.

Now while they were living with the monk on Inish Glora, Lairgren, the king of Connacht, went south to Munster and took a king's daughter for his wife, and through this marriage the last part of Aoife's prophecy came to pass.

When the new queen arrived in Connacht, she heard about the music of the wonderful swans who lived on the Lake of Birds. She told her husband to bring them to her so that she could hear them for herself. Lairgren refused for he knew that the saint would not allow the swans to leave his island. But his wife was determined to hear them and she threatened to leave her husband and go back to her father's house if her wish was not granted. This would have been a great disgrace for Lairgren, so he sent a message to the hermit ordering him to send the swans to his court as a gift for the new queen. The saint refused and the messenger reported this to the king. Lairgren was furious that his orders had been ignored, and he went in person to the Lake of Birds. The hermit saw him coming over the water and put the swans into the little church for safety. Then he went down to the shore to meet the king.

'Is it true that you turned my messenger away and would not grant the favour I asked?' the king demanded.

'It is true,' said the holy man. 'I refused the king's messenger and I will refuse the king himself. The children of Lir have found sanctuary in my church and there they will stay!'

Lairgren pushed the monk aside and stormed into the church. He seized the chains that linked the swans to one another and dragged the frightened creatures out of the church. The terrified swans struggled with all their strength, frantically beating the air with their wings, but Lairgren pulled them away from the door and towards the water. He had only taken a few steps when the tumult behind him stopped and he turned round quickly to see why. As he looked, the plumage of the swans fell away and lying on the ground, chained together, were four people, ages old, a frail wrinkled woman and three feeble old men. Filled with horror at what he saw Lairgren rushed to his boat and fled from the place with the hermit's angry words ringing in his ears.

The monk hurried to the side of the four, frightened, old people lying helpless on the ground and tried to comfort them. Fionnuala, who knew her life was coming to an end, asked the saint to baptize her brothers and herself. He sprinkled water on their heads from the Lake of Birds and blessed them. When this was done Fionnuala said to him, 'We are dying. My kind friend, we are as sad to leave you as you are to see us go. Bury us here where we found peace. When we were swans, I sheltered my brothers under my wings, Conn at my right side, Fiacra at my left and Aed beside my breast, so let us lie like this in our grave.'

Then the children of Lir died peacefully, the saint at their side, and were buried as Fionnuala had requested. Over their grave the hermit raised a stone and on it, in ogham script, he carved their names.

Over Nine Waves:
the Milesians Come to Ireland

Aᴼᴼᴿ ᴛʜᴇ ʙᴀᴛᴛʟᴇ ᴏꜰ ᴍᴏʏᴛᴜʀᴀ, the Fomorians did not return to Ireland to harry the people. The powerful Tuatha De Danaan were the rulers now, and the country was at peace. Ireland was a beautiful country, the coastline fringed with high mountains and below the wooded slopes lay deep valleys, fertile plains and marshy bogs. The rivers and lakes were full of fish, cattle grazed on the plains and herds of pigs rooted for acorns in the oak forests. Bees hummed among the heather in the bogs and the woods rang loud with birdsong. The weather was not too hot in summer, nor too cold in winter, so crops grew abundantly and there was plenty of food. The island wasn't overcrowded and there was room enough for everyone.

In the north of Spain lived another tribe, the Sons of Mil. The Milesians were skilled in magic too, and for generations had been a wandering people. They had travelled to distant places, and had gone as far as Greece and Egypt. At last they had settled in Spain, and Bregan, one of their kings, built a tower so high that from it the Milesians could see great distances in every direction. One clear day a learned magician called Ith climbed the tower and in the north-west he saw a shadowy outline. As he stared, he thought he could see an island with high mountains hazy in the distance. The longer he looked the clearer the outline became until he was sure another country lay on the horizon. He quickly came down from the tower and ran to tell his brothers what he had seen. He tried to persuade them to go with him to find out what this distant island was like but, as he described what he had seen, they laughed at him.

'You have seen nothing but stormclouds piling up on the horizon. We will not risk men and ships on these stormy waters to follow a mirage!' his brothers mocked. But Ith's son and a few others believed his story so they made ready for the expedition and set sail.

It was indeed a stormy journey and sometimes Ith feared his brothers might have been right, but he kept to his northerly course. After several days he and his companions saw a coastline faint on the horizon. As they sailed closer they saw how beautiful the island was and, praising Ith, the Milesians rowed into a sheltered bay and pulled their ships ashore.

They made their way without any hindrance through the country, until they came to where the leaders of the Tuatha De Danaan were gathered.

The three kings who ruled Ireland at the time were brothers and when Ith arrived at their fort at Aileach they were quarrelling among themselves as to who had seized the greatest part of their father's wealth and lands. Ith was amazed that such a disagreement should take place in a land where was plenty for all.

'Settle your differences,' he told them. 'There is no need for brothers to quarrel over such things. You should treat each other fairly. Your father has been generous to you and the land you have inherited is beautiful. It has fertile soil and the waters teem with fish. You have grain and honey and salmon to eat. The weather is comfortable. You don't suffer from too much heat or too much cold. This lovely island can give you everything you need.' The kings stopped arguing to listen to Ith's wise counsel and, having delivered his judgement, Ith returned to his ship.

But Ith's praise of their land disquieted the kings. They were afraid that he meant to take it for himself, since he had praised it so much. In their alarm they forgot the quarrel they had with one another and together they made a plot to kill Ith. They sent some soldiers after him and before he reached his ship they ambushed him and left him fatally wounded. His son and his companions, though wounded themselves, carried their leader to the boat and made for home as fast as they could, but when they reached land Ith was dead. They brought him ashore, lamenting his death, and showed his body to his kinsmen. Ith had been a wise and just man and his murder angered the Milesians. They resolved to sail to Ireland and take revenge for the treachery of the Tuatha De Danaan.

Then the Sons of Mil and their neighbours, the Gaels, sent

messengers far and wide to all the countries they had visited over the years. They told their allies the story of Ith's death and recruited warriors everywhere they went. They returned to their own country with a huge army and built ships, laid in supplies and got ready for the expedition. A great host of people, Milesians and Gaels, assembled in Brigaton, chiefs and warriors and with them ordinary people, men and women both.

They set sail in a huge fleet, sixty-five ships in all, and on the day before the first day of May they saw the island rise slowly out of the sea ahead of them. Then they raced each other, sailing and rowing with all their strength, to see who would be first to set foot in Ireland.

This time the Tuatha De Danaan were expecting them. They hurried to the shore and watched helplessly as the Milesian fleet approached with great speed. The De Danaans had made no armed preparations for war so their leaders asked their magicians to use their druidic powers to halt the approach of the invaders.

The druids began to work their spells and the outline of the shore began to shimmer and waver, until the Milesians saw land and sea swirling together in one confusing mass. The approaching ships were completely engulfed in a mist. Cloud closed round them and the sailors lost their bearings completely. Three times they circled the island, frightened and helpless. At last, through a break in the fog, they saw an inlet into which the fleet could sail and here they anchored.

Disembarking quickly, glad to be ashore, they began to march to Tara to confront the three De Danaan kings. On the way they met the three queens of Ireland, Eiriu, Fodla and Banba, who prophesied to them that the island of Ireland would belong to them and to their children for ever. This gave the Milesians encouragement and they pressed on with renewed will. At Tara, they found the three kings who had killed Ith in council. The Milesians chose Amergin, a poet and one of their leaders, to meet the De Danaan kings and give them an ultimatum. Amergin went into the hall where the kings were in council and told them the choices they had: to give over their country peacefully, or to fight to keep it. The loss of their homeland was the price they would have to pay for the murder of Ith.

Though they were not ready for battle, the Tuatha De Danaan had no notion of handing over their land without a struggle, so they played for time. 'Let your poets and wise men make an offer,' they said, 'but it must be a fair offer, otherwise our druids will kill you with their spells.'

So Amergin made his offer.

'We will go back to our boats and retreat from the shore over the distance of nine waves. Then we will come back over the nine waves, disembark and take this island by force if need be. But if you can prevent us setting foot on the shore, we will turn our boats homewards and we will never trouble you again.'

The Tuatha De Danaan were pleased with this offer. They were sure that their druids' power was strong enough to prevent the Milesians landing, so they agreed to the terms.

Amergin and his companions put out to sea over the space of nine waves and then turned to approach the shore. Immediately a huge storm blew up and gravel on the sea bed rose to the surface with the force of the wind. Waves rose in front of the boats as tall as the cliffs along the strand. In the tempestuous breakers the boats were pitched and tossed. They lost sight of each other in the deep troughs and were driven westward and scattered in every direction until they were exhausted. Many, many boats foundered in the boiling sea.

Amergin and the other leaders knew that the storm was not a natural one, but one called up by the power of the druids. They did not know how far from land they had been driven, so Amergin's brother climbed to the top of the mast to see if land was visible over the towering waves. He was flung from the mast by a fierce gust of wind and crashed to his death on the deck below. The people in the boat were terrified and angry. They ranted at Amergin and begged him to use his powers to calm the sea and save them. Amergin, buffeted by the winds and waves, made his way forward and clinging to the prow, his voice rising above the roar of the waves, he invoked the spirit of the land of Ireland, calling out to it, praising its beauty. Instantly there was a lull in the wind, the dreadful noise ceased and the sea became calm. Swiftly the boat headed for land over nine waves, with Amergin like a figurehead leaning forward in the prow. As soon as the keel of the boat touched bottom, Amergin jumped out and waded ashore. He put his right foot on dry land at Inver Sceine and then, standing on the shore of Ireland, he chanted this poem,

> 'I am the wind on the sea.
> I am the wave of the ocean.
> I am a powerful bull.
> I am an eagle on the rock.
> I am the brightness of the sun.
> I am a fierce wild boar.
> I am a salmon in the pool.
> I am the wisdom of art.
> I am a spear, sharp in battle.
> I am the god that puts fire in the brain.'

Other ships pulled ashore and the men and women who had survived the storm disembarked. They were grateful to be alive and more willing than before to fight the Tuatha De Danaan whose magical powers had cost them so many lives. They fell into formation and marched to meet their enemy.

The Tuatha De were dismayed to see the Milesians land in spite of their druids' efforts and they hastily marshalled their forces. Then they too marched to battle.

The first skirmish was won by the Gaels and Milesians but the Tuatha De mustered again and on the plain of Tailtinn faced the invaders. It was a fierce battle. The Milesians, remembering Ith and their lost kinsmen, fought fiercely. The Tuatha De Danaan, knowing their territory was at stake, fought to the death. The three De Danaan kings and their three queens were killed in the battle and when their followers saw this happen they lost heart. They were pushed back to the sea by the triumphant Milesians. They too had suffered losses, but they had won the battle for the land.

Then the Milesians divided Ireland into provinces: Ulster in the north, Munster in the south, Leinster in the east and Connacht in the west and, at the centre, Tara. Each province had its own king, chiefs and champions, but the High King, who lived in Tara, ruled the country, helped by the provincial kings and chiefs.

As for the Tuatha De Danaan, though they had been defeated by the Milesians at the battle of Tailtinn, they did not leave Ireland. They went underground to inhabit the mounds and earthworks known as *sidhes* that are scattered all over the country. Above them, in the upper kingdom, the human inhabitants of Ireland, the descendants of the Milesians and Gaels, lived and died, helped and sometimes hindered by the People of the Sidhe. From time to time, down through the ages, these mysterious, imperishable people entered the world of mortals. Sometimes they fell in love with human beings and at other times they held humans in thrall with their beauty and their haunting music. But their kingdom was that Happy Otherworld under the earth and they always went back there to the Land of the Ever Young.

The Voyage of Bran

THERE WAS A GATHERING OF CHIEFS one day in the fort of Bran, the son of Febal. They had come from neighbouring forts with some of their followers to celebrate the great feast of Bealtaine, which falls on the first of May.

As his guests listened to the musicians and poets, and cheered on the champions, and ate and drank their fill, Bran himself left the gathering to get away from the noise. The guards opened the gates of the fort and let him out on the ramparts where he stood looking across the plain he knew so well, glad of the silence and glad to be alone. Suddenly, at his back, he heard music. Not the sound of the harps he had just left, but a music stranger and sweeter than anything he had ever heard. He turned round to see who the musician was who could make music so plaintive and beautiful, but he saw no one on the deserted ramparts of his rath. The music sounded behind his back again, and he turned swiftly towards the sound. Again there was no one there and once more the music came from behind him.

Bran was bewildered at first, but then he realized he was listening to the music of the Sidhe and became afraid. He had heard about the music from the Happy Otherworld that lay beneath the grassy mounds where the banished Tuatha De Danaan lived. He had heard people tell how snatches of it were blown in from the sea and it was said that the music was so sweet that women in pain and wounded men found peace as they listened to it.

As he listened, enthralled, the mysterious sounds soothed him until his fear left him and he became drowsier and drowsier. Then he could stay awake no longer and, lying down on the grassy slope, he fell asleep.

When Bran awoke it was to the ordinary, happy sounds of a spring day all around him; there was not even an echo of the strange music in the air. He sat up and as he looked round the familiar place something gleamed in the grass beside him. It was the branch of an apple tree.

Bran gazed at it, spellbound. The bough was made of silver that shone with a frosty brightness and half-hidden in the leaves a sprig of apple blossom glinted like glass. Lifting the branch carefully, he returned to the fort to tell the gathering about the mysterious music he had heard and to show his guests the marvellous bough. A silence fell as Bran entered the hall carrying the jewelled branch aloft. People gazed at it in amazement and delight, wondering where it came from. As Bran opened his mouth to tell them how he had found it and to describe the music he had heard, a woman appeared out of nowhere and stood in the centre of the room. She was wearing clothes that were different from anything anyone there had ever seen and she was so beautiful that the company held its breath. Since the gates were locked and guarded, the crowd realized that this woman in their midst could not be a mortal. They stared in awe at this woman of the Sidhe, one of those ageless ones who lives under the great mounds and under the water of rivers and lakes. They had heard about those beings who visit the world of men in human form from century to century, but who are not human, for they possessed that gift that mortals yearn for, the gift of eternal youth. Turning towards Bran the woman began to sing these words:

'This silver apple branch comes from a distant isle, the playground of the horses of Manannan Mac Lir.
In the south of the island is a glorious plain raised high by four shining columns.
Huge crowds hold their games on this silver-white plain, boats race against chariots, and the blossoms fall from the trees.

From one ancient tree, a chorus of birds sings out the hours.
All is harmony and peace in this fertile, well-tilled land.
Music sweetens the ear and colour delights the eye.
Brightness falls from the air and the sea washes against the cliffs like a crystal veil.

In this fair island there is nothing rough or harsh.
No weeping or sobbing is heard there and treachery is unknown.
There are no cries of lamentation or grief, no weakness or illness.
No death.

On the plain of the sea, golden chariots rise with the tide towards
the sun.
On the broad plain, the plain of sport, silver and bronze chariots
shine out.
Horses of many colours race on the margin of the waves, horses
that are yellow, gold and crimson and horses that are as blue as
the sky.
At sunrise a fair man appears lighting the level lands.
On the sea-washed plain he rides, stirring the sea till it looks like
blood.

A band of strangers will come to this island over the waves.
They will hear the music which comes from a stone, music that
swells with hundreds of voices.
Those sailors will know neither illness nor death.
Fortune will bring them to the Island of Women and for them there
will be no ebb tide.

Though all can hear me, Bran, my song is for you,
Don't let tiredness delay you.
Don't wait to drink wine.
Begin the voyage across the clear sea to the beautiful land I have
promised.'

As her song ended the branch in Bran's hand began to move. He
tightened his grip on it, but it leapt from his grasp and into the
woman's outstretched hand and she and the glittering bough disappeared.

Bran wasted no time. He gathered together a company of sailors,
thirty in all, and the next day they set sail. They rowed without rest
for two days and two nights, taking turns at the oars, skimming
over the white crests of the waves. They met no other boat and saw
no sign of land or life in all that time. Then suddenly, on the

horizon, the crest of the waves got higher and higher and they saw a chariot coming towards them, drawn by a big horse whose mane was tossing in the tide. In the chariot they saw the god of the sea, Manannan Mac Lir. As Manannan came closer to the boat he began to sing:

'Bran's boat skims over calm waters.
Bran's ship is revelling in a clear sea, but to me, in my chariot, it is a flowery plain.

In my gentle land, the home of Manannan Mac Lir, sea horses glisten in the sun, and rivers pour forth honey.
Flowers are growing where Bran sees waves.

Bran sees the speckled salmon that are calves and lambs to me and one horse only, coming towards his boat.
But there are many others beside it, invisible to him.

His boat is sailing through an oak wood.
There's a fragrant fruit grove at the curragh's prow, an orchard of blossom and fruit.

The scent of vines hangs in the air and the golden leaves that shine in the sun will never fall

I am Manannan, son of Lir.
In human shape I appear to Bran, my chariot speeding over the waves.

Row steadily, Bran, row steadily over my kingdom and you will reach the Land of Women before the setting of the sun.'

Manannan Mac Lir and his chariot disappeared under the waves and Bran and his companions rowed on.

Soon after the visitation of the sea god, they reached an island and Bran ordered the sailors to row all round it before he would put to shore. Crowded on the beach were a great number of people pointing and laughing at the strangers.

'I am Bran, son of Febal,' he called out above the noise. 'We have been on the sea now for three days since we left our home in

Ireland. We are looking for the Island of Women.'

There was no reply. Instead the laughter got louder. Bran circled the island again and its strange inhabitants never stopped gaping at them, great gusts of laughter coming out to the boat.

One of Bran's crew was chosen to go ashore on this Island of Joy so the boat pulled into land. No one put out a hand to help pull it ashore and the laughter continued without a pause. The moment the sailor set foot on the land, he too began to laugh and gape and point at Bran and his crew. He joined the crowd on the seashore and though Bran called his name over and over again, he didn't answer but stared at them as if he had never seen them before and his laughter became loudest of all.

Bran circled the island again and again and when the boat came alongside the laughing sailor, his crewmates called him by name and urged him to leave the island and join them on the boat. Each time he stared and laughed in turn, as if they were complete strangers. As they went round the island for the last time, the sailors called out to their companion that they were leaving the island and begged him to come aboard the ship, but he gave no sign that he heard a single word. Sadly they turned their boat away from the staring crowd and set course for the open sea.

As evening approached and the light began to fade, they saw in the distance the misty outline of another island. They pulled harder on their oars and soon arrived at the shore. They saw a landing place and beside it stood a woman. Then they knew they had come to the Island of Women that Manannan Mac Lir had promised them.

'You are welcome here, Bran son of Febal,' the woman said and she waved them to the landing place. Remembering the fate of the sailor on the Island of Joy, Bran kept the boat offshore and wouldn't let its prow come into contact with the land. Suddenly the woman threw a ball of thread straight at his head. Instinctively Bran put up his hand to stop it and it stuck to his hand. He tried again and again to throw it back to her but could not. The woman still held on to the other end of the thread and now she began to pull steadily on it. Fine and delicate though the thread looked, Bran and his boatload of sailors found themselves being pulled slowly but surely to land.

Bran got out of the boat as if in a trance, and his sailors came behind him. Like sleepwalkers they followed the woman up from the shore until they came to a large house full of women. Inside a feast was straight away put in front of them. After days on ship's rations the sailors ate hungrily but no matter how much they ate their plates remained laden. When at last they could eat no more, the leader of the women brought them to a dormitory. Each man had a bed to himself and they stretched out gratefully and were soon asleep.

In the morning another feast was waiting. All day long there was music, games, drinking, the company of the women. They could have anything they wanted, and time flew past. They forgot Ireland, their families, their abandoned companion on the Island of Joy; they forgot everything except the pleasure and comfort that was theirs on the Island of Women.

Bran and his men lived in great contentment for a year until Nechtan, one of the sailors, felt a wave of homesickness come over him and a longing for his old life. He told the others of his sadness but they wouldn't listen to him. They said they would never leave the pleasures of the Island of Women. They told him to forget about home. The women on the island joined in to persuade Nechtan to stay but, in spite of all this pleading, his longing became stronger and he became more and more persistent in his request to return to Ireland.

Reluctantly Bran agreed to bring Nechtan home and they all got ready to depart. The night before they were to leave, the leader of the women came to Bran and warned him that if he returned home he would regret it for the rest of his life. When Bran heard this he made up his mind to stay. He told his followers of his change of plan and they were delighted. But Nechtan would not be appeased. He reminded the others of their former lives and insisted that they take him home. His constant complaints made his companions restless, so Bran decided to go.

'If you must go,' the leader of the women said to him, 'pick up your companion from the Island of Joy, but when you reach Ireland on no account set foot on the soil'

The women accompanied Bran and his sailors to the quay to take their farewells and sadly they left the place where, for a year, they had been so happy.

When they reached the Island of Joy their companion saw them coming and this time he detached himself from the gaping, grinning crowd, waded out to the boat and climbed in. His friends welcomed him with delight and then turned the boat into the open sea and set sail for home.

After three days at sea they arrived at the coast of Ireland at a place called Srub Brain. A man was standing at the quay and as the boat approached the land, he came over to help to pull the boat ashore, but Bran kept his distance. As their boat stood out from land a crowd gathered. One of them called out to Bran, 'Who are you and what is your business here?'

Bran answered, 'I am Bran, son of Febal. I left Ireland a year ago, but now I have returned . . .'

A gasp of astonishment rose from the people on the land.

'We have heard of Bran, son of Febal,' said one. 'He set out hundreds of years ago in a curragh to seek a magic land called the Island of Women. He has not been heard of since, but the Voyage of Bran is a story known to all of us. It is one of our oldest tales.'

At that Nechtan could bear it no longer. He leapt over the prow and waded to the shore. As soon as his foot touched the earth he turned into a handful of dust the same as if he'd been buried there for centuries.

A cry rose from Bran and his men as they saw the fate of their friend. They remembered what the woman of the Sidhe had foretold and realized they were doomed to sail the seas for ever. From the boat, they told their adventures to the people on the shore, and a scribe wrote it down. Then they said goodbye, turned their boat round and headed out to sea.

The watchers on the shore looked after them until they could see them no longer. And since that day no one has seen or heard of Bran and his companions.

FAME OUTLIVES LIFE

———

*The Ulster
Cycle*

The Weakness
of the Ulstermen

CRUNNCHU, a wealthy farmer, lived in a lonely place up among the hills of Ulster. He was dedicated and hardworking and soon became rich. He had plenty of stock and servants to attend him. His wife and he had four sons but his wife died when the children were still young and for years Crunnchu lived without a woman around the place.

One day as he was resting alone in his house, a tall young woman came into the hall where he lay. She was richly dressed and stately and there was a great dignity and confidence about her. She walked into Crunnchu's room as if she owned it. She did not speak to him but walked over to the hearth, sat down and calmly began to poke the fire. She sat all day there at the fireside and spoke to no one.

As mealtime approached she rose and went directly to where the cooking utensils were kept, as surely as if she'd put them there herself. She brought down a kneading trough and a sieve and began to prepare the evening meal. When it was ready Crunnchu and his family and the mysterious visitor ate the meal together in silence and afterwards the woman took a pail and went out to milk the cow. When she came back to the house she went straight to the kitchen and there, for the first time, she broke her silence as she instructed the servants. Then she returned to the hall where Crunnchu sat and took the seat beside him. When bedtime came and everyone went to their quarters, the woman stayed behind to make the fire safe and set the place in order for the night. Then she went to Crunnchu's room and lay down beside him. And so she became Crunnchu's wife and they lived happily together for many years. They loved each other and worked harmoniously together getting more prosperous all the time.

One day there was a great fair in Ulster. There were many such assemblies at that time where both men and women went to be entertained with games, contests and races. Crunnchu decided to attend the gathering and told his wife of his intention.

'Don't go!' she said to him, 'in case you let slip that I am with you here. If you mention my name to a soul our time together will be over.'

'I will not utter a word about you,' Crunnchu promised, and off he went to the assembly.

It was a marvellous occasion. A huge crowd had gathered and the king and queen were there and with them the champions and heroes of Ulster. There were tournaments and contests, feats of strength and skill, processions and games, but the climax of the meeting was the chariot race.

The king's magnificent chariot was brought to the field and his two fastest horses were yoked to it. All the other charioteers made ready their best horses to race against it, but the king's team won easily and the crowd roared with delight. Then the bards came out and began to praise the king and queen. Next they praised the poets and druids, then the champions and fighters. After that, the royal household and all the people assembled at the fair. Lastly they praised the king's horses and everyone joined in.

'These two horses of the king's are the best in the country!' they said to one another. 'Never before have a better pair raced. They are the fastest in Ireland!'

In his excitement Crunnchu forgot his promise. 'My wife can run faster than the king's horses!' he shouted out.

The king heard what Crunnchu said and was outraged. 'Seize the man who dared to say that!' he bellowed. 'Send for his wife and hold him here until she comes and races against my horses. *Then* we'll see who wins the race!'

Crunnchu was bound and held prisoner while messengers were sent to bring his wife to the meeting.

When the king's messengers arrived at Crunnchu's fort his wife welcomed them and asked why they had come.

'We've come to take you back with us to the fair,' they said. 'Your husband boasted to the king that you could run faster than his horses and now you must prove his word true. Until you do that your husband will remain a prisoner.'

The woman sighed in dismay. 'Oh, Crunnchu! What a foolish thing to say!' she murmured to herself. Then she turned to the messengers. 'As you can see for yourselves I'm going to have a child any day now. I'm in no condition to run a race. I am not going to the assembly!'

'That's bad news for your husband then!' said the messengers, 'The king will have him killed!'

When she heard this the woman was distraught. 'Then I'll *have* to go with you,' she said and she got into the chariot and went to the fair.

The crowd gathered round to look at her and because of her pregnant condition she felt humiliated under their stares.

'It is not right that I should be brought here in this state,' she cried, 'to be stared at by this crowd. You are disgracing me. Why was I brought here?'

'To race against the king's horses!' the crowd shouted at her.

'Can't you all see that my baby is due at any moment?' she cried. 'I cannot run a race!'

'Draw your swords and kill her husband!' the king commanded the messengers.

When she heard this, the woman turned to the bystanders in great distress. 'One of you, please help me!' she cried. 'A mother gave birth to each one of you so remember her and help me now!'

No one moved. The frantic woman turned back to the king. 'Have pity on me!' she pleaded. 'In a short time my baby will be born and *then* I'll race against your horses!'

'I can't wait!' said the king. 'You will run that race *now* or your husband will be killed!'

'Shame upon you all,' the woman said, 'for showing no respect or pity for me at this time! You will pay a heavy price for your cruelty.'

'What is your name?' the king demanded.

'My name and the name of the child I am carrying will stick to this place for ever!' she said. 'I am Macha, a daughter of Ocean. Now bring the horses here and I'll race against them!'

The horses were led out and Macha raced against them and out stripped them easily. Just as she reached the end of the course she fell to the ground and before the horses had finished the course, she gave birth to twins, a daughter and a son. As her twins were born Macha let out a loud scream and the strength of all the men who heard it suddenly ebbed away. They became like Macha lying on the ground, helpless and weak with labour pains.

Then Macha spoke again. 'From this day on you will be afflicted by this weakness because of your cruel treatment of me. At the hour of your greatest need, when you are under attack, every Ulsterman will become as defenceless and helpless as a woman giving birth to a child. For five days and four nights you will remain in that state and your descendants will be afflicted by the same weakness for nine generations!'

Both of these prophecies came true. Ever afterwards the place was known as Emain Macha, which means 'the Twins of Macha'. It was there that Conor Mac Nessa and the Red Branch warriors lived and there too that the great hero Cuchulainn grew up and trained in arms. And the Ulstermen *were* punished for their cruelty to Macha. For many years after that they lay powerless at the time of their greatest danger. Women and children were free from Macha's curse, but Cuchulainn was the only man to escape the weakness and that was because Lugh, his father, like Macha herself, was one of the Tuatha De Danaan. It was Cuchulainn who stood alone against the Men of Ireland when Medb mustered her forces and moved against Ulster to capture the Brown Bull of Cooley. As the Tain Bo Cuailgne, that famous cattle raid, took place, all the other Ulstermen lay in Emain Macha, weak and helpless, as Macha had foretold.

The Birth of Cuchulainn

CONOR MAC NESSA, king of Ulster, had a sister whose name was Dechtire. She lived in his fort at Emain Macha with fifty young girls as companions. One day, without any warning, they all disappeared completely. Neither the king nor any member of his household saw them go nor knew anything of their whereabouts.

For three years nothing was heard of them, until one day a large flock of birds flew across the country and landed at Emain Macha. As Conor and the Ulstermen watched helplessly the birds ate everything that grew round Emain Macha until not a blade of grass was left in a field nor a green leaf hanging on a tree. The land was devastated. Conor grew more and more angry. At last he ordered his chariot to be brought so that he could follow the birds and hunt them down. He was accompanied by his most important followers: Fergus Mac Roi, who had once been king himself, Amergin, the poet, the champion Conall Cearnach and Conall's mother, Finnchoem. With him too went Blai, the king's quartermaster, Sencha the Wise, chief judge of the Ulster court, and the satiric poet Bricriu Poison-Tongue. Other members of his household went as well.

The birds rose into the air as the large troop led by the king came galloping out of the fort. They flew south across Slieve Fuad heading in the direction of the Boyne river, where the great mound dwellings of the Tuatha De Danaan were clustered. The king and his followers raced after them unhindered and unchecked for in Ireland in those days there were no fences, ditches or stone walls, just wide open plains. But though the king's company galloped fast, the birds were always just ahead of them, graceful and beautiful. The birds, two by two, were joined together by a silver chain and they flew in companies of twenty with a leader at the head of each flock. As daylight began to fade three birds broke away from the group and led the king and his company towards Aengus Og's

69

tumulus at Brugh na Boinne. Just as they reached the river a heavy shower of snow fell and they lost sight of the birds. Conor ordered his men to dismount, unyoke the chariots and find some shelter for the night.

Fergus Mac Roi set off and found a little house. It was small and poorly furnished but the couple were welcoming so he returned to tell the king. The whole company pressed into the house to find a space for the night.

But Bricriu felt it was a very poor place, cramped and foodless, and he went out to look further. As he wandered round in the dark he heard a strange, low sound. He couldn't see what the source of the noise was, but he walked in the direction it came from. Suddenly he saw a large, spacious, well-lit house. He went to the door and looked in and there before him was a handsome couple, a young warrior richly dressed, strong and straight, and at his side a beautiful woman.

'You are welcome, Bricriu,' said the man. When he heard the warrior call him by name, Bricriu realized that he was one of the Tuatha De Danaan. And as he looked at the beauty and splendour of the young man he knew he was facing Lugh of the Long Arm, one of the most important personages from the Land of the Ever Young.

'You are welcome a thousand times over,' said the woman at Lugh's side, smiling with delight.

'Why does your wife greet me so warmly?' Bricriu asked.

'It is on *her* account that I have welcomed you,' Lugh replied. 'Has anyone been missing this while from Emain Macha?'

'Dechtire, the king's sister and her companions have been missing these last three years,' said Bricriu.

'Would you recognize them if you saw them?' Lugh asked the Ulsterman.

'Unless the years had changed them, I would,' replied Bricriu.

'They are here in this house,' said Lugh. 'The woman by my side is Dechtire herself. It was she and her companions who took on the shape of birds and went to Emain to lure Conor and the Ulstermen here to Brugh na Boinne.'

Bricriu looked at the woman and saw that it was indeed Dechtire.

Then Dechtire gave Bricriu a cloak with golden fringes and he started back to join his companions.

On his way back, Bricriu, a perverse and mischievous man, was fingering the lovely mantle when he began to think to himself that Conor would give a large treasure to recover his sister Dechtire and the lost girls. He said to himself, 'I won't mention that I've found Dechtire. I'll just say that I've found a rich house full of beautiful women, where we can all spend the night.'

Conor was delighted when he heard this news and without delay he and his companions went with Bricriu to Lugh's house. The woman who had greeted Bricriu was not there to greet the king because she had retired to give birth to a baby but they were made welcome by Lugh and retired for the night.

Next morning Lugh had gone but there in their midst was Dechtire and her newly born son. Gathered around her were the fifty girls who had been spirited away from Emain Macha.

Everyone knew that this child, the son of Lugh, was destined to be a great hero so they took counsel with each other about how he would be raised. Conor said the child should be given in fosterage to Finnchoem, Dechtire's sister, and Finnchoem was delighted to be chosen.

'He will be as precious to me as my own son, Conall Cearnach here.'

'He's as nearly your son as he can be,' said Bricriu. 'He's your sister's son.'

But the others objected to this for they all wanted a hand in rearing this chosen child.

'*I* should foster the boy,' said Sencha the judge. 'I am a skilful warrior, strong and fast in combat, but I am also a learned judge, wise and wary in disputes. Only the king may speak before I speak and he listens to my advice and accepts my arbitration, so he alone has more right than me to foster this child!'

At this Blai, the quartermaster, rose up to speak. 'Let me rear the child!' he said, 'and he will want for nothing. My house is so well stocked that I could feed the province of Ulster for a week and hardly notice it. If he comes to *me* he will be reared like a prince!'

'You are a presumptuous crowd!' said Fergus. '*I'm* the one to foster this child. I am the trusted envoy of the king and second only to him in richness and rank. Moreover I am a famous champion, battle-hardened and brave and a good craftsman as well. And I am just: I protect the weak, terrorize the tyrant and support the oppressed. I would be a worthy guardian of this child.'

'Now that you've all had your say,' Amergin said, 'perhaps you'll listen to *my* claim. I can rear the child as if he were a king. Men praise my bravery, my honour, my wisdom, my good luck, my venerability, my fame, my lineage and my eloquence. I am famous for all these things. Though I am a poet, I can still fight any man. I am beholden to no one but the king and I take orders only from him!'

'We will never be able to judge between ourselves!' said Sencha, 'so let Finnchoem take care of the child till we reach Emain Macha then Morann can judge between our claims.'

So Finnchoem took the child and they all set out for Ulster. Morann was consulted and pronounced the judgement that they *all* should share in the child's upbringing, each one teaching him his special skills. He said to the king, 'You, Conor, will be his special patron for he is your sister's child. Sencha, you can make an eloquent orator out of him. Blai, you can provide for his material needs. Fergus can take him on his knee, Finnchoem feed him and Conall Cearnach can be a brother to him. For this child is destined for greatness. He will be praised by warriors, sages and kings. He will be a hero to many. He will be the champion of Ulster and avenge her wrongs. He will defend her rivers and fords, he will fight her battles!'

Then Finnchoem and Amergin took the child to Dun Breth on the Plain of Muirthemne. Dechtire, the baby's natural mother, married Sualdam Mac Roich and they helped to rear the child as well. He was guided by his fosterers who taught him their special arts. He stayed at Dun Breth in a house made of oak until he was five years of age and the name he was given was Setanta.

The Boyhood Deeds
of Cuchulainn

THE BOY WAS CALLED SETANTA for the first five years of his life. He lived with his parents on Muirthemne Plain getting care and instruction from those who had been close to him when he was born.

When he was in his sixth year Setanta heard about the boy troop that Conor Mac Nessa had established at the Red Branch head-quarters at Emain Macha. These boys were specially selected by the king and they trained in martial exercises and were highly skilled with javelin, spear and sword. They played games as well, especially hurling. Conor was so proud of the achievements of this élite troop that he would spend a third of his day watching them training at arms and playing hurley on the green at Emain Macha. Another third of the day the king would spend playing chess. The last third in feasting and entertainment.

Setanta was determined to join these trainee warriors at Emain Macha and meet his uncle, Conor Mac Nessa, so he asked his mother if he could go to join the boys and play games with them.

'You're too young, son,' Dechtire told him. 'You'll have to wait for a champion or one of Conor's messengers to escort you to Emain Macha and protect you from the boys.'

'I can't wait that long!' exclaimed Setanta. 'I'm going *now* so just show me which direction I should take.'

'You head north,' said his mother, 'but you have a long tiring journey ahead of you and between you and Emain Macha lies steep Slieve Fuad.'

'I'll take my chance!' cried Setanta and away he went carrying his bronze stick and ball, his javelin, a toy spear and a small wooden shield. He made up games to shorten the journey. He hit the ball with the hurley stick and drove it a great distance. Then he flung the stick itself after the ball. Next he would launch his javelin on the same course and lastly the spear. As they flew through the air, Setanta would race after them, snatch the hurley, the ball and the javelin off the ground and pluck the spear from the air before it fell. In this way he soon reached Emain Macha.

The boys, one hundred and fifty in all, were on the green when Setanta arrived. Some were practising their fighting skills and others were playing hurley. Their captain was Folaman, Conor Mac Nessa's son. Setanta rushed headlong to join in the game. He got the ball and, dodging round the astonished boys, slipped it past them and scored a goal. Folaman was angry at the intrusion and he called the boys who were standing open-mouthed to gather round him.

'No one has a right to join our group and interrupt a game like this without having the manners to ask our permission!' he said angrily. 'It is an insult to us. Come on, we'll all attack him together and kill him. He deserves it. He's a nobody, some minor chieftain's son. A nonentity, otherwise he would have been given safe-conduct here.'

The boys flung their hurleys at Setanta's head, but he ducked and dodged so that not one of them struck him. When the balls showered down on him he fielded them with his arms and fists and elbows. They cast their spears at him but he deflected them all with the toy shield. Suddenly a war spasm came over the boy. His face became distorted and discoloured with anger, his eyes squinted and rolled, his mouth gaped wide open and his teeth were bared, his hair stood straight up on end and round his head played a bright circle of light.

In this frenzy, Setanta rushed at the crowd of boys and knocked to the ground fifty of them who were far bigger than he. He chased five others through the hall where the king and Fergus were playing chess and took a short cut by jumping across the board set out between the two men. Conor grabbed the child by the arms. 'Hold on, young man!' he said. 'This is rough treatment you're giving these boys!'

'They deserve it!' countered the boy. 'I'm Setanta, the son of Sualdam and your sister Dechtire. I've come a long way to join them and a strange welcome I've got!'

'Don't you know the rules of the group?' demanded the king. 'These boys are forbidden by a most solemn code to allow a newcomer to join them until he has first of all claimed their protection.'

'I didn't know that at all,' said Setanta, 'otherwise I would have done what is required.'

Conor called the boy corps to order and explained this to them. He asked them to take Setanta under their protection. They agreed and so Setanta was allowed to join their ranks.

No sooner had they restarted the game than Setanta attacked them anew. Fifty more boys fell to the ground when he charged. Their fathers thought their sons were dead but it was fear of Setanta that had put most of them to the ground.

'What are you doing *now*?' yelled the king. 'What's wrong with you!'

'I'll fell every one of them,' Setanta yelled back, 'until they agree to come under *my* protection in the same way that I came under *theirs*!'

The terrified boys agreed and placed themselves under the protection of Setanta, though he was not yet seven years old.

Culann's Hound:
Cuchulainn Gets His Name

SETANTA stayed with the boy corps, practising games and learning fighting techniques. He could take on the whole troop in a game, and win. One day, after he had beaten them all, the boys ganged up to attack him. Setanta defended himself, knocking fifty of them to the ground. Then he ran for refuge to the king's chamber and hid under Conor's couch. Because of his treatment of the boys, Conor, Fergus and other Ulstermen ran to the chamber and surrounded the royal platform. Thirty men sprang on to the couch, but Setanta lifted it off the ground with the thirty men still on it, and carried it on his shoulders to the middle of the house. Seeing this, Fergus and the king thought it best to intervene and make peace between Setanta and the other boys and settle the matter. This they did, and harmony was restored to Emain Macha.

Setanta slept on a special bed the king had made for him. It was supported by a huge stone at the head and another at the foot. One morning one of the king's men went in to rouse Setanta and the boy, alarmed to be awoken so suddenly, knocked the man cold with his fist. After that no one dared go near him when he was asleep.

When Setanta was nearly seven, Culann, a smith, came to Emain Macha to offer hospitality to the king.

'I am not rich,' he told Conor, 'I have no lands or inherited wealth. Everything I possess I earned with the tongs and the anvil. I want to honour you by welcoming you to my fort, but I beg you to limit your guests so that I can provide enough food for the feast.'

So Conor picked only the most famous and powerful of his household to go with him to Culann's feast.

It was the king's habit to visit the boy corps before leaving Emain Macha, so he went out to the field where they were playing games. He arrived in time to see Setanta play on his own against the whole one hundred and fifty boys and beat them. While he watched, they changed to shooting goals. Setanta put every ball past the troop and then, while in the goal alone, stopped every ball that his companions drove at him. After that he wrestled with the whole troop and tumbled them all and finally, in the stripping game, he took the cloaks and tunics off all of them, while they could not even take the brooch from his cloak.

Conor was delighted and amazed at the boy's prowess. He realized what a great champion Setanta would make and the warriors who were watching the young prodigy agreed. The king went over to the boy and spoke to him.

'I'm going to a feast tonight with a number of my most prestigious followers. I would like you, Setanta, to come too, as an honoured guest.'

'I want to finish the game,' the boy replied. 'I'll follow after you when I've played enough.'

The king accepted this answer and he and his followers set off in fifty chariots to Culann's fort. When they arrived they were greeted by the smith and brought to the hall where the feast had been laid out. When everyone was seated, Culann said to Conor, 'Is all your party present? Or is there someone else still to come?'

'No one,' replied the king, forgetting the arrangement he had made with Setanta.

'Then I'll let loose the hound,' the smith said. 'He's a savage animal that I got from Spain, and he's so strong that it takes three chains to hold him back and three men hanging on to the end of each chain. But he guards my stock and cattle well. I'll shut the gate of the enclosure now and let the animal free outside the walls.'

The fierce hound was let loose and it made a swift turn around the walls of the fortress. Then it lay down on a hummock where it could keep watch on the whole place. It crouched there, its head on its paws, savage and vigilant, ready to spring.

At Emain Macha, Setanta and the boys played until it was time to disperse, then all the others returned to their homes. Setanta set out alone for Culann's stronghold on the Plain of Muirthemne. He shortened his journey by hitting the ball with the hurley stick then casting the stick after it so it struck the ball before it fell. He kept up this game all the way and soon he was close to the smith's house.

When the hound saw the boy come racing over the green towards him, it let out a blood-curdling howl that rolled and echoed across the plain. All who heard it froze with dread but Setanta didn't even break his stroke at the sound. The hound leapt forward to tear the child apart, its massive jaws wide open. Setanta hurled the ball with all his strength down its gullet and so great was the force of the ball that it carried the animal's entrails out through its body. Then Setanta seized the hound by the hind legs and dashed it against a rock so hard that its body broke in fragments that scattered the ground. As the hound's savage roar echoed round the hall Conor started up in horror. When he could speak he said, 'It's a tragedy that I came here tonight!'

'Why is that?' the warriors asked fearfully.

'Because my sister's son Setanta was to follow me to the feast. And the roar of the hound is his death knell!'

The Ulstermen rose like one man and stormed out of the fort. Some went through the gates, but others swarmed over the ramparts in their haste to find the boy. Fastest of all was Fergus Mac Roi and he was the first to reach Setanta.

When he found the boy alive, standing over the remains of the hound, he lifted him on his shoulders and carried him back to Conor who still sat in the hall, too appalled to move. Fergus placed Setanta on the king's knee while the warriors let out shouts of jubilation and relief.

But Culann, the smith, remained outside for some time, heart-broken, looking down at the broken carcass of his hound. When at last he came back into the feasting hall, he addressed Conor and his retinue.

'It is indeed a tragedy that you came here tonight. And it was ill luck for me that I invited you at all. I'm glad for your mother's sake that you're still alive, boy, but I am ruined! Without my fierce hound to guard us, my household and my land will be raided and my flocks will be carried off. He saved us all from danger. Little boy, when you killed that hound you killed my most valued servant, and you've left me without protection.'

'Don't be angry, Culann!' Setanta said. 'I'll make it up to you.'

'How will you do that, child?' said the king.

'I will find another dog of the same breed and I'll rear him up until he can give you the same protection as the one I've just killed. In the meantime, Culann, *I* will protect your flocks and herds and lands. I will guard the whole Plain of Muirthemne, and no one will attack or rob you while I am on guard. I will be Culann's hound!'

'That's a fair settlement,' said the king.

'No wise man could do better,' said Cathbad the druid. 'And from now on, Setanta, your name must be Cuchulainn, the Hound of Culann!'

'I prefer my own name. I'd rather be called Setanta, son of Sualdam!' the boy protested.

'Don't say that,' Cathbad replied. 'In days to come the name Cuchulainn will be famous throughout Ireland and Scotland.'

'Then I'll take the name!' Setanta said stoutly and from that moment on he was known as Cuchulainn.

Cuchulainn
Takes Up Arms

WHEN CUCHULAINN was seven years old, he was playing one day in the north-eastern corner of Emain Macha. Across the compound, at a fair distance, he could see Cathbad the druid teaching druidic lore to eight elected pupils. One of the students asked Cathbad what omens, good or bad, were predicted for that day. Cathbad answered, 'Whoever takes up arms today will become the most famous warrior in Ireland. Though he will have a short, swift life, stories of his exploits will be told for ever.'

Across the distance between them, Cuchulainn heard this judgement and instantly threw away the toy weapons he had been playing with and ran to Conor Mac Nessa's room. 'All honour to you, heroic king!' he said.

'That's the greeting of someone who wants a favour,' smiled Conor. 'What is it you want, little boy?'

'To take up arms,' said Cuchulainn.

'To take up arms,' said the king, surprised and amused. 'Who put *that* notion into your head?'

'Cathbad the druid,' Cuchulainn replied.

The king thought for a moment or two. 'Cathbad would not give you false advice, child,' he said, and gave Cuchulainn two spears, a sword and a shield.

Cuchulainn took the weapons and practised with them, bending them, shaking them and swishing them through the air. He tested and balanced them, twisting and flexing the blades until they broke into fragments. The king gave him a second set and these too broke under the force of Cuchulainn's strength. Fourteen sets of weapons were destroyed in this way. In the end Cuchulainn said to the king. 'These weapons are not good enough for me. Give me some that will do justice to my skills!'

So Conor gave him his own weapons. Cuchulainn bent the blade of the sword until the tip met the hilt and this time the weapon took the stress. He shook and brandished the spear, testing its strength, and it too held fast. So did the shield. 'Now *these* are weapons worthy of me!' he said. 'I salute the king who owns them and the land and people he rules.'

Just then Cathbad came into Conor's room and saw Cuchulainn in battle gear. 'Is that child over there taking up arms?' he asked in surprise.

'He is indeed!' replied Conor.

'It's a sorry day then, for his mother's son!' exclaimed the druid.

'What are you saying?' demanded the king. 'Wasn't it *you* who advised him to take up arms!' He turned to Cuchulainn. 'You misleading little devil!' he shouted. 'Why did you tell me a lie?'

'Don't be angry with me,' Cuchulainn begged. 'I didn't tell a lie. It *was* Cathbad who put the idea of taking up arms into my head. I heard him telling his pupils that glory would follow the boy who took up arms today, even though his life would be short. Cathbad said he would be famous throughout Ireland and for all time. That's why I came to you!'

'I did indeed make that prophecy,' said Cathbad, 'and it *will* come true. You will be the most honoured and glorious hero in Ireland, but remember, your life will be brief.'

'I don't care about that!' Cuchulainn cried. 'I would happily live for one day only if my name and fame live after me.'

'Get into a chariot then, lad, so my word can be proved true,' said the druid.

A chariot was brought round and Cuchulainn seized it by the shaft and shook the frame so fiercely that the shaft broke and the chariot crashed to the ground. Another chariot was brought round and the same thing happened, until seventeen chariots lay splintered on the ground.

'Conor, my master, these chariots are no good to me. Bring round one that's worth having!'

Conor called his own charioteer, Ibar, to his side and said to him. 'Catch my own two horses and yoke them to my chariot and let him try *those*!'

Ibar did as he was ordered and Cuchulainn swung on the chariot shaft and shook it violently but it stood the strain. 'Now you could be proud of *this* chariot!' Cuchulainn announced.

'I *am* proud of it!' Ibar retorted. 'And now we'll turn the horses out to graze!'

'Not yet, Ibar,' said the boy. 'Drive me round Emain Macha first.'

Ibar got into the chariot with Cuchulainn and they did three circuits of the fort.

'Now! Out of the chariot, child, while I let the horses loose to graze,' said Ibar.

'Too soon for that,' said Cuchulainn. 'I know the horses are precious to you, but I'm precious too! Drive round to the boys' camp so they may congratulate me on taking up arms.'

When the boys saw Cuchulainn approaching in the king's chariot they sent a cheer into the air. 'Cuchulainn has taken up arms!' they yelled. 'Cuchulainn has taken up arms!' They crowded round the chariot wishing Cuchulainn luck and success in striking the first blow. 'We hope you are always victorious, Cuchulainn,' they said, 'even though we all think you have taken up arms too soon. Now you'll leave us and we'll miss your competition and your company.'

'I won't be leaving for good,' Cuchulainn told them. 'I only took up arms today because it's a lucky day.'

'*Now*, little boy,' said Ibar, 'we'll let the horses loose to graze.'

'By no means!' said Cuchulainn. 'Whip them up and off we go!'

'Where to?' asked the charioteer.

'As far as this wide road ahead will take us!' shouted the child.

'You're a real joker!' said Ibar, and off they went.

They galloped on towards Ath na Foraine, the look-out fort on Slieve Fuad.

'Why is it called that?' Cuchulainn asked Ibar.

'It's called that because every day one of the bravest Ulster warriors goes there and guards the province. If anyone crosses the boundaries bearing arms he is challenged to a fight. If a poet passes the fort on his way out of Ulster and is dissatisfied with the welcome he has received at Emain, the man on duty will compensate him and comfort him. If the poet's on his way in, heading for Conor's fort the champion will guarantee him safe-conduct and be rewarded with poems and songs in his honour.'

'Do you know who's on duty today, Ibar?' asked the boy.

'I do,' said Ibar. 'The foremost warrior of them all, Conall Cearnach.'

'Then head for the look-out fort!' ordered Cuchulainn.

At the water's edge they came on Conall. He looked at the boy in full battle gear. 'Has that child taken up arms?' he asked in disbelief.

'He has indeed,' the charioteer replied.

'Then I wish you victory and triumph,' said Conall. 'Though I think you're far too young to bear arms.'

Cuchulainn ignored this. 'What are you doing here, Conall?' he asked the champion.

'I'm here to protect the province of Ulster.'

'Go home, Conall. Let me take over the job for today,' said Cuchulainn.

'I think not, little son!' said Conall. 'You might be able to deal with a poet, but you would be no use at all against a fighter!'

'Then I'll keep going southwards to Lough Echtra. I believe another warrior takes up a stand there on the border. I might yet redden my hands with first blood before the day is out!'

'I'm coming with you, child, to keep you out of harm's way,' Conall said.

'I don't need you!' retorted Cuchulainn. .

'I'm coming with you whether you like it or not!' countered Conall. 'If any harm came to you, Conor Mac Nessa and the Ulstermen would blame me!'

Before Conall had time to yoke his horses Cuchulainn lit off as fast as the wind towards the border. He heard Conall's chariot racing after him and he knew that if a chance to fight arose Conall would not let him take it, so as soon as Conall's chariot drew abreast, Cuchulainn put a stone in his sling and let fly at it. The stone smashed through the shaft and brought the chariot to the ground. Conall was flung out dislocating his shoulder in the fall.

'Why did you do that?' Conall roared in a fury.

83

'I was only testing the accuracy of my aim,' replied the boy.

'Bad cess to you and your aim!' Conall yelled. 'I'm going no further. Even if an enemy should try to cut your head off, I'll make no move to save you!'

'The very thing I planned!' Cuchulainn said. 'You'll *have* to turn back for I know you Ulstermen are prevented by your military code from travelling in a faulty chariot.'

Conall turned back to the look-out fort on Slieve Fuad, and Ibar and Cuchulainn headed south till they came to Lough Echtra and there they stayed beside the lake.

As it began to get dark, Ibar said to Cuchulainn, 'I know it's not my place to mention it, but I think it's time to get back to Emain Macha, son. It's all right for you. You have a place reserved for you between King Conor's feet, but I have to take my chances among the servants and messengers of the household. It's high time I got back to scramble among them for my share!'

'Fetch the horses, then,' Cuchulainn said. The charioteer did so and they set off northwards towards home.

'What is the name of that high mountain, Ibar?' Cuchulainn asked. 'And what is the pile of white stones on the summit?'

'That's Slieve Mourne and the pile of stones on the top is Finncairn, the White Cairn.'

'It must be pleasant up there,' said Cuchulainn. 'Please bring me to Finncairn, Ibar,' he coaxed the charioteer. 'After all, this is your first outing with me!'

'You're a stubborn nuisance!' said Ibar. 'As you say, it's my first outing with you, boy, and, if I'm lucky enough to see Emain Macha again, it will definitely be my last! But if you stop pestering me I'll take you to Finncairn.'

When they reached the monument they looked down at the country spread out below them.

'Point out the landmarks to me,' said Cuchulainn, 'because I don't know this countryside at all.'

So Ibar pointed out Breg Plain, and the hills and forts near by, and in the distance the shining waters of the River Boyne and Aengus's fort at Brugh na Boinne.

'And this here?' asked Cuchulainn, pointing to a fort in the distance. 'Whose fort is that?'

'That is the fort of the three sons of Nechtan. A dangerous place. Nechtan himself was killed by Ulstermen and his sons boast that they have left more Ulstermen dead than are alive at this moment.'

'We'll go there!' said Cuchulainn.

'Are you mad?' said the charioteer. 'Whoever goes there it won't be me!'

'It *will* be you. You'll come with me dead or alive!'

'We may go there alive,' said Ibar, 'but we'll end up dead.'

When they reached the green in front of Nechtan's fort, Cuchulainn jumped from the chariot and ran up to the standing stone that was implanted in the ground. Around the pillar was an iron band. Carved on the band was a message from the sons of Nechtan to anyone who read the words, challenging him to single combat.

Cuchulainn read the message, then put both arms round the pillar and with all his might he wrenched it out of the earth and threw it into a small lake near by.

Ibar was terrified. 'You might have left it where it was, Cuchulainn!' he said. 'You'll get what's coming to you for doing a thing like that. A speedy end!'

'Give me peace!' said Cuchulainn. 'Put the rugs and covers over me. I'm going to sleep. Now don't wake me if only one man comes near. It's not worth it. But if there are more, then I'll get up.'

'You're on dangerous ground, my friend.' Ibar warned.

As the boy slept, Ibar sat in mortal dread, the horses' reins in his hands. Before long one of the sons of Nechtan came out on to the green.

'Don't dare to unharness those horses!' he cautioned Ibar.

'I have no intention of doing that,' the charioteer replied. 'As you can see I'm holding the reins.'

'Whose horses are they?'

'They're Conor Mac Nessa's piebald horses,' Ibar replied.

'I thought they were,' said Nechtan's son. 'What are Conor's horses doing on my territory?'

'A young boy took up arms today, hoping for good luck, and he has come here to show off his form,' Ibar answered.

'He won't find good luck here. If he were old enough to fight I'd have him sent back dead to Conor!' the man said angrily.

'Well, he's *not* old enough to fight,' said Ibar. 'It's out of the question. He's only seven years old.'

Crimson with anger, Cuchulainn threw off the covers. 'Of course I'm old enough to fight!' he yelled.

'It's a pity you said that!' said Nechtan's son menacingly.

'It will be a bigger pity for you when you meet me at the ford! But go and get your weapons. I don't attack unarmed men.'

As the man raced off to collect his weapons, Ibar said to Cuchulainn, 'You'd better be careful, child! You've just challenged Foill Mac Nechtain and he cannot be pierced by a sword or spear.'

'Then I'll put out his brains!' said the boy. As Foill raced back to attack him, Cuchulainn hurled an iron ball at his forehead and killed the man. Then he cut off Foill's head and set it at his feet.

Tuachell Mac Nechtain came rushing out of the dun. 'I suppose you're bragging already about what you've just done!' he roared.

'To kill just *one* man is nothing to boast about!' Cuchulainn shouted back.

'You'll never kill another! I'll see to that!' the man yelled.

'Get your weapons, then!'

As the man hurried off to get his weapons, Ibar said to Cuchulainn, 'Look out for this fellow. If you don't get him with the first blow, you'll never get him at all.'

'I'll use Conor's sword and I'll put his heart through his body at the first thrust!' Cuchulainn boasted, and that's what he did before Tuachell had time to draw his sword. Then he cut off his head as well, and laid it beside his brother's on the ground.

Out on to the green rushed the youngest son of Nechtan and yelled at Cuchulainn, 'My brothers were fools to fight you on the grass here. I'll fight you in deep water. Come down to the river!'

'This is Fannall Mac Nechtain and look out for him!' Ibar said to Cuchulainn as they ran down to the river. 'Fannall means "swallow" for like a swallow or a weasel he can travel across water. The best swimmer in the world cannot contend with him!'

'That's no threat to me!' Cuchulainn said. 'Do you know the River Callan that flows through Emain Macha? Well, when my companions get out of their depth there, I can take one on each of my shoulders, two more on my hands and tread water so lightly that my feet hardly get wet.'

Fannall Mac Nechtain jumped into the river and Cuchulainn leapt in after him. He grabbed Fannall and forced him down under the water. Then he cut off his head with Conor's sword and brought it to the riverbank as Fannall's body was carried away by the current. After that Cuchulainn and Ibar looted Nechtan's fort and filled their chariot with the spoils. They tied the heads of the three brothers to the front of the chariot and turned for home. They galloped like the wind across Breg Plain until they reached Slieve Fuad.

At the foot of Slieve Fuad, they startled a herd of wild deer who darted off when they heard the chariot approaching.

'What sort of strange, restless cattle are these?' Cuchulainn asked Ibar in wonderment.

'They're not cattle, they're wild deer,' Ibar told him. 'They live in the wild places on Slieve Fuad.'

'Whip up the horses and I'll catch one!' Cuchulainn commanded, and Ibar did so. They raced after the herd but the king's fat, well-fed horses couldn't overtake the deer and the chariot wheels bogged down in the soft ground. Cuchulainn leapt across the boards and raced after the deer on foot. He caught two of the biggest, handsomest stags, brought them back to the chariot and tied them to the shafts at the back. Then they whipped up the horses and got out of the bog.

As they were crossing Slieve Fuad, a flock of swans flew past them.

'What kind of bird are those, Ibar?' asked the boy. 'Are they tame or wild?'

'They're swans and they're wild,' Ibar told him. 'They fly inland to feed on the plains and rivers of Ireland.'

'Which would be the best thing to do?' Cuchulainn asked. 'To bring the birds back to Emain alive or dead?'

'It would be a real marvel if you could bring them back alive. Others can bring them back dead, but it's rare to bring one back alive.'

Cuchulainn set a stone in his sling and brought down twenty-four birds from the flock.

'Get the swans, Ibar!' he commanded.

'I can't get out of the chariot,' the charioteer said. 'The horses are galloping flat out and I daren't let go of the reins. The wheels are as sharp as scythes and they'd cut me down if I try to get over the side, and if I try to get out the back, past the stags, they'll gore me with their horns!'

'You're not much of a champion, Ibar!' said Cuchulainn. 'I'll tell you what I'll do. I'll control the horses with a full stare so they won't break their gallop when you drop the reins. Then I'll stare at the stags and subdue them in the same way so that they'll be cowed and lower their heads and *then* you can step out over their antlers!'

He turned a dark, intense stare on the horses and, though Ibar dropped the reins, the team galloped steadily on. He turned the same steady fierce look on the stags and the animals lowered their horns. Then Ibar stepped over the antlers of the wild deer and gathered up the swans which were lying stunned on the ground. The birds revived immediately and Cuchulainn tied them to the back of the chariot. In this way they covered the rest of the ground until they reached Emain Macha.

From the ramparts, Levercham, Conor's messenger, spied the strange chariot approaching the fort and was aghast at what she saw. She ran in to the hall of the Red Branch where Conor and his companions sat and cried out, 'There's a chariot coming here very fast and it's a terrifying sight. It's decorated with bleeding heads. Above it flies a flock of great white birds and racing behind it, tied to the chariot, are two fierce, wild stags tossing their antlers. Most terrifying of all is the warrior himself! He is in some sort of battle frenzy. A war warp has contorted his face and a hero light is spouting out of his head. If he cannot be stopped, he will redden the soil of Emain Macha with the blood of the boy troops!'

'I know well who that chariot fighter is!' Conor exclaimed. 'He's my sister's son. He took up arms today and set off to the borders of Ulster to bloody his weapons with first-wounding. He's inflamed with battle frenzy and if he's not stopped, he'll slaughter all his companions.'

Conor, with Mugain his wife and the other women of the household, hastily put together a plan to seize Cuchulainn and cool his lust for blood.

As the boy veered his chariot round and round outside the ramparts of Emain Macha, keeping the left side turned in insult towards the fort and challenging and threatening everyone inside, the gates were suddenly opened. Cuchulainn galloped towards the ramparts ready for a fight. Instead of armed warriors, seventy women headed by the queen herself walked out, baring their bodies as they did so.

'These are the warriors you will fight today, little boy!' Mugain called out.

When Cuchulainn saw the naked women coming towards him he was covered in confusion and hid his face from them in shyness and embarrassment. He bent down to press his forehead against the chariot headboard, and as he did so the king's men seized their chance. They jumped on him and carried him to three vats of cold water that had been prepared to extinguish his battle frenzy.

They lowered him into the first vat and it erupted with a blast of steam so powerful that the hoops flew off and the staves burst apart. They placed him in the second vat and it boiled over with bubbles as big as fists. When they doused him in the third vat the water became too hot to touch, but it cooled Cuchulainn down and he was restored to his normal self. Then, when he was dressed in his richest clothes, he sat down in his usual place at Conor Mac Nessa's feet. The king stroked his head and the whole company gazed in wonder at the boy who had triumphantly taken up arms and defeated the most formidable warriors though he was only seven years old.

The Wooing of Emer

CUCHULAINN grew up at Conor Mac Nessa's court at Emain Macha near Armagh. Conor was a powerful and well-loved king and there was peace and plenty in Ulster and the province came to be rich and prosperous. Conor's hospitality was as great as his wealth and in his banqueting hall, richly decorated in silver and bronze, were held many feasts and entertainments. There was music, poetry, storytelling and singing, and there, between ropes stretched from wall to wall, the chariot warriors performed athletic feats of balancing and juggling and skilful play with swords and spears.

One night the chiefs of the Red Branch had gathered for a feast and were drinking from the huge vat that held enough wine to keep them satisfied the evening long. Conall Cearnach, Fergus Mac Roi, Laoghaire, Dubhtach, Scet, the greatest Ulster warriors were present, and there too was the youngest of them all, Cuchulainn. They took turns on the ropes, displaying their skills, but Cuchulainn outshone everyone. The women of Conor's household loved to watch him do his chariot feats. He was swift, light and well built; he was wise and kind; he spoke sweetly to them and he was the handsomest of all the men. He was prudent, too, unless battle frenzy came over him, as it did on the day he took up arms, and he was a skilled chess player and a good judge. He had all these gifts and the gift of foresight as well.

The other men became jealous of Cuchulainn because he was too young, too daring, too handsome and too popular with the women, so they decided to find a wife for him. If he had a wife, they told themselves, their own wives and daughters would pay less attention to him and be less in danger from his charms. Moreover, since it was foretold that his life would be heroic and short, it would be as well if he had a son as soon as possible, for only Cuchulainn himself could father a child as gifted as he.

So Conor sent nine men into each province to look for a woman, the daughter of a king or chief, who would make a worthy wife for Cuchulainn. A year to the day later the messengers returned, and not one of them had found a girl whom Cuchulainn would marry. Cuchulainn decided to take the matter into his own hands. He and his charioteer, Laeg Mac Riangabra set off to a place called the Gardens of Lugh to visit a girl Cuchulainn knew. This was Emer, the daughter of Forgall the Wily, and she was the most beautiful and accomplished woman in Ireland. Because Laeg was the best charioteer in the country and no one could touch them for speed, in a very short time they arrived at Forgall's fort.

Emer was seated on the green in front of her father's rath, surrounded by the daughters of the local landowners. She was teaching the young women embroidery when she heard in the distance, the drumming of hoofs, the rattle of weapons, the clanging of metal, and the rattle and hum of a chariot approaching at full tilt.

Emer said to her sister, Fial, 'Go and see who it is who is coming here at that reckless speed.'

Fial ran to the road to look. 'I see two fine, lively horses,' she said, 'a black and a grey. They are yoked to a high wooden chariot with wicker-work sides. The harness and fittings are made of silver and the chariot poles are bronze. In the chariot is a dark, melancholy man, the handsomest man in Ireland. He is wrapped in the folds of a crimson cloak fastened with gold and his weapons are silver and bronze. There is a red-haired charioteer beside him.'

Moments later, Laeg pulled the team of horses to a halt and Cuchulainn vaulted out of the chariot, his eyes alive with excitement as he looked at Emer. The girl lifted her beautiful face to look at the visitor and saw that it was Cuchulainn. 'May the road you travel be smooth and may you be safe from every harm!' she greeted him. 'Where have you come from, and why are you here?'

Cuchulainn did not give Emer a straight reply. His answer was a riddle that Emer alone could understand and she answered him in the same strange way. She knew from his words that he had come to court her and since she admired and loved him she was pleased.

Then Cuchulainn began to press his suit. 'I was reared at Conor's court,' he told her, 'and not among the servants in the kitchen. My companions have been chiefs and champions, warriors and druids, judges and poets. From them I have learnt hospitality and benevolence, battle skills, champions' honour, wisdom and sound judgement and the recital of stories from memory. My father is Lugh and my mother the king's sister Dechtire. I am the most respected and beloved hero in the kingdom, the Hound of Ulster, and I fight for the honour of all who live there. Now, what about you, Emer, how were you brought up?'

'I was brought up to respect the old values. I am well behaved and modest, graceful and beautiful and equal in rank to a queen. I am the most praised and admired woman in Ireland.'

'We seem well matched then,' said Cuchulainn. 'Why don't we join together. You are the first girl I have met who could match me riddle for riddle!'

'One last question,' said Emer. 'Have you got a wife already?'

'No!' he answered. 'You're the only woman I love.' As he spoke he looked at Emer's breasts curving above her dress and said softly to her, 'I see a sweet place, a sweet resting place!'

'No one rests there until he has killed a hundred men at each ford from the Ford of Scemen to Banchuin,' Emer replied.

'I see a sweet resting place!' Cuchulainn repeated.

'No one rests there unless he has slain a group of three times nine men while leaving the man in the middle of each group alive,' Emer told him.

'I will rest in that sweet place!'

'No one will rest there who does not stay awake from February to May and from May to November.'

'I'll do everything you've asked,' Cuchulainn promised.

'If you do, then we'll join together and be like one,' Emer promised.

Then Cuchulainn said farewell to Emer and Laeg and he set off for Emain Macha.

'What was all that about?' asked the charioteer. 'I couldn't make head nor tail of it, and neither could any of Emer's companions.'

'That's why I spoke in riddles. Can't you see I am courting Emer? I disguised my words so that the girls would not realize this. If Forgall knew I was after his daughter he would not consent to the match at all. Now I'll tell you what we said to each other.' All the way back to Emain Macha, Cuchulainn shortened the journey by explaining to Laeg what Emer and he had meant by their riddles.

When Emer's companions went home that night, they told their parents of the strange meeting between Emer and the handsome young man who had come to the Gardens of Lugh in a splendid chariot. They described how he had spoken to Emer in riddles that no one but she could understand and how she had answered him in the same way. They had talked together for a good while, the girls said, before the young warrior had headed northwards towards the Plain of Breg.

The next day the girls' fathers went to Forgall and told him what they'd heard.

'It could be no one else but that misshapen madman from Emain Macha,' Forgall said angrily. 'He came here to court Emer and the girl has fallen in love with him. That's what the wordplay was all about. But they won't get away with it. I'll put a halt to his gallop!'

So Forgall went to Emain Macha with two friends disguised as messengers from the king of the Gauls bringing tributes of wine and gold to Conor Mac Nessa. Conor received the visitors and gave a feast in their honour. There was the usual entertainment and the chariot warriors did their rope feats and displayed their battle skill. Conor praised his champions to the guests and talked about the expertise and bravery of Conall, Cuchulainn and others. Forgall agreed they were all great champions, especially Cuchulainn, but he told Conor that they could be even better.

'Send your heroes to Scotland to train with Donall the Destroyer and when Donall has taught them everything he knows, they can go further west to Skye, the island home of Scathach the Shadowy One. That mysterious woman warrior can train them in the special fighting skills she has learnt, and reveal to them secrets of war and weaponry that only she knows. Not only is she fierce and powerful but she can foretell what is to come. Under Scathach's tutelage they will become the best warriors in Europe.'

When they heard this, Conor, Conall, Laoghaire and Cuchulainn decided to go to Scotland, and Forgall was well pleased. He hoped that Cuchulainn would take his advice and become so involved in Scathach's wars that he would be killed in action.

Before he left for Scotland, Cuchulainn slipped away secretly to tell Emer where he was going and why.

'The man who gave you that advice was no Gaulish messenger!' Emer exclaimed. 'It was my father, Forgall, in disguise. He wants to separate us and he'll have you killed if he can. So be on your guard!'

Cuchulainn thanked Emer for the warning and they parted, making promises to be faithful to each other as long as they both lived.

In Scotland, Donall the Destroyer taught the king and his three chariot-chiefs many feats of endurance and nimbleness. He showed them how to balance on a spear point and dance on a heated flagstone. And when he had instructed them in all he knew, Donall sent them on to Scathach's camp on the island of Skye to perfect their knowledge.

They set off for Skye, but before long Conor, Laoghaire and Conall got so homesick for Emain Macha that they left Cuchulainn to go on alone and they turned back for Ireland. Cuchulainn was sad and lonely without his friends and he didn't know how to get to Scathach's camp.

As he wandered helplessly over the rough terrain, suddenly there appeared in front of him a large beast like a lion. Cuchulainn was terrified as the fierce creature came towards him but, although it eyed him, it did him no harm. It turned around then and walked ahead of him and whichever way he turned, it turned too until Cuchulainn realized it was guiding him. He leapt on its back and it took him to an island in the middle of a loch. There it disappeared into a deep glen and Cuchulainn went on alone, wandering around until he met a youth who told him the way to Scathach's camp.

'But between it and you lies the Plain of Ill Luck,' warned the young man. 'For the first half of the plain your feet will stick fast

94

and on the second half the blades of grass will be like knives and you will have to walk on the sharp points. But I know a way to get across the plain safely. Roll that wheel in front of you for the first half and walk in the tracks that it makes and you will not get bogged down. When you reach the sharp grass roll this apple in front of you and follow its path over the flattened grass till you get to the other side of the plain.'

Cuchulainn thanked the boy, took the wheel and the apple and following his new friend's instructions crossed the plain safely and reached Scathach's training camp.

When he arrived at the camp there was no sign of the woman warrior. 'Where is Scathach?' he enquired of the young men who had gathered round.

'She's on that island there,' her pupils said, pointing out to sea.

'How can I get there?' Cuchulainn asked.

'Across the Pupils' Bridge,' they told him. 'But you can only cross the bridge if you're trained and proven in the use of arms.'

The Pupils' Bridge was arched, high in the middle and low at both ends. When a person stepped on one end the other end would rise up and pitch him off. Cuchulainn didn't know this and as soon as he stepped on the bridge he was flung off. The other boys roared with laughter. He tried again and again but each time, in spite of his efforts to keep his balance, he was thrown back while the trainees who were watching jeered and mocked him. Then Cuchulainn went into his war warp. As the battle spasm seized him, he did his hero's salmon leap on to the middle of the bridge and then off at the other side before the bridge could rise and toss him off. Safely on the island, he went directly to Scathach's fort. There he hammered the door with his spear and broke it in two.

Scathach knew that only a fully trained warrior could have reached her door so she sent her daughter, Uathach, to see who the champion might be. The moment Uathach set eyes on Cuchulainn she fell in love with him and persuaded her mother to take him in and train him in her most secret ways of war. After three days Uathach directed Cuchulainn to go to the hidden place where Scathach trained her sons, Cuar and Cat, and to spy on them.

95

Cuchulainn did what Uathach had advised and from watching the Shadowy One train her sons he learnt her secret and mysterious war tactics. Then Scathach gave Cuchulainn a javelin called the Gae Bolga, the deadliest weapon of all. She taught him how to cast it with his foot so that it never missed its mark.

While Cuchulainn was living in Scathach's camp his companion-in-arms was another young Irish warrior whose name was Ferdia, son of Daman. The two became great friends, sharing excitement and danger, well matched in every way. They were as loyal and as close to each other as brothers.

At that time Scathach and her people were at war with a tribe whose leader was Aoife, a woman warrior so fierce that even Scathach feared her. The two armies met to fight but because Scathach was afraid that Cuchulainn might be killed in battle she gave him a sleeping draught that would keep a man asleep and out of danger for twenty-four hours. But after just one hour the effects of the potion wore off and Cuchulainn sprang into the fray. For two days he fought and killed many of Aoife's men including her three sons. Then Aoife challenged Scathach to present a champion to meet her in single combat and Cuchulainn volunteered to go.

'What are the things that are most precious to Aoife?' he asked Scathach as he got ready to fight.

'More than anything else in the world, she loves her horses, her chariot and her charioteer,' Scathach told him.

Then Aoife and Cuchulainn met in a hand-to-hand sword fight. Skilled as Cuchulainn was, Aoife was more skilful still. She struck the blade off Cuchulainn's sword and left him with only the hilt in his hand. As she closed in for the kill, Cuchulainn shouted out, 'Oh look! Look, quick! Aoife's chariot has fallen down the mountainside and the horses and charioteer with it. They'll all be killed!' Aoife whirled round when she heard this and Cuchulainn jumped on her, seized her round the breast and pinned her arms to her sides. He hoisted her over his shoulders and ran with her to Scathach's lines. There he threw her on the ground and, grabbing a sword, held the point against her heart.

'A life for a life, Cuchulainn!' Aoife cried.

'Only if you grant me three demands!'

'Say what you want in one breath and you can have it,' she said.

'That you do not make war on Scathach again, that you stay with me tonight and that you bear me a son.'

'I promise those three things,' agreed Aoife, and she made peace with Scathach and spent that night with Cuchulainn.

Shortly after this Aoife told Cuchulainn that the last part of the bargain would be fulfilled and that she would give birth to his son. When he heard this news Cuchulainn was delighted. He took a gold thumb ring off his hand and gave it to Aoife.

'When this ring fits my son's hand send him to Ireland to search for me. I will recognize him by the ring. Give him the name Connla, but tell him to reveal it to no one. Tell him to step aside for no one and refuse no one who challenges him to a fight.'

After they had made this agreement, Aoife went back to her own territory and Cuchulainn stayed with Scathach and Uathach till he recovered from the wounds he had received in the fight. Then word came to Scotland that he was needed in Emain Macha and he set sail for Ulster.

While Emer still waited in the house of Forgall her father for Cuchulainn's return and Cuchulainn was with Scathach in Scotland, Lugaid, a king from Munster, brought twelve of his chariot-chiefs to Tara to marry twelve young women who lived there. Lugaid himself was not married, and when Forgall heard this he made a plan. He hurried to Tara and told Lugaid that the best maiden in Ireland, a woman perfect in every way, was still unmarried and was living in his house. Then he promised Emer to him and a match was arranged. Lugaid and his entourage came to Forgall's house for the marriage feast and Emer was brought to the banqueting hall to meet the king she was to marry. As she passed in front of Lugaid to sit by his side, she took his face between her hands and held it tight. She swore to him that she loved only Cuchulainn and that she was under his protection. She told Lugaid it would be dishonourable of him to take her against her will and warned him that Cuchulainn would surely have his revenge for such an insult. Lugaid dreaded Cuchulainn's anger so he dared not force the issue. Making his excuses to Forgall, he left his house and made straight for home.

When Cuchulainn returned to Emain, Conor gave him a hero's welcome and at the great feast in his honour Cuchulainn entertained all present with stories of his adventures in Scotland. Then he set off to try and abduct Emer from her father's house and bring her to live with him. Forgall had expected this and his stronghold was so well fortified that for a year Cuchulainn could not even get near the place.

After a year Cuchulainn decided to take Emer by force and his scythed chariot was made ready. When he arrived at Forgall's house he did his hero's salmon leap across the three outside ramparts and landed inside the dun. Three groups of warriors charged at him, nine men in each group. He dealt three mighty blows with his sword, killing eight men in each group but leaving the man in the centre alive. The three survivors were Emer's three brothers. Forgall tried to escape by jumping out over his own fortifications but he stumbled and fell to his death.

Then Cuchulainn seized Emer and her weight in gold and sprang with his burden out of the stronghold and away. A great clamour went up from Forgall's followers and his guards poured out of the fort to hunt down Cuchulainn and Emer. At every ford between Scemen and Banchuin, Emer got out of the chariot and Cuchulainn turned back and raced towards his pursuers sending sods flying in every direction. His scythed wheels and his sharp weapons cut through his enemies and he left a hundred men dead at each foray. In that way he completed the tasks Emer had set him and they reached Emain Macha before nightfall. Emer was brought into the House of the Red Branch to Conor Mac Nessa and his assembly and they welcomed her into their company. Then she and Cuchulainn became man and wife and went to live in Dun Dealgan, Cuchulainn's own inherited stronghold, and they were not separated until Cuchulainn's death.

Bricriu's Feast

BRICRIU POISON-TONGUE spent a whole year preparing a great feast for Conor Mac Nessa and his followers. At his fort at Dun Rudraige he had a special mansion built after the fashion of the Red Branch hall at Emain Macha, but surpassing it in grandeur and magnificence: its architecture was more splendid, its design more artistic and its furnishings and materials even costlier. Pillars and walls, lintels and doorways were richly carved and decorated and screens were overlaid with gold. At the front of the hall a balcony was raised high and on it stood the king's seat. Encrusted with jewels of every colour, this throne shone so brightly it turned night into day. Around the platform were arranged the twelve seats of the twelve tribes of Ulster.

Then Bicriu had a platform made for himself on the same level as the king's throne and the seats of the greatest Ulster heroes. It too was richly furnished and decorated but it was separated from the main hall by large glass panels. Bricriu was notorious for causing strife among the guests at any feast he attended and he knew the Ulstermen would not let him stay among them at the banquet.

When all the preparations were made, the furnishings in place and lavish amounts of food and drink on hand, Bricriu went to Emain Macha to invite Conor and the principal Ulster champions and their wives to the feast. Conor accepted the invitation and agreed to go on the condition that his followers were willing to attend the feast as well. The rest of the Ulster chiefs did *not* want to go to Bricriu's house because they mistrusted him and his mischievous tricks. On their behalf Fergus went to Conor to tell him this.

'We don't want to go to Bricriu's feast,' Fergus said, 'for we know he will set man against man and at the end of the night the dead will outnumber the living.'

Bricriu overheard what Fergus said to Conor. 'It will be worse again if you *don't* come!' he said darkly.

'What will happen if we don't go?' Conor asked.

'I will set warrior against warrior until they kill each other.'

'We will not be blackmailed by you!' retorted Conor.

'I will set father against son, mother against daughter, wife against wife till their very mother's milk turns sour,' Bricriu threatened.

'In that case we'd better go,' said Fergus.

Before they set out, Sencha, the judge and the wisest man in Ulster, called the Ulster chiefs together in council to make plans for protecting themselves against Bricriu's malevolence. They decided they would go to the feast if they could get a guarantee from Bricriu that he would leave the feasting hall as soon as the banquet was ready. Bricriu agreed happily to these terms and the Ulster court set out in a great cavalcade to go with him to the feast. Immediately, Bricriu set about thinking of a way to cause bad blood among his guests. It wasn't long till a plan had formed in his head and he could begin his mischiefmaking.

He drew alongside Laoghaire the Triumphant and greeted him fulsomely. 'Laoghaire,' he said, 'you are a brave warrior. You're the scourge of Ulster's enemies. You are the most senior of all the Ulster champions. Why, then, is it that the champion's portion is not given to *you* at Emain Macha?'

'It would be if I wanted it!' Laoghaire retorted.

'Well, if you *do* want it, take my advice. When the champion's portion is offered at this feast of mine, let your charioteer bring it to *you* and it will be yours from then on. And, believe me, the champion's portion at Bicriu's feast is worth having! There's a huge cauldron big enough to hold three stout men and I have filled it with strong wine. By way of food I have a seven-year-old boar that has from birth been fed on only the best: fresh milk and fine meal in springtime, curds and sweet milk in the summer, nuts and harvest wheat in autumn and beef broth during the winter. As well as that there is a seven-year-old bull which has never grazed in poor, heathery upland slopes but has eaten only the sweetest lowland meadow hay and corn. There are also a hundred honey-soaked wheat cakes, with a quarter-bushel of wheat in each one. No mean portion! And it should be *yours*, Laoghaire!'

'It had better be mine or there'll be blood spilt!' Laoghaire exclaimed. And Bricriu went off laughing to himself.

A little while later Bricriu drew close to Conall Cearnach. He flattered him with fine compliments, told him the same story as he had Laoghaire and gave him the same advice. When he was satisfied that Conall felt slighted and aggrieved and would fight for his right to the champion's portion, Bricriu was well pleased and made his way to Cuchulainn's side.

He greeted Cuchulainn with the most extravagant praise of all, and spoke to him of the injustice of the champion's portion not being awarded to him.

'How can any one deny it to *you*, Cuchulainn? You are the acknowledged champion and darling of Ulster. You have defended her borders. You have held back her enemies single-handed. You have succeeded where others have failed. Everyone knows your achievements surpass theirs, so why is the portion not yours by right?'

As Cuchulainn listened to Bricriu's insinuations and instructions he grew angrier by the minute. 'I swear by the gods of my tribe I'll take the head of anyone who dares to claim the portion before me!' he burst out at last.

Well satisfied with his day's work, Bricriu left Cuchulainn and mingled with his guests until they reached his banqueting hall.

When they arrived at Bricriu's fort, the Ulster visitors settled into their quarters, Conor and his men on one side of the building, the queen and the chieftains' wives on the other. Bricriu oversaw the food and wine being set out while musicians and players entertained the visitors. When the banquet was ready, Bricriu and his wife took leave of their guests as agreed. But just as they were leaving, Bricriu turned to the assembly. 'The champion's portion is over there!' he announced. 'It is a magnificent one. Only the greatest champion deserves it. Make sure it goes to the right man!' With that he and his wife climbed up to the glass viewing room above the hall.

When the servers were ready to allocate the champion's portion, the three charioteers rose to claim it for their masters as they had been instructed.

'Bring the champion's portion over here to Cuchulainn, where you all know it belongs!' Laeg shouted.

When they heard Laeg's words, Laoghaire and Conall sprang to their feet and seized their weapons.

'That's not true!' they roared and made for Cuchulainn. They jumped over tables in their haste to get to the middle of the hall and there they both laid into him. Cuchulainn defended himself fiercely with his sword and shield. So violent was the mêlée that one half of the hall blazed like the sun, lit up with the sparks from their swords, while the other half was white as snow with enamel dust from their shields.

Conor and the other Ulster chiefs sat aghast at the injustice of the fight but were too frightened to intervene. At last Sencha the judge stood up and roared, 'Stop the fight! Two men against one is shameful.'

Then Conor commanded the warriors to put down their weapons and Fergus stepped between them. They stopped at once.

'I'll settle this dispute for now,' Sencha said. 'Will you abide by my judgement?'

'We will,' the three warriors said.

'We will divide the champion's portion between the whole company tonight and tomorrow we will go to Cruachan and let Aillil, king of Connacht, choose the champion from among you.'

Peace was restored and the food and wine was divided equally among all.

Watching these developments from his balcony, Bricriu was not pleased. He was dismayed to see the feast continue harmoniously and fell to plotting another way to disrupt it. He decided it was time to incite the women and set them against each other as he had done with the men. He pondered how best this could be done. Just as he had hit on a plan, Fidelma, the wife of Laoghaire, came out of the hall and Bricriu went down to her side.

'I'm the lucky man tonight to meet someone as distinguished as *you*, Fidelma!' he said. 'The wife of Laoghaire, the daughter of Conor Mac Nessa, the king himself! You must surely be the fore-most woman in Ulster for nobility, beauty and intelligence. You should take second place to none. Let me tell you a secret. If you are the first to re-enter the hall tonight you will be the considered first in rank among the Ulster women from now on.'

Fidelma was flattered and pleased. She thanked Bricriu for his advice and promised to act on it and Bricriu smiled to himself.

Just then Lendabar, wife of Conall came out of the hall with her companions and Bricriu approached her.

He flattered her even more extravagantly than he had Fidelma and told her to be sure to be first back into the feast and she would hold that position thereafter. Lendabar vowed to do as Bricriu had advised and Poison-Tongue moved away, laughing quietly to himself.

Then he sought out Emer, Cuchulainn's wife, and greeted her warmly. He spoke to her effusively of her lineage, beauty and learning and of her unquestionable right to be the first lady in Ulster after the queen herself. His blandishments and flattery reached new heights as did his pleasure when he noted Emer's determination to be first back to the hall. Then he returned to his balcony to await developments.

The three noble women and their entourages strolled about companionably in the evening air until they all met together at the same spot, three ridges away from the feasting hall. They talked happily together, each one confident that Bricriu had spoken to her alone. When the time came to return to the feast the three women began to walk in step, slowly and sedately, towards the hall. At the first ridge their progress was stately and serene. By the second ridge their steps had become shorter and quicker. At the third ridge, the one next to the house, the race was on. They hitched their skirts around their hips and ran at full tilt trying to outstrip each other and be the first through the door.

As the women raced against each other towards the house, they made so much noise with their feet and their voices that the men inside thought chariot-chiefs were raiding the place. They sprang for their weapons, striking each other in their befuddlement and confusion till Sencha called them to order.

'Stop! Put down your swords! This is not the arrival of an army: these are your own women you hear. This is Bricriu's work! He has set your wives against each other outside the hall. If he gets inside with the women there will be carnage. Shut the door quickly!'

The doorkeeper got the door closed just as Emer, fastest of the women, arrived. She shouted to be let in first, ahead of the other women. When they heard Emer demand this, Conall and Laoghaire ran to the door to open it for *their* wives so that *they* might be first. Conor was frightened that another fight would break out and he ordered the warriors to return to their places. When the company was calm again, Sencha told them that it would not be a war of arms that would settle the matter, but a war of words.

Outside the doors each wife in turn praised her husband. Each commended her husband's character and person and paid tribute to his courage, skill, deeds, lineage and virtue, each one hoping to out-praise the other.

When the three warriors heard their wives complimenting them in such glowing terms, each was determined that his spouse would be the first to enter and claim the highest rank. Laoghaire and Conall hacked at the walls to force open an entrance for their women, but Cuchulainn simply wrenched one side of the hall up by the foundations and held it so high that the stars in the sky were visible beneath it, and so Emer stepped into the house first. Then Cuchulainn let the building fall with such a mighty crash that the foundations sank seven feet into the ground. Bricriu's balcony sloped at such and angle that he and his wife slid out of it and landed among the hounds in the ditch below. Bricriu climbed out of the mud, furious and dishevelled. When he saw his house at a crazy angle he ran inside to protest, but he was in such disarray and so caked with mud that no one recognized him until he started to harangue them.

'It was a sorry day I prepared a feast for you Ulstermen!' he shouted. 'Look what you've done to my precious house! I'm giving you a choice: you either set it straight at once or you go! There'll be neither food nor lodging until it's back in order!'

When they heard that there would be no more food or drink till the house was put to rights, the Ulstermen got up and pulled and heaved and pushed at the walls but to no avail. They badly wanted the feast to continue so they sent Sencha to plead with Cuchulainn to straighten the house.

The young champion was very tired because he had spent the whole day breaking in the Grey of Macha. That morning the wild horse had come to him out of a lake in Slieve Fuad and when Cuchulainn had jumped on its back it had bolted and raced off, circling Ireland until darkness fell. Then, with Cuchulainn still clinging to it, it had stopped, broken in and obedient, as exhausted as its rider. Cuchulainn was still weary after that gallop, but at Sencha's request he rose and tried to raise the foundations of the house. He tried again and again but he couldn't budge it. Then his war warp came over him. His hair stood up straight, rooted in blood, his face distorted and his body arched and stretched like an extended bow, and he heaved the house aloft in one movement and set it straight again. Then the spasm left him, he regained his normal appearance and they all settled down to continue the feast.

But Bricriu had sown the seeds of dissension among the warriors and the quarrel about the champion's portion came up again. The next morning, therefore, they set out for Connacht to let Aillil and Medb, the rulers of the western province, settle the matter. Across Ireland they drove with the three contenders at the head of the band. The chariot wheels threw clods up into the air and the thunder of hundreds of hoofs rolled ahead of them to Cruachan. Inside the fortifications, Medb heard the sound and looked up at the blue sky in puzzlement.

'Thunder in a cloudless sky? That's strange!' she exclaimed.

Her daughter, Finnabair, went to a vantage point overlooking the plain and she saw clouds of dust on the horizon as the chariots approached.

'Mother!' she shouted. 'A chariot is racing towards us pulled by two powerful dappled horses. The man in it has long plaited fair hair. He's wearing a cloak made of rich scarlet cloth and he's carrying a five-barbed spear.'

Medb looked up in alarm. 'That sounds like Laoghaire the Triumphant, and he will cut us off at the ground like leeks being sliced out of a drill unless he can be settled.'

'There's another chariot behind him, coming just as fast. It's pulled by a pair of broad-chested bays. They are being goaded on by a man with long wavy hair and a shining pale face with high colour on his cheeks. He's carrying a shield and a spear.'

'That man is Conall Cearnach, and he will leave us all like gutted fish on a slab unless we can cool his anger.'

'And here's another chariot!' Finnabair shouted. 'It's drawn by two magnificent horses, one grey, the other black. The chariot is made of wood and wicker on iron wheels. It has a copper frame, a silver shaft and gold-mounted harness. It is covering ground like a hare. The dark man in the chariot is the most beautiful I've ever seen, though he looks sad. He is dressed in a red tunic embroidered in gold and is wrapped in a linen cloak. The cloak is fastened with a heavy gold pin and his chest is heaving with exertion. A freckled, wiry, red-haired charioteer is goading on the horses, while the warrior does acrobatic feats and salmon leaps in the chariot behind him.'

'The others were just spits of rain before a downpour!' Medb exclaimed. 'That is Cuchulainn, the Hound of Ulster, and he will grind us the way a mill grinds malted wheat unless we can calm him down.'

Immediately the queen ordered three vats of icy water to be set out to cool the battle fever of the three warriors. And when they drew up outside Medb's fort they were seized and submerged in the vats until their frenzy had ebbed away.

When this was done, the Ulster chiefs, led by Conor, were invited into Cruachan by Aillil and Medb and were entertained lavishly for three days and three nights.

Aillil asked Conor why they had come to Cruachan and Conor told him about the dispute regarding the champion's portion and how Sencha had deemed that he must settle the dispute. Aillil was very disturbed when he heard this. He knew that if he chose one of these three powerful champions he would make enemies of the other two. He asked Conor to allow him three days and three nights to consider the matter. Conor agreed and returned with his retinue to Ulster leaving the three champions behind in Connacht.

That night, as Cuchulainn and the other two sat down to their meal, three druidic cats were let loose and went scratching and spitting for the warriors' food. Conall and Laoghaire leapt for the rafters and swung themselves on to them and stayed there while the cats devoured their food. Cuchulainn stayed where he was and, though his sword could not harm the magic creatures, sat his ground wide awake all night long, keeping the fierce creatures at bay. At daybreak the demonic cats disappeared. When Aillil saw this he declared that the champion's portion should go to Cuchulainn. Conall and Laoghaire disagreed. 'We don't test our skill against magic beasts,' they said. 'We test it against men.'

Aillil was distracted with worry and for three nights could not eat or sleep. He was sitting disconsolately in his chamber with his back against the wall when Medb came into the room.

'You're a coward,' she scolded. 'If you can't choose between them, I will! Laoghaire is as different to Conall as bronze is to silver. And Conall is as different to Cuchulainn as silver is to gold.'

Then she called Laoghaire to her and gave him a bronze cup with a silver bird on the base. 'This cup is a token of our judgement that you deserve the champion's portion. Take it back with you to Emain Macha but say nothing to anyone and show it to no one till the time comes when the champion's portion is to be allocated.'

After this she sent for Conall and she gave him a silver cup with a gold bird chased on the bottom. She told him that the goblet was a guarantee that he had been judged the champion and swore him to secrecy as she had Laoghaire.

Finally she sent a messenger to Cuchulainn's quarters to ask him to join her. He was playing chess with Laeg when the messenger arrived with Medb's request that he should come to the royal quarters. Cuchulainn's reply was to brain the messenger with a chess piece. So Medb herself went to his room and put her arms around his neck to coax him out of his rage.

'Tell your lies to someone else, Medb!' said Cuchulainn angrily.

'This is not a lie,' she whispered in his ear. 'You are the greatest hero in Ulster and to you should go the champion's portion without question. And your wife should have precedence over all the women of Ireland.'

Then from her robes she took out a magnificent gold cup, a jewel-studded bird on its base, and put it in front of Cuchulainn. 'This is the proof of my judgement,' she said and gave him the same instructions as she had given the other two. Cuchulainn drank wine from the cup as the others had done and Medb went away content.

The next morning, before they left Aillil's court, the three Ulstermen entertained the women of Cruachan with tricks and juggling to delight them. Cuchulainn took embroidery needles from fifty of the women and flung them into the air. As they fell the point of one needle linked into the eye of the next to form a shining unbroken chain and the women thought this was the best trick of all. Then the three Ulster chariot-chiefs set off for Emain Macha.

That night, as the meal was served, the champion's portion was carved but it was given to no one. Dubtach, a senior warrior, was impatient with the whole affair by then. He said crossly to Conor, 'Give the portion to some of the other champions. These three here have arrived back from Cruachan without any proof of Aillil's decision!'

At that, Laoghaire sprang up holding aloft the bronze cup. 'Give the champion's portion to me! Here is proof of Aillil and Medb's decision,' he shouted.

'Not so fast!' Conall roared, brandishing his silver cup. 'It goes to me! My cup is worth more than Laoghaire's.'

Then Cuchulainn took from the folds of his cloak his golden goblet studded with jewels and held it aloft. 'If there is any justice, I should get the portion. This is the best token of all,' he said.

The three men were so furious at this turn of events that they drew their swords and would have attacked each other had not

Sencha pointed out that they *all* been duped by Medb. So yet again the champion's portion was cut up and eaten by the whole company and not awarded to one man alone.

But the matter did not rest and the struggle for supremacy between the contenders went on and on. The three champions went through many other tests and ordeals to settle the question but each time, though Cuchulainn proved himself the best, the other two would not agree and they trumped up excuses to deny him his portion. In the end, however, the affair was resolved and this is how it happened.

One evening when the Ulstermen were tired after a great tournament, they left the playing fields and went into the Red Branch hall for a feast. Conor and Fergus presided over the gathering, but of the three foremost champions only Laoghaire was present. When the feast was nearly over and darkness was drawing in, a giant figure appeared at the end of the hall. He was a monstrous creature and he terrified the assembly as he lumbered up the room. His yellow eyes were the size of cauldrons and each finger was as thick as a normal man's wrist. He wore an old skin tunic and over it a rough brown cloak. In one huge hand he carried a cudgel the size of a mature tree and in the other an axe with a blade so sharp it could cut hairs floating across it in the wind. No one stirred as he moved among them up to the front of the room. He shambled over to the fire and addressed Conor Mac Nessa.

'I have come here on a mission,' said the giant, 'for I know that the Ulstermen are world-famous for their courage, dignity and magnanimity. I have travelled the world on this quest of mine, through Africa, Europe and Asia. But I haven't found a man who will do what I ask, not in Greece, nor in Scythia nor in Spain. Will any one *here* do what I request?'

'What *is* your request?' Fergus asked.

'To find a man who will make a pact with me and keep his word,' replied the giant.

'That shouldn't be hard!' the king exclaimed.

'Harder than you think,' the giant said, 'because my quest is this. I'm looking for a man who will agree to cut off my head tonight and let me cut off *his* head tomorrow.'

There was complete silence in the room.

'Conor and Fergus are exempt because of their rank as kings,' the giant went on, 'but is there anyone else present who will make this pact with me?' Still no one spoke. The giant sighed. 'Just as I expected! Where are those who claim the champion's portion? Won't one of *those* heroes pledge his word? Where is Laoghaire the Triumph?'

'Here I am!' Laoghaire roared. 'And I accept your challenge! Bend down and put your neck on the block. I'll cut off your head!'

'That's easily said! But what about tomorrow night?'

'I'll be here,' promised Laoghaire.

The huge man bent down and with one blow of the axe Laoghaire cut off the giant's head, burying the blade in the block. A torrent of blood flowed across the floor and the head rolled against the wall. Then, to the horror of the crowd, the giant rose, gathered up his head, his axe and the block, held them against his chest and with blood gushing from his neck walked out of the room.

The following night as darkness fell the giant returned to the banqueting hall. His head was back in place and in his hands he carried his cudgel, axe and block. He stared around the room, looking for Laoghaire but Laoghaire was nowhere to be seen. The giant let out a great resigned sigh and issued his challenge again. This time it was Conall who agreed to the pact. He gave his solemn word to be there on the following night, took up the axe and with one swift stroke severed the giant's head from his body. Once more the giant picked up his bloody head and departed.

When the giant returned the next evening great crowds had gathered in the Red Branch banqueting hall, but Conall was not among them. When he discovered this the giant laughed contemptuously. 'Ulstermen, you're no better than anyone else in spite of all your talk!' he jeered. Then he spied Cuchulainn in the middle of the throng. 'What about the fierce Cuchulainn?' he roared. 'Can *he* keep a bargain?'

'I want no bargain with you!' Cuchulain shouted and he grabbed the axe from the giant's hand and struck off his head with such force that it bounced to the ceiling. Cuchulainn hit it another huge blow and crushed it but the giant rose to his feet, took up his shattered head and went out.

The next evening every warrior in Ulster was in the house of the Red Branch to see if Cuchulainn would be there. Sure enough, Cuchulainn was present, but he was dejected and scared. He would not speak to anyone and his comrades were full of distress that his end should come so early and in such a way. Suddenly the giant appeared at the far end of the hall. 'Where is Cuchulainn?' he demanded.

'Here I am,' Cuchulainn answered in a low voice.

'You haven't as much to say for yourself tonight!' said the giant. 'I can see you are scared to die! But at least you have kept your word.'

The giant pointed to the block and Cuchulainn knelt down and put his head on it. 'Stretch out your neck!' the giant commanded.

'Kill me quickly and don't torment me any longer,' Cuchulainn begged.

'Your neck is too short for the block.'

'Then I'll make it as long as a heron's neck!' Cuchulainn cried and he contorted his body and stretched his neck till it reached the end of the block.

No one moved as the giant using both hands, raised the axe so high it struck the rafters. The swish of his cloak as it swung into the air and the hiss of the axe as it came down filled the hall with a sound like wind through trees on a stormy night.

The axe swung down towards Cuchulainn's neck as everyone watched aghast, but it was the blunt side of the blade that landed on the warrior's neck and it came down so gently that it barely marked him.

'Stand up, Cuchulainn,' the giant said. 'You are the champion of Ulster. No one is your equal for bravery, honesty and honour. From now on your supremacy must go unchallenged. You must be awarded the champion's portion and your wife must take first place in the banqueting hall. I am Cu Roi and I swear by the oath of my people that whoever disputes this, puts his life in danger.' And with that the giant disappeared.

The Death of Connla

CUCHULAINN killed his only son and this is how it came about. When he left Scotland to come back to Emer and to Ulster, he left behind him Aoife who was expecting his child. Cuchulainn gave the woman warrior a gold thumb ring and talked to her about the child that she would bear him.

'Call our son Connla,' he said, 'and when he's big enough send him to Scathach on the Isle of Skye to train in arms. As soon as this ring fits him, send him to find me. He must step aside for no one, he must tell his name to on one, and he must refuse no one who challenges him to single combat. Only when he has been overcome by another warrior may he declare himself.' Then Cuchulainn took his leave of Aoife and returned to Scathach's camp for a while before returning to Ulster.

Seven years to the day after that, Connla came to Ireland to find his father. Cuchulainn was with Conor Mac Nessa and the other Ulster warriors at a gathering on Tracht Eisi, the Strand of the Tracks, when they saw a little bronze boat with golden oars coming across the water towards them. Standing up in it was a young boy. As he skimmed across the waves he fired stones from a sling at the seabirds flying around the boat. He would take aim at a bird and bring it down at his feet, still alive. Then he would revive it and release it back into the air. He would tune his voice to a pitch so piercing and high that the bird would fall stunned for a second time and then he would revive it again.

'Well now,' said Conor, 'I pity the unfortunate country he's heading for! And I *fear* the country he's coming from! If a small boy can do these things, the grown men from that place would grind us all to dust! One of you hurry out and meet the boy. Don't, on any account, let him land here!'

No one moved but at last someone asked, 'Who should go out to meet him?'

'Who else but Condere?' said the king.

'Why Condere?' asked the others.

'Because he's a reasonable and persuasive man,' replied Conor.

'I'll go,' said Condere.

Condere reached the water's edge just as the boy's skiff touched the shore. The boy let down the golden oar and made to jump out of the boat.

'Come no further, young fellow,' Condere said, 'until you've told me your name and your destination.'

'I tell no one my name,' said the boy, 'and I stand aside for no one.'

'Don't dare set foot on this land until you've told me your name and where you're going!' Condere warned.

'I'm going where I have to go,' said the child and tried to pass.

'Take care, son,' Condere persisted. 'Listen to me and do what I ask and the men of Ulster will welcome you. Gathered here are the greatest heroes of the Red Branch: the king, Conor Mac Nessa, Sencha the wise judge, Amergin the poet, and Conall Cearnach, master of the Ulster heroes. They were watching your skilful feats and they admire you, even though you're still too young to grow a beard.'

'I am honoured by your eloquent speech and this is my answer,' said Connla. 'Step aside. No man stands in my way and I refuse no challenge. I'll tell my name only when I'm beaten in single combat. But even if you had the strength of a hundred men you couldn't stop me.'

'I won't try to stop you. Someone else can,' said Condere and he walked back to Conor and the other champions and told them what the boy had said.

'No one makes light of Ulster's honour while I'm around!' Conall Cearnach roared. 'I will not stand for it!' He strode down to meet the boy. 'You play pretty good games, little fellow,' he said.

'I do indeed!' said the boy and put a stone in the sling and shot it into the air. It roared like thunder as it rose and the force of the noise threw Conall to the ground. Before he could rise the boy tied up the warrior's arms with his shield strap.

Conall, furious and humiliated at this treatment, shouted to the others to overcome the boy while Connla stood and laughed at the shamefaced men on the shore.

Cuchulainn, who stood on the strand with his wife, Emer, beside him, watched all this until he could stand it no longer. He started to move towards the boy, practising the feats Scathach had taught him as he advanced. Emer threw her arms round her husband's neck and tried to stop him.

'Don't go down there,' she pleaded. 'That is your own son on the strand. Please don't go near him or challenge him. It would be a tragedy indeed if you were to kill your own flesh and blood. Turn back, Cuchulainn! Take heed of my warning! I beseech you to listen to me! When that boy tells his name, I know what it will be. It will be Connla, your only son and the only son of Aoife.'

'Let me go, Emer!' Cuchulainn said. 'No one can stop me now. Even if he *is* my son I will kill him for making fun of the Ulstermen.' He went down to the boy and said, 'You're having good sport here, boy!'

'*I* am, but *you're* not!' replied the child. 'I've outfaced two of you already and I still haven't told my name.'

'You will tell your name to me or I'll kill you.'

'Well, so be it!' said the boy, and drew his sword. Quickly Cuchulainn drew his sword too, and they began to fight. With one stroke of great precision the boy shaved Cuchulainn's head without drawing blood.

'This mockery has come to a head!' Cuchulainn cried. 'We'll wrestle now!'

'Wrestle!' the boy exclaimed. 'I can't even reach your belt!'

Then he climbed up on to two pillar stones, lifted Cuchulainn off his feet and wedged him between them. He pushed with such force that his feet drove into the standing stones as far as his ankles and the tracks are still there on Tracht Eisi, the Strand of the Tracks, to this day.

When Cuchulainn had freed himself from the pillar stones they raced down to the sea to fight in the waves and twice the boy held Cuchulainn under the water until he was almost drowned. Then Cuchulainn's battle frenzy came over him and he took the Gae Bolga with his foot and sent it through the water at the boy. It tore into his body, its barbs opened out and the breakers turned red with blood.

'Now that's one trick Scathach *didn't* teach me!' the boy said. 'You have killed me!'

'I have,' said Cuchulainn, bending down in the water to lift the boy in his arms. And at that moment he saw his own thumb ring on Connla's hand. He carried the boy to where Conor and the Ulstermen stood and laid him on the ground in front of them. 'Here is my son for you, men of Ulster,' he said.

'Your own son?' they cried out in horror. 'No, no! It can't be true!'

'It's true!' the dying boy said. 'My name is Connla. If I'd been allowed even five years among you, I would have conquered the world for you. Conor, because of my prowess your kingdom would have reached to Rome. But since this is how it ends, point out the famous men standing round that I may say farewell to them.'

One after another the Ulster heroes knelt down and Connla embraced them. Last of all, Cuchulainn knelt beside his son, full of desolation and remorse, and Connla died in his arms. The Ulstermen set up a sorrowful lament for Connla and Cuchulainn. Then they made a grave for the boy and set a stone above it. All of Ulster mourned the tragedy. For three days no one dared to go near Cuchulainn, so terrible was his despair, and not even a calf was let near a cow to feed during that time.

Deirdre of the Sorrows

ONE DAY CONOR MAC NESSA, king of Ulster, came to the house of Felimid, his bard, whose wife had prepared a great feast for the king's company. They ate and drank their fill and the hall was full of the sounds of entertainment.

Felimid's wife oversaw the feast, moving among the guests the whole night long until at last they began to fall asleep. Then she made her way, heavy-footed, to her own quarters because her baby was ready to be born. As she passed through the middle of the house the child in her womb gave a shriek so loud that everyone started up in alarm and the warriors seized their weapons and rushed to the main hall to see what had made the unearthly cry. Nobody knew or could tell what it was till Felimid came from his wife's chamber and told them that it was his unborn child who had screamed.

'Bring your wife here and let her tell us how she interprets this strange happening,' the company said.

Felimid's wife came before the warriors, distraught and frightened.

'What caused our child that is still unborn to scream out?' Felimid asked her. 'It made my blood run cold to hear the sound, it was so piercing and so full of foreboding.'

His wife did not know how to answer him. She too was filled with dread at the loud shriek that had come from inside her body. 'No woman knows what sleeps in her womb,' she told him.

Then she turned fearfully to Cathbad the druid and asked him to tell her the cause of this strange happening. 'Cathbad, you are a wise, generous man and you can foretell the future, please tell me what lies inside my womb.'

The druid answered, 'The infant who has just screamed from your womb is a girl. She will grow up to be a beautiful woman with shining eyes and long, heavy fair hair. Her cheeks will be pink flushed under her white skin. Her lips will be as red as strawberries and she will have teeth like pearls. She will be straight and tall, fed on the fat of the land. Queens will envy her and kings desire her.'

Then the druid laid his hand on the woman's belly and the baby in the womb kicked beneath his hand. 'Yes, it is a daughter lying here. She will be known as Deirdre and because of her there will be great sorrow in Ulster.'

Shortly after this Felimid's wife gave birth to a baby girl. Cathbad took the baby in his arms and prophesied over her.

'Fair daughter of Felimid, O Deirdre of the Sorrows, you will be the envy of women and in your life time you will bring wars to Ulster. O exquisite maiden, woman as vivid as a flame, the beauty of your face will bring jealousy to the hearts of men and exile to the three sons of Usnach. Because of your beauty, violent deeds will bring about the destruction of a king's son. The powerful king of Ulster himself will witness a fierce and terrible deed. Your grave will be a lonely mound, and your story told for ever!'

'Kill the child,' the warriors shouted, 'so that Ulster may be spared!'

But Conor Mac Nessa held up his hand, 'No,' he said, 'I will take this child and I will give her in fosterage to someone I trust and when she grows up she will be my wife.'

The king's decision did not please his followers but they were afraid to argue with him.

So Deirdre was raised as Conor wished and she grew more beautiful each day until she surpassed every woman in Ireland. Conor built a fort in a place apart for her so that none of the Ulster chiefs would see her and want her for themselves. Her foster father was the only man, besides the king, who saw Deirdre's beauty. A poet called Levercham, a powerful woman whose anger the king feared, stayed with her and was Deirdre's nurse and teacher.

One winter's day Deirdre's foster father was skinning a calf to provide veal for the table and the blood flowed out across the snow. As Deirdre watched from her window a raven swooped down to sip the blood.

Deirdre turned to her nurse and said, 'Look, Levercham, I could love a man like that, with hair as black as the raven, and skin like the snow and cheeks as red as blood!'

Levercham answered, 'Well, good luck is yours, Deirdre, for not far from here, in Emain Macha, just beyond this enclosure, is a man like that. He is called Naoise, one of the sons of Usnach. These three brothers are warriors of such courage and skill that if they stood back to back they could hold off all the warriors in Ulster. They are so swift that they can overtake wild animals, and take down deer like hunting dogs. And when they sing together, their song is so melodious that women and men lulled by the music fall silent and peaceful, and cows' milk increases by two-thirds. Ardan, Ainnle and Naoise, these are their names, but Naoise is the strongest and most beautiful of the three.'

'If that is so,' said Deirdre, 'I will not have a day's good health till I see him.'

Not long after this, when the snow had cleared and spring had come to Emain Macha, Deirdre heard beautiful singing coming from the ramparts of the fort. She stole out for she knew that it must be Naoise. She walked past him without glancing in his direction, but Naoise saw her and was so struck by her beauty that he stopped in the middle of his song. He looked at her but she passed him by as if he wasn't there, and then he shouted out so that she could hear him, 'This is a fine young heifer passing me by!'

'Heifers are bound to be fine when there are no bulls about !' Deirdre retorted.

'You have the pick of the herd,' said Naoise, realizing that the beautiful girl must be Deirdre. 'You have Conor for yourself!'

Deirdre turned round then, and looked at Naoise. 'If I had my choice between a fine young bull like you and an old one like Conor I would settle for *you*!'

'But you can't settle for me,' said Naoise. 'You are promised to the king. And don't forget what Cathbad prophesied about you.'

'Are you turning me down?' Deirdre shouted at him.

'I am indeed!' replied Naoise.

In a fit of passion, Deirdre ran up to Naoise and grabbed his head between her hands, holding him by the ears. 'May mockery and disgrace fall on this head,' she cried, 'unless you take me with you!'

Because he was terrified of Conor Mac Nessa's anger, Naoise struggled to free himself from her headstrong hold. 'Go away from me, Deirdre!' he shouted at her. 'Leave me alone!'

'Too late for that. I'm putting your honour at stake. You must take me with you,' said Deirdre, holding him fast.

Naoise began his loud chant that signalled danger and when the Ulster warriors inside Emain heard the sound they seized their weapons and got ready to fight each other. Ardan and Ainnle ran out to their brother to stop him singing.

'What are you doing?' they yelled at him. 'Do you want to bring about the destruction of the place?'

So Naoise told them about Deirdre and what she had said to him and how she had put a *geis*, a most solemn bond on him, to take her with him or lose his honour.

'It will bring destruction on us all,' they said. 'But as long as we're alive we cannot allow you to be disgraced. We'll all leave together and take Deirdre away to another country where Conor can't find us.'

The brothers gathered together a band of warriors, one hundred and fifty strong, the same number of women as well as servants and dogs, and when darkness fell the sons of Usnach fled with Deirdre from the province of Ulster and the anger of the king. Other kings made them welcome and for a while they wandered around Ireland going from one king's protection to another's, but they were harried by Conor's men. They escaped ambushes and treacherous traps until they could stand it no longer and left Ireland for Scotland.

They set up camp among the wild mountains and glens and lived on the game they caught. When winter came and the game was scarce, they stole cattle for food. These cattle raids angered the people of the place and a huge crowd of the men gathered together and marched on Naoise's encampment to kill him and his followers.

The sons of Usnach, seeing the men advance, fled to the king of Scotland to seek protection and offered to fight for him in exchange for food and sanctuary. The king was glad of the services of such great soldiers and gladly took them into his service.

In their encampment, they built their houses in a circle and because they remembered Cathbad's warning they built a secret house for Deirdre in the centre so that no one would see her. They were afraid that there would be killing on account of her great beauty.

But the king's steward rose early one morning and stole into the brothers' encampment. He found Deirdre's hiding place and saw Naoise and Deirdre asleep there. Like everyone else who saw her he was struck by the girl's beauty and he ran in great excitement to tell the king.

'Until this day we have never found anyone worthy to be your queen,' he said to the king who had just awoken, 'but now I know where there is a woman worthy to be queen of the whole world! She is in a secret room with Naoise. Kill him while he's still asleep and make the woman your wife!'

'I won't do that,' the king said. 'We'll try a different way. Every day when Naoise is out, go secretly to the girl's room and tell her that the king of Scotland loves her. Ask her to leave Naoise and come here to me and be my wife.'

The steward did as he was told. Every day, in secret, he wooed Deirdre for the king, and every night, when Naoise returned, Deirdre told him the whole story.

So now that this ploy had failed the king tried another one. He arranged dangerous missions for the three brothers. He sent them into the front line of battle, and set traps for them so that they would be killed, but through their skill and bravery the three brothers emerged safe from every perilous situation. At last Deirdre was given an ultimatum by the king; she must come to him willingly or she would be taken by force and the three brothers would be killed.

That night Deirdre warned Naoise of the danger and urged him to escape. 'If you stay till tomorrow,' she told him, 'by nightfall you'll be dead. I hate to leave Scotland. I love its lochs and mountains and its purple valleys. It has become a home from home for me but we must go!'

As they got into the boats that were to take them away, Deirdre looked back at the place she had grown to love and began to sing a song in praise of the mountains and lakes of Scotland. As the boat drew away from the shore, she named the hills and the wooded glens, the lochs and inlets, lamenting her departure and remembering her happiness with Naoise in that place.

Once more Deirdre and the sons of Usnach were fugitives. They stole away with their followers and hid on a remote island from where they could see both Ireland and Scotland.

When the news reached Emain Macha that Deirdre and Naoise had left Scotland and were on the island, the Red Branch warriors went to Conor to put the brother's cause before him. 'This is Deirdre's doing, not theirs,' they told him. 'It would be tragic if their enemies killed them in a foreign land because of a headstrong woman. You should forgive them and allow them to return here unharmed.'

'Let them come back then,' said the king, 'and tell them I will send someone to guarantee their safety.'

When the fugitives got this message they were delighted at the prospect of returning home to their country and their companions. They sent back a message to Conor thanking him for his pardon. They asked for three of Ulster's most famous champions, Fergus, Dubtach and Cormac, the king's son, to guarantee their safety, and Conor agreed.

But the king still wanted Deirdre for himself and laid a trap for the sons of Usnach.

He ordered Fergus to make sure that Deirdre and the three brothers and all their household came directly to Emain as soon as they arrived in Ireland. He gave instructions that on no account were they to eat or drink *anywhere* until they ate and drank with him. Then he ordered Borrach, a chief whose fort lay on the route to Emain Macha, to prepare a lavish feast in Fergus's honour. 'He will not refuse your invitation. Remind him of his *geis*.' Conor advised the chief for he knew that there was a bond on Fergus that he must never, under pain of death, refuse to attend a feast that had been prepared in his honour. Borrach did as he had been instructed and when Fergus arrived at the stronghold invited him to the feast and reminded him of his *geis*. Fergus turned pale with anger at Borrach's words. 'You had little call to make me choose between my fate and my honour!' he shouted. 'It's a cruel choice! I have given my word to accompany Deirdre and Naoise and their followers to Emain without delay but I cannot refuse your hospitality, unwelcome as it is!'

Naoise and Deirdre were alarmed when they heard that Fergus had to attend Borrach's feast and that they had to go on to Conor's fort without him.

'Are you forsaking us for a meal?' they said bitterly.

'I'm not forsaking you,' Fergus said. 'I'll send my son Fiacha with you to ensure your safe-conduct.'

So Deirdre and the sons of Usnach, accompanied by Fiacha, set off for Emain Macha, while Fergus, Cormac and Dubtach went to Borrach's feast.

When the travellers arrived at the king's fort, another band of visitors was already with Conor. This was Eogan, son of the king of Fernmag who had been a longstanding enemy of Conor's. Eogan had come on his father's behalf to make peace with the king of Ulster, and Conor, seeing his chance, had accepted his offer on the condition that he would kill the sons of Usnach.

As Deirdre and the brothers stood on the green at the centre of Emain Macha, the women of the king's household came out and sat on top of the ramparts to watch. Conor's bodyguard of hired soldiers made a circle round him. Eogan of Fernmag began to move towards the sons of Usnach, and Fergus's son Fiacha, sensing treachery, went up to stand beside Naoise.

As Eogan came close, Naoise went to greet him, In reply Eogan drew his sword and drove it through Naoise's body breaking his spine. As Naoise fell, Fiacha caught him in his arms and pulled him down to shield him with his body but Eogan killed them both. He killed Naoise through the body of Fiacha. Then Conor's mercenaries closed on Ainnle and Ardan and their followers and hunted them like hares from one end of the green to the other and killed them all.

Deirdre was seized, her hands were tied behind her back and she was handed over to Conor.

Fergus was already on his way to Emain Macha when he heard of the murder of his own son and of the sons of Usnach. He was mad with anger at Conor's treachery. He and the two other warriors, Dubtach and Cormac, who had promised safe-conduct to Naoise swiftly gathered their army and made a surprise attack on Conor's fort. Hundreds of Conor's soldiers died in the raid and Fergus set fire to Emain Macha.

Then Fergus fled to Connacht to Aillil and Medb, the king and queen of that province, for he knew they would give him sanctuary. Fergus brought a large band of his soldiers into exile with him and they made raids on Emain Macha. Every night for sixteen years there was bloodshed and suffering in Conor Mac Nessa's territory in revenge for the death of the sons of Usnach.

After the death of Naoise, Deirdre was kept in Conor's house for a year. In all that time she was never once seen to smile or laugh. She hardly slept at all and the little food she ate barely kept her alive. She crouched in her room, never raising her head from her knees. When Conor brought musicians to play for her, she wouldn't listen to their songs. Instead she recited a poem lamenting Naoise's death. When the king tried to comfort her she accused him bitterly of Naoise's murder and threw his love back in his face.

Conor became more and more angry at the rejection and at Deirdre's defiance. 'Of all that you see, Deirdre, what do you hate most?' he asked her one day.

'I hate you, Conor, and I hate Eogan who killed Naoise,' Deirdre answered.

'If that's the case,' said Conor, 'you can spend a year with him!' and he handed her over to Eogan.

Next day the three of them drove out to the fair at Emain Macha. Deirdre was behind Eogan in his chariot. Alongside was Conor. Deirdre could not bear to be between her two tormentors and she made a vow that she would not look at them together, so she kept her eyes cast down, fixed on the earth.

'Well, Deirdre,' Conor taunted her, 'here you are where you can eye us both, like a ewe between two rams!'

There were galloping past a huge boulder as the king spoke these mocking words and, hearing them, Deirdre leaned out of the chariot, dashed her head against the rock and died.

Cuchulainn and Ferdia's Fight
at the Ford

MEDB was the proud and headstrong queen of Connacht and her husband was called Aillil. As the couple lay in bed one night, their pillow talk turned to the wealth they both had. They argued about which of them was the richest. They compared their lands, their dwellings, their furnishings, their precious vessels, their jewellery, their clothes, their flocks of sheep and their herds of cattle. All these things were matched and measured and found to be equal except for one thing: in Aillil's herd there was a magnificent bull called the White-Horned and Medb had none to touch it. When she heard that an Ulster chieftain called Daire, had a bull as powerful and majestic as Aillil's, Medb was determined to get the bull and bring it back to graze with her own herd in Cruachan. She sent her messengers to Ulster to negotiate with Daire about acquiring his bull, the Brown Bull of Cooley, but the man would not part with it and when diplomacy failed Medb decided to make a raid on Ulster and take the animal by force. She called the kings of the other parts of Ireland to help her invade the province, and troops from Leinster and Munster went to Connacht to join forces with her. Fergus Mac Roi, the powerful Red Branch warrior, sided with Medb as well. Though he was an Ulsterman he had become an enemy of Conor Mac Nessa's because of the king's cruel and treacherous treatment of Deirdre and the sons of Usnach.

A great army of the men of Ireland assembled at Cruachan ready to march on Ulster and capture for Medb the Brown Bull of Cooley. The queen herself took command of the army, and Fergus, who knew the territory and the route to Ulster, was chosen as the chief scout and guide. Medb waited until Macha's curse had come on the Red Branch warriors and they were stricken by birth pangs, and lay helpless as infants or women in childbirth. Then she moved against Ulster.

But one Ulster warrior was immune to this weakness and that was Cuchulainn. Because his father was Lugh of the Tuatha De Danaan, Macha's curse did not affect him. Cuchulainn was still only seventeen as Medb's army began the Cattle Raid of Cooley, but he was already one of the greatest warriors of the Red Branch. Even in childhood his courage and ferocity were famous. Later, as a youth he had gone to Scotland and had learnt special secret battle skills from Scathach, the fierce woman warrior of Skye. Thus it fell to Cuchulainn to defend the province of Ulster on his own. For three months, single-handed, he harried the men of Ireland as he waited for Conor Mac Nessa and the Red Branch heroes to be freed from Macha's throes.

As Medb's scouts made incursions into Ulster, Cuchulainn stalked them and beheaded them. When she sent companies of soldiers against him, he defeated them, slaughtering as many as a hundred a day, and when she sent her greatest champions to meet him in single combat at the ford, he killed them one by one.

The men of Ireland had a meeting to decide who would go out to the ford next and fight Cuchulainn since he had killed so many of their champions already. They agreed unanimously that Ferdia, the son of Daman, was the only one strong and brave enough to face Cuchulainn. He had been trained in arms with Cuchulainn in Scathach's camp, so he knew the same secret tactics. They were perfectly matched in battle except for one thing; Cuchulainn had the Gae Bolga, the deadly weapon that Scathach had given him. This spear was cast with the foot and never missed its mark. When the point entered its target it opened out into thirty barbs, that invaded the whole body, tearing and pulling at the flesh. It could not be pulled out so the victim's body had to be cut open to remove it. Though Ferdia had no weapon to match the Gae Bolga, he had a special horn-skin that no spear could pierce.

Medb sent her messengers to Ferdia in his camp telling him to come and meet her and her commanders. But Ferdia did not want to fight Cuchulainn. He and Cuchulainn had been companions-in-arms. They had defended each other in times of danger and they loved each other like brothers. They were foster brothers, one of the strongest ties of all. Although message after message was sent to him, Ferdia refused to go to see Medb for he knew what she wanted him to do. So Medb sent her druids and her poets to mock him and blame him and to disgrace him in satirical poems and spells. In the end Ferdia agreed to go with them to see Medb and Aillil for he preferred to die with honour and courage in battle than to fall victim to the abuse and derision of the satirists.

When he arrived in their tent he was greeted rapturously by the king and queen. They threw a feast in his honour and all the leaders of the men of Ireland were present. Finnabair, the beautiful, fair-haired daughter of Medb and Aillil sat beside Ferdia and poured great quantities of liquor into his goblet, kissing him each time she filled the cup. She whispered in his ear that he was her darling and of all the men alive he was the chosen one, the only one she loved.

Ferdia was flattered by the attentions of the king's lovely daughter and was happy to be the guest of honour. He soon became drunk and merry and forgot why he had been summoned to the royal quarters. Then Medb spoke.

'Do you know why we sent for you, Ferdia?' she asked.

'I assume I'm here because all the other champions are here,' Ferdia replied, 'for I'm as good as they are!'

'We know you're the *best* champion we have!' Medb said. 'And so we've chosen you to meet Cuchulainn.'

When he heard this, Ferdia's happiness melted like snow off a ditch and he told Medb he would not fight his friend. Medb pressed him again and again to meet Cuchulainn but he would not. Then she offered him great rewards.

'You can have priceless chariots and the swiftest horses and enough tackle and harness for a dozen man if you will agree to fight Cuchulainn at the ford,' Medb promised. Ferdia refused.

'I will give you a tract of land in Connacht as big as the Plain of Muirthemne,' Medb said. 'And you and your family can live in my court in Cruachan for the rest of your lives, free from taxes, and the best of food and drink supplied! And take this,' she said, unpinning a leaf-shaped brooch from her cloak. 'Feel how heavy it is, how beautiful it is! It's made of solid gold!'

But Ferdia steadfastly refused to fight Cuchulainn.

'You can have Finnabair, my daughter for your wife,' Medb pleaded, 'and *my* love for life if you go to the ford. You can have anything you want for you are a great warrior and you alone are equal to Cuchulainn'

'Medb, you're powerful and persuasive but I will not be bribed. If you offered me the sun and the moon still I would not fight Cuchulainn at the ford. Only disaster would come from our meeting. He is a great warrior, greater than me though we trained together and fought together. He is the Hound of Ulster, a fierce fighter, and I would rather fight two hundred men than him. One of us must die if we meet and if I killed my foster brother, I would turn back and kill *you*, Medb, and all your followers!'

But Medb, who knew better than most how to stir up trouble, tried another trick. Ignoring Ferdia's outcry she turned to the assembled company. 'What Cuchulainn said was right after all!' she exclaimed.

'What did Cuchulainn say?' Ferdia demanded angrily.

'He said it would come as no surprise to him if he overcame you in a fight wherever or whenever you would meet.'

'He had no right to say that!' Ferdia burst out. 'For he knows me well enough to know I'm a good fighter and that I'm not afraid to fight and never have been. I wouldn't degrade him like that, so tomorrow morning to save my good name I'll be the first man out and in front of you all, I'll fight Cuchulainn!'

Medb was pleased when Ferdia shouted out this promise and all the other warriors there as witnesses.

'I knew you were no coward,' she said, 'and you're sure to win. It's right that you, like Cuchulainn, should put your loyalty to your country above friendship.'

Among the men of Ireland who witnessed all this was Fergus Mac Roi, the Red Branch leader who had fled from Emain Macha and joined forces with Medb after avenging the deaths of the sons of Usnach. Fergus was one of Cuchulainn's foster fathers and he loved him like a son. He was dismayed as he watched Medb trick Ferdia into going to the ford to meet Cuchulainn and he left the assembly and went back to his own camp and told his companions of his fears for Cuchulainn. He knew that Ferdia was the one man who could match Cuchulainn's fighting skills and he knew too that Ferdia was hungry for battle now that he had been goaded by Medb's lies and taunts.

'Go and warn Cuchulainn that there's danger in store for him tomorrow,' he told his messengers. 'Tell him that his foster brother is coming out to fight him. Try to persuade him not to come to the ford tomorrow morning!'

'Fergus, even if you were at the ford yourself we'd be afraid to go near Cuchulainn and give him a message of that sort!' they protested.

'I'll go myself then,' said Fergus. 'Get the horses and chariots ready!'

Fergus took his huge curved shield, his silver spear and his sword in its scabbard of chased silver and stepped into his magnificent chariot. As he approached the river, the copper chariot and the shining weapons flashed in the evening sun. Laeg, Cuchulainn's charioteer and faithful guard, saw the light in the distance and told Cuchulainn about the splendid warrior who was approaching.

'It's not hard to say who *that* is,' said Cuchulainn. 'It could be no one else but Fergus, my foster father, who has come out here to warn me about the battle against all the men of Ireland!'

At the ford, Fergus got out of his chariot and Cuchulainn greeted him.

'You're welcome here, Fergus my friend! If I could, I would prepare a hero's feast for you of fish and waterfowl, a salad of cress and seaweed, and a drink of cold water.'

'That's the meal of an outlaw!' said Fergus.

'It is indeed,' said Cuchulainn. 'That's what I have become.'

'I didn't come here for hospitality,' said Fergus. 'I came to tell you who is coming to fight you tomorrow morning.'

'Tell me who is that?' asked Cuchulainn.

'I'll tell you,' said Fergus. 'It's your friend Ferdia who's coming to the ford. Your foster brother, your brother-in-arms, your equal in courage and skill.'

'As sure as I live it's an encounter I dread,' Cuchulainn cried, 'not because I *fear* Ferdia, but because I *love* him. I would almost rather he killed me than that I killed him!'

'For that very reason be on your guard! You have every reason to fear Ferdia. He is by far the greatest warrior you have met so far in this war, and the greatest you will ever meet. He is as skilled as you are. Moreover he has his horn-skin protection and when he fights no weapon can pierce it. He is as ferocious now as a lion and he will overwhelm you like a tidal wave!'

'Don't say that!' Cuchulainn said. 'For I swear in the name of my tribe, the people I am defending at the ford, that I will overcome Ferdia. I will pierce him as if he was a rush softened by river water. For months now, on my own, I have faced the onslaught of the four provinces of Ireland without once stepping back, and I assure you I will not step back now!'

'I hope with all my heart that it will turn out like that,' said Fergus. 'Though I joined Medb's forces because of Conor's treachery, I want you to win, Cuchulainn, but the fight will be hard and bitter!'

Then Cuchulainn embraced Fergus and thanked him for coming to warn him and Fergus returned to Medb's camp. When Fergus had gone Laeg turned to Cuchulainn.

'What will you do tonight?' he asked him.

'What indeed!' said Cuchulainn.

I'll tell you,' said Laeg. 'Tomorrow Ferdia will come to the ford to attack you. He will be bathed and rested, his hair will be plaited and dressed and he will have a great crowd of Medb's followers with him to be spectators at the fight. So you should go to your wife, Emer and let her make you ready for battle so that tomorrow you'll present yourself to him as well groomed and ready as he.'

Cuchulainn took Laeg's advice and went to Emer's house to spend the night.

As for Ferdia, when his outburst was over he left the feast and went back to his tent to tell his companions how he had promised to fight Cuchulainn the next morning and to show them the favours he had got in return. His friends were dismayed at this news. They knew that when the two greatest champions in Ireland met, one or both of them would die. They had seen the fearful work that Cuchulainn had done in the past months and in their hearts they were afraid that it would be Ferdia who would fall.

Ferdia, still half drunk from the feast, slept heavily for the first part of the night but woke up early, anxious and frightened at the promise he had made and the thought of the battle ahead of him. He was afraid that after he had faced Cuchulainn, whatever the outcome, his life would not be his own. His charioteer was frightened as well and advised Ferdia not to go to the ford.

'Keep quiet!' Ferdia snapped. 'I made a promise in front of all the men of Ireland that I would fight Cuchulainn, and I must keep my word. To tell you the truth I would almost rather he killed me than that I killed him!'

Then Ferdia tried to comfort and encourage his charioteer by describing how he would overcome Cuchulainn in battle and they set off for the ford.

When they arrived there dawn had not yet broken so Ferdia tried to get some more sleep. 'Make a bed for me in the chariot,' he said, 'and I'll try to get back to sleep, for I got little enough last night.' So the servant unyoked the horses and made a bed for his master and Ferdia slept fitfully till dawn.

The sun was well risen when Cuchulainn arrived at the ford. He waited till then for he did not want the men of Ireland to think that fear had woken him early. When it was broad daylight he ordered Laeg to harness the horses and yoke them to his chariot. 'Hurry up, Laeg,' he said, 'for the man who is waiting for us has been up a long time!'

Then Cuchulainn, the champion of the Ulstermen, and Laeg, his skilful charioteer, got into the chariot and set off for the ford. As they sped along, the air around Cuchulainn's head shrieked with the war cries of the Tuatha De Danaan. When he set out to fight, these war demons rallied round their kinsman, striking even greater terror into the minds of his opponents who were terrified already by his fearsome reputation.

As he clattered towards the ford, the uproar around his chariot was tumultuous. Shields clashed, spears rattled, swords thudded and armour clanged. The ropes strained and hissed, the wheels rumbled and the chariot creaked. The thunder of the horses' hoofs and Cuchulainn's deep loud voice vibrated in the clamorous air around his head.

Ferdia's charioteer heard the tumult and ran to wake his master. He shook him and said, 'Ferdia, rise up at once! They are coming to meet you at the ford. I hear the sound of a silver-yoked chariot. It is driven by a reckless charioteer and in it there is a tall warrior. He is coming fast down the road, he is heading for victory. It is that fierce fighter, the Hound of Ulster, who is galloping south-wards, swift as a hawk. He comes bloodstained from battles to do battle again! I pity the man who has to meet Cuchulainn. I knew it in my bones, I foretold it, that some day we'd meet him in battle. Now I hear him and he hears us. It is Cuchulainn, the Hound of Emain, the defender of Ulster!'

'Stop praising Cuchulainn,' Ferdia said, 'and help *me* now! Get ready my weapons. I'll soon lower his pride and his triumph. Others may have failed but I'll succeed!'

Cuchulainn arrived at the north side of the ford and stopped. Ferdia faced him from the opposite bank.

'You're welcome, Cuchulainn!' shouted Ferdia.

'I don't trust your welcome any more!' Cuchulainn shouted back. 'And anyway, Ferdia, it is for *me* to welcome *you*. Not the other way round. After all it is you who has come to the borders of my homeland to challenge me. *I* should be doing the challeng-ing! You have driven away our women and children, our horses and herds!'

'What brought you here to fight me?' Ferdia shouted. 'Don't forget that when we were together in Scathach's place you were my serving man. You sharpened my weapons and made my bed for me.'

'True enough!' Cuchulainn yelled back. 'But that was then. Things have changed now. I was only a strip of a boy then. Young and small. That's why I was your servant. Today there is not a warrior anywhere who can match me!'

'Foolish, rash Cuchulainn! What bad luck brought you here?' Ferdia lamented.

'You'll be lucky to see home again,' Cuchulainn roared. 'I'll cut you till you reek with blood. I'll fell you. You'll die trying to defend yourself. You're facing your doom at this ford, and at the hands of a great champion!'

'Stop boasting, Cuchulainn,' said Ferdia. 'Before morning your head will be on the point of my spear!'

'Oh, Ferdia,' said Cuchulainn, 'when we were at Scathach's we set out together to face all sorts of dangers. You were my companion, dearer to me than any brother. We shared the same bed. I'll miss you! You shouldn't have come to challenge me here because of false promises. Medb has promised you Finnabair, but you will never have her. She's been promised to fifty men before you and she's destroyed them all. They died at my hands, and you will too, Ferdia!'

'That's enough talk,' said Ferdia. 'Choose the weapons we're going to fight with today.'

'You make the choice,' said Cuchulainn. 'You were here first.'

'Do you remember the throwing feats we learnt at Scathach's?'

'I do,' said Cuchulainn. 'They were the last feats we practised.'

'Then they'll be the first feats we use today,' said Ferdia.

They both lifted their small, sharp-edged throwing shields, their small ivory-handled swords and their light ivory darts. All morning they skimmed the shields and cast the spears at each other and the small darts hummed through the air like bees on a sunny day. But skilfully as they threw just as skilfully they parried and the weapons were blunted against their long shields.

'No one will win at this,' said Ferdia. 'What will we use now?'

'It's still your choice till nightfall,' Cuchulainn replied. 'You were the first at the ford.'

'Well then,' said Ferdia, we'll take our heavy javelins and fight with them.'

They hurled the javelins at each other till nightfall but skilfully as they parried just as skilfully they threw and they wounded each other until they bled.

'We'll stop, Cuchulainn,' said Ferdia.

'I agree,' said Cuchulainn.

They tossed their weapons to their charioteers who caught them and took them away. Then Cuchulainn and Ferdia waded into the middle of the ford to greet each other. They put their arms around each other's neck and kissed three times in acknowledgement of their friendship. Then the two warriors went back to their own side of the river and lay down on the beds of rushes that their charioteers had made for them. The physicians and healers came to dress their wounds with herbs and potions. For every herb and healing plant that was applied to Cuchulainn's gashes, the same amount was sent across the ford to Ferdia so that none of the men of Ireland could say that Cuchulainn had won because of his advantages in the matter of healing.

In the same way half of the food and refreshing drinks that were brought to Ferdia was sent across the ford to Cuchulainn, for only a small band of dwellers on Breg Plain supplied Cuchulainn with food, while Ferdia had the four provinces of Ireland providing for him. That night the horses of both warriors grazed in the same paddock and their charioteers sat round the same campfire.

Next morning Cuchulainn and Ferdia went to the ford to start fighting again.

'*Your* choice of weapons today, Cuchulainn,' said Ferdia.

'Since we had no decisive win from casting our weapons yesterday we'll use spears today and come closer,' said Cuchulainn. 'Maybe the thrusting of spears will decide between us.'

They buckled on their broad shields and moved closer to each other, gripping their spears. They lunged at each other, driving the spears past their shields, finding their mark all day long till by nightfall the holes in their bodies were so big that birds could have flown through them, carrying blood and loosened flesh into the air.

When the long day was over and evening came at last, the charioteers and horses were weary and the champions were exhausted.

'Let us stop now, Ferdia. If our horses and men are as spent as this, what about ourselves?'

Ferdia agreed and they both threw aside their weapons and their charioteers caught them. They put their arms around each other and embraced. Their horses were led to the same paddock and their exhausted charioteers slept round the same fire. That night the physicians and healers came to minister to the warriors but their injuries were so great that no herbal dressing or healing plant, no potion or ointment could close the wounds or staunch the blood. Instead, they used charms and spells and incantations. Half of these were sent across the ford to Ferdia and in return Cuchulainn got half the food that the men of Ireland had brought to Ferdia as a mark of their respect.

The next morning, as they approached the ford, Cuchulainn noticed that Ferdia had changed. His hair had become darker, his eyes were dull and listless and he seemed weaker in his movements. Cuchulainn was full of pity for his friend.

'Oh, Ferdia,' he called across the water, 'if this is the state you're in, you're doomed! You should never have come here for Medb or Finnabair's sake. You'll bring about your own death.'

'We all die in the end,' Ferdia called back, 'no matter how brave and proud in battle we may be. But I must fight you, foster brother, or lose my good name throughout Ireland. Don't blame yourself for my death, Cuchulainn. Medb, not you, betrayed me.'

'My heart is tight, the blood runs cold at having to fight you in this state, my friend,' Cuchulainn said.

'No matter,' said Ferdia. 'I'll fight you anyway. What weapons will we use?'

'Your choice,' said Cuchulainn.

'Very well,' said Ferdia, 'we'll use our swords today. Maybe that will bring an end to this.'

So they took up their full-length shields and their heavy hard-hitting swords and they raced at each other. They hewed and hacked and sliced until lumps of flesh as big as a child's head flew into the air from their shoulders and thighs. So it went on all day until Ferdia called a halt. This time there was no embrace. They staggered wearily away from each other, sad and despondent. Their charioteers sat at separate fires that night and their horses were penned in different fields.

Next morning Ferdia rose early. He knew that today the battle would be won or lost and he came alone to the ford. He put on his richest battle gear. Next to his skin he wore a silk tunic edged in gold. Over that he buckled an apron of pliant brown leather and on top of that again he hung a stone as big as a milestone. Over all he put a strong iron apron to protect him from the Gae Bolga. On his head he placed his crested helmet, enamelled and jewelled with rubies, crystals and amethysts. He carried a strong sharp spear in his right hand and in his left, a curved gold-hilted sword. Across his back he slung a huge shield deeply engraved round a great gold central boss. Then he started to leap and dance through the air doing marvellous turns with his weapons. He performed miraculous, perilous feats that no one had taught him, not even Scathach or the other champions who had fostered him, stupendous tricks that he had invented on the spur of the moment as he screwed up his courage to fight Cuchulainn.

The Ulster champion arrived at the ford in the middle of this display. He watched Ferdia's gymnastic leaps, his fierce play with his weapons, his amazing demonstrations of balance and strength and he said to Laeg, 'Now you can see what I'm up against! These thrilling moves of Ferdia's could defeat me, so taunt me and mock me if you see me falter; then my battle frenzy will fuel my anger. If I'm winning, praise me and encourage me, in case pity for Ferdia should make me lose heart!'

'I'll do as you say, Cuchulainn,' said Laeg.

Then Cuchulainn put on his battle gear and as Ferdia watched across the ford he too performed thrilling acrobatic leaps and manoeuvres that he had not learnt from Scathach or anyone else but rose out of the exultation of the moment. Ferdia watched these feats and feints and knew that before the day was over they would be turned on him.

'What weapons, Cuchulainn?' he asked.

'We'll use the feats of the ford today,' said Cuchulainn.

When Ferdia heard this his heart was heavy for he knew it was by these feats that Cuchulainn had defeated all his enemies.

A furious combat began, a struggle between the two great

champions of Ireland, two battle-hardened, fierce warriors, heroes in both their camps.

At first they stayed apart and hurled spears and darts at each other across the ford. By midday they were both inflamed by the fight and as the battle fury rose in them, they moved closer for hand-to-hand combat. Cuchulainn sprang to the boss of Ferdia's shield to strike him from above. Ferdia gave the shield a mighty heave with his forearm and set Cuchulainn spinning like a stunned bird to the bank of the ford. Again Cuchulainn leapt from the bank to the boss of the shield to reach over the rim and strike at Ferdia's head. With one thrust of his knee, Ferdia tossed him off the shield as if he were a baby.

Laeg saw that Cuchulainn was in trouble.

'What's this, Cuchulainn! Ferdia has tossed you in the air like a mother tossing her baby. He has flung you away from him like water out of a cup. He has drilled through you like an awl through wood. He has tied you up in knots like a creeper choking a tree. He has dropped on you like a hawk on a sparrow. You're grist to his mill. From now on you can make no claims as a fighter, you spoilt little sham!'

Wild with rage at Laeg's taunts and Ferdia's mastery, Cuchulainn sprang into the air with the speed of a swallow in flight and lit on the boss of Ferdia's shield for the third time. Ferdia gave the shield a strong, disdainful shake as though nothing had landed on it and flung Cuchulainn backwards again across the ford.

Then Cuchulainn's war warp contorted him. He swelled up in his spasm like a huge bladder full of wind. He changed colour and his face became mottled and distorted. He arched his deformed body like a grotesque bow and towered over Ferdia, huge and terrifying as a Fomorian giant.

They began to fight. Their foreheads met above and their feet met below and their hands met in the middle, hacking and stabbing at each other over their shields. They fought so closely that their shields split with the impact. They fought so closely that their spearheads bent in their staves and the rivets burst out. They fought so closely that demons shrieked from the hilts of their swords and the points of their spears and the rims of their shields. They fought so closely that their trampling feet forced the river off its course. The riverbed became dry enough to sleep in and the only water that fell round them poured from the combatants themselves. The battle was so intense that the chariot horses reared in a frenzy and bolted, ripping free from their chains and tearing their traces apart. The struggle was so tumultuous that there was panic in the camp of the men of Ireland. The camp followers, the women and children, the old, the weak and the mad were crazed with fear and broke headlong out of the stockade and fled southwestward for Connacht.

Then Ferdia found a gap in Cuchulainn's defence and thrust his sword into his chest. Blood spouted from the wound, and the fighters at the ford slithered in the blood. Ferdia struck again and again until Cuchulainn could bear the thrusts no longer and he yelled at Laeg to get the Gae Bolga. Ferdia heard the name of the weapon he dreaded and he dropped his shield to protect his lower body. As he did so Cuchulainn cast his spear at Ferdia's chest and it went through his heart and halfway out of his back.

Laeg hurled the Gae Bolga downstream to Cuchulainn and he caught it with his foot. Ferdia thrust up his shield to protect his chest but it was too late. The Gae Bolga cast from Cuchulainn's foot smashed through the iron apron and split the huge stone under it into three parts. It drove into Ferdia's belly and the barbs opened out, filling every crevice and cavity of his body.

'You're killed me with that, Cuchulainn!' Ferdia cried out. 'My ribs have been shattered and my heart has burst. It was treachery that brought me here but it was *you* who killed me. My blood is on your hands!'

Cuchulainn ran towards Ferdia and caught him as he fell. He carried him and all his gear across the ford so that he would die on his territory and not on Medb's. He laid Ferdia down on the ground and collapsed beside him. He lay in a faint beside Ferdia's head, overcome with grief.

Laeg saw Cuchulainn lying prone and so did Cuchulainn's forces. They fell into battle formation and as they prepared to attack, Laeg ran up to Cuchulainn and shook him back to his senses. 'Get up, Cu!' he shouted. 'Get up! The men of Ireland are preparing to attack. Rise up or they will kill you!'

'Oh, Laeg, why should I bother to rise? Why should I bother, now that Ferdia is dead?' came the response.

Laeg begged and pleaded with his master, but Cuchulainn would not listen to him nor answer him. Instead, he bent over his dead friend, talking as if he were still able to hear. 'Oh Ferdia, if only you had listened to the pleading of your friends! If only you had taken their advice! They reminded you of our friendship. They warned you about this battle. They knew I would beat you. You should have listened to them. You were my dearest comrade, Ferdia. Ever since our time together at Scathach's you have been my truest friend, the companion I loved most. You were the handsomest lad, the bravest soldier, the best fighter that I ever met. I thought our friendship would never end. And that it should end like this! You, killed, and I your killer. And that I should have to live on! Not since I killed Connla, my own and Aoife's son, have I felt such despair!' Staring into Ferdia's face and rocking with grief Cuchulainn lamented and mourned his friend and cursed the futility of the fight. At last Laeg stepped in to strip Ferdia of his armour. He found Cuchulainn's brooch pinned to his tunic and handed it to Cuchulainn.

'So this is what he fought for!' Cuchulainn said bitterly. 'This and Finnabair's false promise. Dear friend, it was a futile, fruitless meeting. And it was an unequal fight!'

Then Laeg cut Ferdia open to take back the Gae Bolga and when Cuchulainn saw his weapon covered in Ferdia's blood, he was overcome once more. He sobbed bitterly for Ferdia and made for him a litany of love and loss.

At last Laeg made himself heard. 'We must go now, CuCu!' he said. 'We must leave the ford at once.'

'Yes, we'll go now, Laeg, and leave our friend here. But I tell you, every battle, every struggle I ever had was like a child's carefree game compared to this fight with Ferdia at the ford.'

The Death of Cuchulainn

BY THE TIME he was twenty-seven Cuchulainn had many enemies. Chief among them was Medb of Cruachan. The warrior queen had not forgotten her defeat at his hands during the Tain Bo Cuailnge, the Cattle Raid of Cooley, and she was biding her time and plotting her revenge. But Cuchulainn had other enemies as well. He had killed many warriors since he had first taken up arms and now their sons were determined to avenge their fathers' deaths. Erc, son of Cairbre, and Lugaid, son of Cu Roi, were implacable foes but the most fearsome of all were the children of the magician Calitin.

Cuchulainn had killed Calitin and twenty of his sons during the *Tain* and when news of his death was brought to Calitin's wife she gave birth to six children, three daughters and three sons. These children were monstrous and misshapen and Medb took them from their mother to Cruachan where she reared them carefully to play their part in Cuchulainn's downfall. They learnt charms, spells, witchcraft and incantation from the druids at Cruachan and in order that they might learn more magic, Medb sent them far away to the East. There they were taught powerful spells by the magician friends of their father, Calitin, and they returned to Medb perfected in those arts.

The children of Calitin came back to Cruachan riding a fierce wind of their own making and landed at Medb's rath. Medb looked out and saw the venomous children on her ramparts and welcomed them home. With these powerful allies at her side, she sent messengers round to the men of Ireland to persuade them to muster once more. She stirred up old hatreds and grievances and the enemies of Ulster rallied to her cause again. Then she planned the downfall of Cuchulainn. When the warriors of Ulster lay powerless under Macha's curse, every man of the Red Branch as helpless as a woman

141

in labour, Medb led her forces north once again. As soon as she had crossed the Ulster border, she set fire to raths and forts until the province was filled with smoke and flames.

The news of Medb's invasion was brought to Conor Mac Nessa and the king knew that Cuchulainn was the quarry Medb was hunting. He sent a messenger to Cuchulainn in his fort at Dun Dealgan ordering him to come at once to Emain Macha. In this way he hoped to protect Cuchulainn against Medb and be protected by him in turn if Medb reached Emain Macha.

Levercham, the king's messenger, was sent to Dun Dealgan to bring Cuchulainn back. She found him on Baile's Strand hunting seafowl. He was letting fly at the birds with sling and stone again and again, but he missed each time and the seafowl flew on unharmed. This disturbed Cuchulainn because he had never missed his target before and he knew his loss of aim was a bad omen. He was sad as well because it was on his mind that on this strand he had killed Connla, his son. When Levercham delivered Conor's message to him, Cuchulainn became even more dejected. He did not want to leave his home territory at all but he had no choice but to obey the king's orders, so he went with the emissary to Emain Macha.

When Levercham and Cuchulainn arrived at Conor's fort, Cuchulainn went straight away to the *grianan*, the light sunny room that had been prepared for him. He was joined there by Emer and her companions and throughout the day Conor's finest musicians, poets and wise men entertained him. In this way the king hoped to keep news of Medb's advance from Cuchulainn until Conall Cearnach, the master of the Red Branch champions, had returned from Scotland and the other warriors had recovered from the effects of Macha's curse.

The children of Calitin incited Medb to engage Cuchulainn in battle as soon as possible, so she marched to Dun Dealgan to challenge him. When she found him gone she set fire to Dun Dealgan and the fort and its inmates were destroyed. The children of Calitin promised Medb that within three days they would bring Cuchulainn himself to his doom.

So, summoning a wind, the loathsome brood set off for Emain

Macha where they knew Cuchulainn was being detained. They
landed on the flat land outside the ramparts of Conor's fort and
went to work with the magic tricks they had learnt in the East. They
crouched on the earth and beat it with their feet and fists and tore it
up around them. They flung up showers of dead oak leaves and
scattered the withered stalks of thistles, sending the fuzz balls into
the air. Through their sorcery, the dead leaves and soil and thistle-
down became like a vast army in battle. The clamour of war filled
the plain, the roaring of men and the clash of weapons upon
armour rang out and it seemed as if a vast host of soldiers, multi-
tudes of men, fought furiously as they attacked Emain Macha.
Inside the room where he sat and talked with Cathbad, Cuchulainn
heard the pandemonium. He ran to the window and looked out and
saw a crowd of soldiers attacking Conor's undefended fort. He
flared up with rage and shame that there was no resistance and ran
for his weapons. Cathbad threw his arms round him and begged
him not to go.

'This is the magic of Calitin's brood. These are phantasmagoric
armies. This is an imaginary battle. It is not real; it exists only in
your mind! Through my own powers, I recognize the powers of
others. And this is the work of the malevolent children of Calitin to
lure you to your death!'

Cuchulainn listened to Cathbad's impassioned pleas and heeded
them. He sat down again but immediately a great roar surged
through the room and once more he ran out to see what was
happening. As he appeared on the ramparts one of the witches
turned herself into a crow and flapped over Cuchulainn's head,
mocking him and gloating over the destruction of his fort and
followers at Dun Dealgan. She taunted him and challenged him to
come out and fight his enemies. Cuchulainn tried to go over the
fortifications and join battle, but Cathbad summoned all his druid's
powers and compelled him to listen.

'Wait, Cuchulainn, I beseech you, wait! In three days Clan Calitin's powers will have vanished. In place of this army you'll see
bent stalks and the fuzz balls of thistles, withered oak leaves, the
flukes of autumn and nothing more. Only three short days and

these spells will evaporate. After that it will be the sound of your victories and fame that will fill the air, everywhere and for all time.'

At last Cathbad convinced Cuchulainn that it was witchcraft and spells that were at work and he went back to his sunny quarters where Emer and another woman he loved, called Niamh, were waiting for him. They entertained him and distracted him from the tumult outside and he became calm again. When darkness came, the thwarted children of Calitin withdrew and peaceful night fell on Emain Macha.

While Cuchulainn was asleep, Emer and the women took council with the druids and they decided that Niamh should take Cuchulainn away with her to a secret place and hide him there. This place was called the Glen of the Deaf, for it was so remote and quiet that the sounds of the battle and Clan Calitin's spells could not reach it. When they told Cuchulainn that a feast had been prepared for him at the Glen of the Deaf he was angry.

'This is no time for me to go feasting. The four corners of Ireland are in flames, the Ulstermen are in their pains and Conall is abroad. It's up to *me* to defend Ulster, otherwise I'll be accused of cowardice and be condemned by all!'

Emer pleaded with her husband to listen to her and go to the feast and not to be deluded by his enemies. 'Up to now, my little Cu, I have never stood in your way when you wanted to fight, but this time I implore you to listen to Cathbad's counsel and go with Niamh to the feast in the Glen of the Deaf!'

In the end Cuchulainn consented to leave Emain Macha and under cover of night he stole away with Cathbad and Niamh and her attendants to the Glen of the Deaf.

When day dawned, the children of Calitin sought out Cuchulainn to call him to battle once more. They found his quarters deserted and they knew that Cathbad had hidden him from them. They raised a blast of enchanted wind and riding it they roared over the whole province of Ulster. They peered into every glen and mountain pass, into every woody thicket and hilly hideout in search of Cuchulainn. As they soared over Donegal they saw Cuchulainn's two horses, the Grey of Macha and Black Sainglain, grazing on a patch of grass outside the secret entrance to the Glen of the Deaf. Down they surged, moaning with the wind, and fell to weaving their magic spells again. This time the sound they made was even more deafening and the mountain passes reverberated with the noise. The shrill neighing of horses, the anguished cries of women, the screaming of wounded men and the thunder of drums filled the air and everyone who heard the tumult, even the watch dogs, was terrified.

The instant the awful clamour rose in the air, the women around Cuchulainn began to shout and sing loudly to drown the noise and the musicians beat on their timpans and plucked their harpstrings. But the cacophany was so great that nothing could drown it and Cuchulainn leapt up shouting again that it brought dishonour and disgrace on him to see Ulster laid low, unguarded and undefended. Once more the old druid gathered up all his powers and convinced Cuchulainn that these were the false lures of his enemies seeking his death and persuaded him once more to withstand the deadly temptations of the wizards. Outside, the children of Calitin were wild with rage as they realized that Cathbad's druidic power was stronger than their wizardry. They knew their time and their power was running out and they made a last attempt to draw Cuchulainn into battle. A daughter of Calitin took on the shape of one of Niamh's attendants. She went to the door of the hostel and beckoned to Niamh. Seeing her companion summon her, Niamh and the rest of her attendants went out into the valley. Instantly, the witch threw up a fog between the women and the hostel and they went wandering distractedly through the woods. Then, assuming Niamh's own beautiful form, the daughter of Calitin made her way to Cuchulainn's side.

'Oh, Cuchulainn, go out at once and face the men of Ireland and protect this province or it will be ravaged and you'll be dishonoured! Dun Dealgan is burnt and Muirthemne Plain laid waste. The whole province has been plundered. If you don't check the advance of Medb's army, Ulster will be destroyed and your good name with it!'

Cuchulainn listened to her in amazement. 'Niamh! Niamh! You

above all to say this to me at this fatal time! You! You, who made me swear that I must not face these forces for all the gold in the world!' He turned his face away and said bitterly, 'I was a fool to trust a woman's word but now that you've given me leave, I'll go!'

As he rose he stepped on the hem of his cloak and was pulled back into his seat. He reddened with vexation at his own clumsiness but as he rose the next time, the gold brooch sprang out of his cloak and pierced his foot clean through. 'Bad omens!' Cuchulainn said to himself as he went out and ordered Laeg to harness his two horses and get the chariot ready for battle.

Cathbad followed Cuchulainn outside, beseeching him to wait till nightfall when the evil magic would have run its course, but the warrior would not listen to him. In the meantime Niamh had found her way back to the hostel and was distraught when she heard what had happened. She ran after Cuchulainn to try to stop him. She told him that he had been tricked by sorcery but his mind was so fevered with conflicting thoughts that he would not listen to her. He ran out to where Laeg was trying to harness the horses to the war chariot.

The charioteer called to the Grey of Macha and shook the harness at him but the horse backed away, his eyes rolling with panic. Laeg tried again but this time the Grey galloped off. Laeg's heart jumped with fear, for he knew this was a bad omen. Usually the horse was trembling with eagerness to be away with Laeg and Cuchulainn in the chariot. Then Cuchulainn himself called the horse and, though it came back to him, it still shied off when he tried to yoke it. Laeg went to the other side of the Grey as it backed away from Cuchulainn and spoke softly to it.

'Grey, little pet, listen to me. Today of all days you must do your best!' At this the horse stood still and bowed its head and as Laeg put the yoke around its neck, great black tears of blood fell from its eyes and raised the dust at Cuchulainn's feet. Sick at heart, Cuchulainn and Laeg put on their fighting gear and stepped into the chariot. As they started forward the weapons fell from their places and clattered on the chariot floor and everyone who heard the noise shivered with fear. The women keened a loud lament as the chariot headed southwards towards Muirthemne Plain and Medb's battle lines.

Then the children of Calitin set the grass and leaves alive again and filled Cuchulainn's mind with visions of horror. He remembered Cathbad's words: 'The tumultuous crowds that you see are powerless shadows, vague and misty. The armies that you see are only vaporous shapes. They are feeble and helpless phantoms conjured up to torment you. There is nothing here but grass and leaves!' The druid's words re-echoed in his head, but still he couldn't free his mind from the delusions and temptations of his enemies. He saw Dun Dealgan aflame, and Emain Macha razed to the ground. Worst of all he saw the headless body of Emer thrown carelessly from the ramparts and he was demented with grief and anger. He galloped his team like the wind until he reached Emer's quarters in Emain Macha. He found the fort untouched and Emer, unhurt, came running out to meet him.

'Come in, Cuchulainn, and stay here with me,' she implored him.

'I can't! I must go to Muirthemne to rout Medb's army. Dun Dealgan is in ruins. Ulster is ablaze. I have old scores and new ones to settle with Medb. I thought I saw *this* place sacked and burnt and swarming with enemies and I thought you had been killed!'

'But, Cuchulainn, *nothing* has happened here. You can see that for yourself. These are empty visions, hallucinations, tricks of Clan Calitin to bring about your end. Don't heed them. Don't be tempted by them!' Emer pleaded.

'Don't try to hinder me, Emer. I'll meet Ulster's enemies and attack them. I give you my word on that. My time is up anyway and my fame is secure. Since the day I took up arms, I've never shirked a fight or combat. So it's not likely I'll do so now. Fame outlives life!'

Emer and her companions wailed and wept and wrung their hands but could not prevail on Cuchulainn to stay. He took his farewell of his wife and with Laeg at his side set out for the Plain of Muirthemne.

On their way south they came upon three wrinkled hags, blind in their left eyes, bending over a fire. They were cooking an animal on a spit made of a rowan branch and as Cuchulainn came up to them he saw that the animal was a hound. He made to pass them, for he knew they were not there for any good and moreover there was a *geis* on him forbidding him to eat the meat of a hound since it was his namesake. But one of the crones called out to him, 'Come here to us, Cuchulainn, and do not pass us. Stop and eat with us!'

'I won't stop with you!' Cuchulainn cried.

'You won't eat with us because the food we're cooking is only a hound and this is a poor cooking hearth. If it belonged to an important man you would stop! Shame on you for shunning the poor!' Cuchulainn was stung by these words so he ordered Laeg to pull up the horses. One of the old women gave him the shoulder blade of the hound to eat. She gave it with her left hand and Cuchulainn took it in his left hand. He ate it and put the bone under his left thigh and the hand and the thigh both seized up and lost their normal strength. Then Cuchulainn quickly left the hags and Laeg and he set off again for Muirthemne.

When they came to the river they went to the ford to cross over. They had to stop there for a pale young girl knelt at the ford, her golden hair falling over her shoulders. She was washing blood-stained clothes in the stream, moaning and sobbing all the time. As Cuchulainn watched, she lifted the garment she was washing out of the water and he saw his own tunic in her hands. Blood poured from it into the stream and turned the water red.

Laeg pointed to her. 'That girl over there is the Washer at the Ford, daughter of Badb, goddess of war. She washes the clothes of those who are about to die in battle and the gear she is washing is yours! Turn around, Cuchulainn! Turn around and come back with me to Emer. Forget about Medb and her army!'

Cuchulainn would not listen to Laeg's pleading but ordered him to drive on towards Slieve Fuad, the place where he had first found the Grey of Macha. From the slopes of Slieve Fuad, Cuchulainn saw the men of Ireland waiting for him on the plain below. Resignation and sadness left him, a war frenzy seized him and distorted him and the hero light played round his head like lightning. The noise of his chariot rolled like thunder across Muirthemne Plain.

His three great enemies, Lugaid, Erc and the children of Calitin were waiting for him, and as the roar of his approach surged over the plain they moved their warriors into battle formation, making a solid wall of shields to halt his onslaught.

But Cuchulainn was demonic in his frenzy. His face was grotesque and his body misshapen as he charged at them, crashing through their ranks. His sharp-wheeled chariot and his sword and spear hacked and hewed until the enemy scattered like hailstones in a storm or leaves in a blast. Laeg wheeled the chariot round and drove back through the lines and his master scattered the men of Ireland until their fragments lay across the plain. His horses ground them underfoot like grains of sand and the plain was grey with their brains. When he saw that his troops were being slaughtered, Erc put a plan into action to trap Cuchulainn. He drew up the remains of his army and at either end he put a pair of champions pretending to fight each other. He placed a druid beside each couple as if he were judging the outcome.

As Cuchulainn charged to attack the line afresh, one set of champions started a mock combat and the druid called on Cuchulainn to separate the fighters. Cuchulainn did this by killing each of the combatants with a blow.

'You have separated them all right,' the druid said. 'They'll not harm one another now. Give me your spear, Cuchulainn!'

'I swear by the oath of my people,' Cuchulainn said. 'I need the spear more than you do! The fate of Ulster rests with me today.'

'I will curse and revile your good name if you don't hand it over!'

'I have never lost my good name yet for any act of refusal or meanness,' said Cuchulainn. 'Here it is!' He reversed his spear and threw it at the druid. The shaft went through the man, killing him and the nine men behind him. It landed beside Lugaid, who picked it up.

'Who's name is on this spear?' he shouted to the Calitin clan.

'That spear will kill a king!' they answered. Lugaid took aim and hurled it at Cuchulainn. It missed him but it hit Laeg who was at his side in the chariot. 'I have been badly hurt, Cuchulainn,' the charioteer gasped as his entrails fell out on to the cushions of the chariot. Cuchulainn drew the spear from Laeg's body and laid him on the ground. He embraced his dying friend and took his farewell of him. 'Today, Laeg,' he said sorrowfully, 'I must be champion and charioteer as well.'

Then with the battle fury raging in him stronger than ever he faced the line of enemies afresh. As he made a charge, two more warriors pretended to fight and again a druid called out to Cuchulainn to intervene and once again he had to obey. He sprang on the men and crashed them against rock and killed them.

'Now, give me your spear!' the druid ordered.

'I swear by what my people hold sacred that I need it more than you do!' Cuchulainn protested.

'I will curse your good name then,' said the druid.

'I have saved my good name once today already. I am not bound to do it twice,' Cuchulainn replied.

'Then I will destroy the good name of Ulster.'

'Never has Ulster been belittled on my account,' said Cuchulainn and he cast the spear, butt side first and it passed through the druid's head killing him and the nine men behind him. This time Erc grabbed the falling spear.

'Children of Catilin, who will this spear lay low?'

'It will kill a king,' they chorused.

'You said that about the spear that Lugaid cast,' Erc reminded them.

'What we said was true! Laeg mac Riangabra, king of the charioteers, fell by that cast!'

Erc cast the spear at Cuchulainn but again it missed its mark and plunged into the Grey of Macha's side. The horse let out a shrill whinny of pain and Cuchulainn quickly pulled out the spear. The Grey plunged forwards and galloped off with half the harness hanging from his back and headed northwards towards the lake in Slieve Fuad from where it had come. Urging on Black Sainglain, Cuchulainn cut through the men of Ireland, scattering them like buttercups on Magh Breg.

A third false fight was started and for the third time a druid challenged Cuchulainn to settle it. He killed the third set of combatants as he had the other two and once again the druid demanded his spear or the honour of his name.

'I have paid dearly for the honour of my name today,' Cuchulainn said bitterly. 'I have no need to pay any more.'

'Then I will dishonour your countrymen, your seed and breed,' the druid warned.

'Word of their dishonour at my hands will never go back to my countrymen,' Cuchulainn said. 'Nor for that part will I myself go back to them. My time is up.'

He killed the druid and nine men with the shaft of the spear and tore through the lines of men, scattering them through the air like flakes of snow.

Lugaid again seized the spear from the ground and took aim.

'Who will die by this spear, children of Calitin? You told Erc a king would fall when *he* threw it.'

'That was true. From it the Grey of Macha, king of the chariot horses, received a fatal wound,' Clan Calitin replied.

Then Lugaid flung the spear at Cuchulainn and it found its mark. It pierced the Ulster hero's armour and made such a wound in his belly that his entrails were exposed. Then the Black Sainglain panicked and reared up into the air breaking loose from the chariot. It galloped off, the second half of the yoke hanging from its neck, leaving Cuchulainn, king of the warriors, dying alone beside his chariot.

Cuchulainn's enemies kept watch from a distance. They knew he was close to death, but they were afraid to come near him for the hero light still flickered around his head.

'I'm thirsty,' the dying warrior said. 'I want to go to the lough to get a drink.'

'Go, if you want to,' they shouted, 'but come back to us!'

'Or you can come to *me*!' he answered.

Holding the huge wound in his body together, Cuchulainn started to drag himself towards the lake. He took a drink and washed himself and turned from the lake to die. On the shore, a little distance away, he saw a pillar stone and he struggled towards it and put his back to it for support. Then he took his belt and tied himself to the pillar so that he could die standing up, for he had sworn he would meet his end 'feet on the ground, face to the foe'. Upright and facing his enemies, he called to them to come near him and cautiously they approached and stood round him silently in a circle. They stayed there and watched him but none of them dared lay a hand on him for the hero light still shone round his head.

'Be a man and take off his head!' Erc urged Lugaid. 'He beheaded your father.'

As Lugaid moved towards Cuchulainn, sword drawn, there was a sudden drumming of hoofs and the Grey of Macha, lathered with sweat and blood, flew towards his wounded master and made three deadly onslaughts with its teeth and hoofs against Cuchulainn's enemies. He scattered them like gravel on Baile's Strand. Then the horse made off to Slieve Fuad to die.

For three days his enemies watched Cuchulainn. The ravens of battle, the Morrigu and Badb, hovered around his head and at last the hero light faltered, flickered and went out. As it did so, Cuchulainn let out a great sigh and the pillar stone split at his back. A raven lit on his shoulder and settled there.

'The first time a bird has landed there!' exclaimed Erc. 'It's not a place where a bird would usually perch.' And with that he went up to the stone where the lifeless Cuchulainn, still stood upright, tied to his pillar.

Lugaid drew aside Cuchulainn's hair to bare his neck, but Cuchulainn's sword fell from his hand and took off Lugaid's hand at the wrist. Then Cuchulainn's head was severed from his body and borne to Tara as a trophy and his body, still tied to the pillar, was left on the strand.

THE MUSIC
OF WHAT HAPPENED

―――――

*The Finn
Cycle*

The Boyhood Deeds of
Finn

WHEN CONN OF THE HUNDRED BATTLES was king of Ireland he had at his command an army of fighters and hunters called the Fianna, whose leader was Cumhall, son of Trenmor.

The king's chief druid at the time was called Nuada and this man built for himself a beautiful, white-fronted fort in Leinster. The druid's wife, Almu, asked that the fort be named after her and so Almu it was called. When Nuada died, his son Tadg became a druid in his place and lived on the Hill of Allen in the fort that his father had built.

Now Tadg had a daughter called Muirne who was so beautiful that the sons of kings and chiefs came in great numbers to Almu to ask for her hand. Among her suitors was Cumhall, head of Clan Bascna and leader of the Fianna. He asked repeatedly that Muirne become his wife but was always refused. Cumhall was so determined to have Muirne in spite of the refusals that one day he abducted her from the fort of Almu and carried her off. Tadg was outraged when he heard that his daughter had been taken away by Cumhall and went directly to see the king. He complained bitterly that one of the Fianna, all of whom were bound by a solemn oath to respect women, should have abducted his daughter. He reminded Conn that Cumhall was a kinsman of his and demanded that he be forced to restore Muirne to her family.

Immediately Conn dispatched his messengers to Cumhall and ordered him to send Muirne back to her father. Cumhall sent word back to the king that he would give him anything he asked, anything at all, except the woman. When Conn got this reply to his command he gathered together from the east and the west the Leinster and Connacht chiefs and the soldiers of Clan Morna, and enlisted their help to fight Cumhall.

From Munster in the south, bands of men loyal to Cumhall and the Clan Bascna marched to Leinster to help him. At Cnuca, called Castleknock today, the armies met and a fierce battle ensued. Cumhall fought bravely leading his small force against Conn's bigger army. In the course of the battle, Luchet, a follower of Cumhall's, struck one of the sons of Morna in the face with his spear and blinded him in one eye. For ever after this man was known as Goll (Blind) Mac Morna. Goll was a ferocious fighter and though he was half blind, he killed Luchet. He stripped him of his valuables and carried off his head. Then the followers of Goll Mac Morna turned on the Clan Bascna and routed them. They killed before and behind them and only a few of Cumhall's men escaped the massacre.

After the battle of Cnuca the king rewarded Goll Mac Morna by putting *him* at the head of the Fianna in place of Cumhall's heir. Because of this, and his part in Cumhall's death, a great feud broke out between Goll's tribe, the Clan Morna, and Cumhall's tribe, the Clan Bascna, which lasted for many years.

When Muirne, Cumhall's wife, heard that her husband had been killed in the battle of Cnuca and his followers scattered, she went back to Almu to seek refuge with her father, but Tadg was so angry that she had eloped with Cumhall that he turned her from his door. Muirne made her way to the king's fortress at Tara and asked Conn for his protection, not only from Clan Morna, but from her own father who had ordered his men to kill her. Conn sent one of his servants to bring Muirne to a kinsman's house where she would be safe. There she was received warmly by the family and remained in hiding. Not long afterwards she gave birth to the son of Cumhall, and called him Demne.

Years later, when Demne grew up and was given the name Finn because he had fair hair, he went back to Almu to call his grandfather, Tadg, to account for his part in Cumhall's death. Finn gave the druid a choice: either fight him in single combat or give him the fort at Almu and everything in it to be his for all time. Tadg, who was an old man by now, knew he could not overcome his grandson in close hand-to-hand fighting so he thought it best to move away from Almu and give it to Finn. This he did and Almu became Finn's headquarters. From then on, though Finn and the Fianna roamed the length and breadth of Ireland and made expeditions to Scotland and to the islands, the fort on the Hill of Allen became his principal residence and he always returned happily to the shining white dun that Nuada had built.

While he was a baby, Demne had no home where he could be safe. Goll Mac Morna, having killed Cumhall and been made captain of the Fianna, was determined to kill Cumhall's son as well. He was afraid that one day, when the boy was grown up, he would claim his father's position at the head of the Fianna. Muirne knew that her son was in danger while he was with her and though she was sad to part with her child she handed the boy over to two of her trusted women attendants who had been trained to survive in the wilderness and were skilled trackers. Then she escaped southwards from the territory controlled by Clan Morna and married a king who lived there.

As soon as Muirne's servant women were given the baby they took him away and hid with him in the woods and valleys of Slieve Bloom. There they guarded him closely and reared him and cared for him as if he was their own child.

Six years after she had parted with him, Muirne came secretly to visit Demne in his forest hideout. She wanted to see her son again and make sure he was hidden from his enemies and well cared for by his friends. She moved stealthily from the remote territory where she lived till she came to Slieve Bloom. The hunting bothy her son lived in was made of wattle and mud and was roofed with branches so that it was almost invisible in the depths of the wood, but Muirne found it and went in. The two women recognized her and welcomed her joyfully. They led her into the room where her fair-haired son lay asleep. She lifted him up and, holding him close, hugged him and talked to him. Then rocking him in her arms she sang him a lullaby until he went back to sleep. She thanked the faithful women for the love and protection they were giving her child and told them to look after him till he was able to fend for himself. Then she stole away, slipping from wood to wilderness till she reached the safety of her own territory.

As Demne grew up his guardians taught him about the changing seasons and life in the woods and hills around him. He was hardy in winter and carefree in summer. He became a skillful tracker and hunter; he could outstrip the hare and bring down a stag on his own without the help of a deerhound and he could make a wild duck drop from the sky with one stone from a sling. He was still a young child when he brought home to his fosterers the first food he had caught. He had seen a flock of wild duck fly low over a lake. As they passed above his head he slung a stone at them and sheared the wing feathers off one of the birds so that it fell to the ground, stunned.

As he became more adventurous Demne went further and further afield in spite of his guardians' warnings. The fair-haired forest boy whom they glimpsed through the trees began to be talked about by the huntsmen of the Fianna. Goll Mac Morna heard these rumours and suspected that the child might be the son of Cumhall. He sent his trackers to Slieve Bloom to find his secret camp and flush him out and kill him. Getting wind of Goll's plans, the women sent Demne away from Slieve Bloom in the care of three wandering smiths, with whom he travelled for a time. But the men kept him half starved and his hair fell out for want of proper food. For a while then he was known as Demne the Bald.

One night as the smiths were asleep a robber came upon them. He killed the three men, robbed them and captured the boy. Then he took him south to work in his own house. But the women trackers who had reared Demne heard about his kidnap and came after their ward and found him a prisoner in the bandit's house. They forced the man to hand over the boy and the three of them made their way back to Slieve Bloom.

Some time later, when Demne was on his wanderings, he came out of the forest on to the green of a large fort. There were boys playing hurley on the green and Demne joined in the game. He was the fastest player among them, so the next day, when he returned, he played alone against a quarter of them and won. Then a third of them measured themselves against him but Demne still beat them. Finally they were all ranged against him, but the newcomer took the ball from them all and won the game.

'What is your name?' the boys asked him.

'Demne,' he said and turned away and disappeared into the forest.

The boys told the chieftain who owned the fort about the stranger who had beaten them all single-handed.

'Surely, between the lot of you, you should be able to beat one boy!' the man exclaimed. 'Did he tell you his name?'

'He said his name was Demne.'

'And what does this champion look like?' the chieftain asked.

'He's tall and well built and his hair is very fair.'

'Then we'll give him the nickname Finn, because of that white hair,' said the chief and from that day on Finn, which means fair-haired, became Demne's name.

The chieftain's son incited his companions to turn against Finn so when he appeared the next day to join the game they flung their hurley sticks at him. Finn grabbed a hurley stick from the ground and made a run at the boys, knocking seven of them to the ground and scattering the rest. Then he escaped to the shelter of the forest and back to the bothy where he lived.

About a week after this as he was going for a swim in a mountain lake he heard shouting and yelling from the water. Finn ran to the lough shore and saw the boys from the fort swimming and playing in the water. They challenged Finn to come in and wrestle in the water with them. They wanted to drown him and as soon as he waded in the youths all grabbed him and held him under the water. Finn broke free and held seven of them under the water and then he escaped to Slieve Bloom. The boys hurried back to the fort to tell this latest story about Finn to the household and the story spread like wildfire.

The two women warriors who had guarded Demne so faithfully knew they could keep him safe no longer now that tales of his exploits were on everyone's lips.

'You must leave us now, son. The Mac Morna scouts are on your track, and if they find you they will kill you,' they told him.

Sadly Finn said goodbye to his brave friends and headed south out of the dangerous terrain of Slieve Bloom. He made his way carefully, slipping from wood to wood down through the country until he reached Lough Lene in Kerry. He made his way to the stronghold of the king of Bantry and joined his band of fighters and trackers, but he told no one his name or lineage. Before long it was clear to all that the newcomer had no equal as a hunter. The king observed the young man closely for a while and decided to catch him off guard and trick him into betraying his identity.

'I would have sworn that you were the son of Cumhall,' he said, 'because you're so like him, except that I know he left only one son and he is a soldier in Scotland at the moment.'

Finn made no reply but shortly after that he left the service of the king of Bantry and became a soldier with a neighbouring king. This king noticed the youth's skill at chess and challenged him to a game. Finn won seven games in a row, making his own moves and advising the king on the moves *he* should make as well.

'Who *are* you?' the king demanded.

'I am the son of a poor farmer from Tara,' replied Finn.

'No, you are not!' the king said. 'You're the son of Cumhall! You are called Finn Mac Cumhaill, and you were born to Muirne after your father was killed at Cnuca. Goll Mac Morna is out to kill you. Leave my place at once. I can't protect you against Mac Morna's men and I don't want you killed under my roof.'

Now that the news of his parentage was out, Finn became a fugitive once more. He made his way east to another chief who was loyal to Clan Bascna and would shelter and protect him. The blacksmith of this tribe was called Lochan and he had a beautiful daughter. As soon as the girl saw Finn she fell in love with him. Her father was so taken by the young man that he consented to their union even though he knew nothing about the new arrival, neither who he was nor where he came from. He made two sharp spears for Finn as a gift so that he could protect himself from a fierce wild boar that was terrorizing that part of Munster. As luck would have it, one day when Finn was out alone he was passing through a narrow gap in the mountain when the huge beast came crashing down the mountainside and charged at him. Finn took one of his newly forged spears and thrust it through the boar's body and killed it. Then he brought the pig's head back to Lochan as a bridal gift for his daughter and to this day that mountain is called Slieve Muc, the Mountain of the Pig.

After he had stayed a while with Lochan and his daughter, Finn set off again, this time to find his uncle, Crimhall, son of Trenmor. Crimhall had fought by Cumhall's side at the battle of Cnuca but had managed to escape the slaughter that followed his brother's death and had fled westward to a wild and desolate part of Connacht. There, with the last remnants of Cumhall's followers, he had taken refuge in a remote wood. The younger men looked after their old leader and hunted for food for him.

As Finn was on his way westwards to find his uncle, he heard loud keening and lamenting. He started off in the direction of the cries and saw a woman wailing and swaying with grief. Her face was smeared with blood and tears of blood streamed from her eyes.

'You are covered in blood! What has turned your tears to blood?' Finn cried out.

'I have good cause to cry tears of blood!' the woman said bitterly. 'My only son was ambushed and killed a short while ago by a tall, terrible warrior.'

Finn went quickly in pursuit of the warrior. He soon overtook him and challenged him to a fight. He overpowered the tall soldier and killed him with his spear. A strange-looking pouch made of delicate hide was lying among the dead warrior's belongings and Finn took it with him and went on into Connacht until he found his uncle.

Crimhall was overjoyed when his nephew arrived at his bothy. Moreover he recognized the strange bag that Finn carried. 'How did you come by this?' he asked in astonishment. 'This was stolen from Cumhall by a cowardly warrior called the Grey of Luachra. We trusted him. He was the treasurer of the Fianna, but at the battle of Cnuca it was the Grey of Luachra who dealt your father the first blow and Goll Mac Morna who finished the work. Then the Grey of Luachra slipped away taking his treasure bag with him. How did you get it back?'

Finn told his uncle about the wailing woman he had met and how he had killed the tall man who had slain her son.

'That was the Grey of Luachra you killed,' the old man said, 'and this bag which you have recovered for Clan Bascna is the chief treasure of the Fianna.'

Then Crimhall told Finn the story of the magic treasure bag made from the skin of a crane.

'This crane bag belonged to Manannan Mac Lir of the Tuatha De Danaan. A beautiful gentle-eyed girl called Aoife fell in love with Manannan's son, Ilbrach, and he loved her in return. But another woman loved Ilbrach too, and was fiercely jealous of Aoife. One day she lured Aoife into the water and then she changed the gentle girl into a crane and drove her away from Manannan's island to wander from lough to lough for two hundred years. When Aoife died Manannan took her skin and made a treasure bag of it and he put into it some of the magic hoard of the Tuatha De Danaan. He put into it his own knife and magic shirt, the anvil and leather apron that Goibniu the smith had owned, the king of Scotland's shears and the king of Norway's horned helmet, as well as a belt made of a strip of whaleskin. When the sea is at full tide you can see the treasures in the bag. When the tide turns and ebbs away the crane bag seems empty. By strange turns it came into your father's possession and it stayed with the Fianna until the Grey of Luachra stole it away. It is a good omen, Finn, that it has come back to us again. It means that our tribe, Clan Bascna, will become leaders of the Fianna once again.'

Finn stayed with his uncle and listened closely to his stories about Cumhall and the Fianna. He listened proudly as Crimhall told of their bravery in battle, their skill in the hunt and their mastery of the art of poetry. Fired by these tales he determined to overthrow Goll Mac Morna and become the leader of the Fianna as his father had once been. But he knew he would not be safe until he could gather around him a band of men strong enough to challenge Goll for the captaincy. And he knew he would not be considered worthy to take command of the élite band of men until he was as good a poet as he was a warrior and hunter.

So he left Crimhall and headed eastwards towards Leinster to the place where there lived a poet and teacher called Finnegas. Now Finnegas had spent seven years camping near a pool on the River Boyne. The red-speckled Salmon of Knowledge lived in this pool and it had been prophesied that whoever ate one of these fish would possess understanding of everything in the world, past, present and future. This was because the salmon ate the berries that fell from a magic rowan tree overhanging the pool and acquired the wisdom of the world from them.

When Finn arrived at Finnegas's house, the poet had just caught one of the salmon from the well. The learned man was overjoyed that, at last, all knowledge would be his. He gave the fish to Finn and ordered him to cook it but he warned him that he was utterly forbidden to taste even the smallest morsel. Finn made a fire and cooked the salmon for Finnegas and as he lifted it off the spit the skin of the fish seared his thumb. To ease the pain Finn put his thumb in his mouth. Then he brought the fish to the poet. Finnegas looked at his pupil as he handed him the salmon and noticed a change in him.

'Are you sure you haven't tasted any of the salmon, my lad?' he demanded.

'No,' said Finn, 'but I burnt my thumb on the skin of the fish and put it in my mouth to soothe it.'

The poet let out a groan. 'What is your name?' he asked the boy.

'My name is Demne,' he replied.

'Your name is Finn!' said the poet. 'It was prophesied that a fair-haired man would eat the Salmon of Knowledge, and you are that fair-headed Finn. So the eternal knowledge is *yours* now, not mine. You may as well eat the whole fish, Finn!'

And so Finn did and from then on, at moments of great significance and danger, when he put his thumb in his mouth whatever he needed to know was revealed to him.

Finn stayed with Finnegas on the banks of the Boyne learning the art of poetry. And to prove to his teacher that he had mastered that difficult art he composed his first poem in praise of early summer, the season he loved best of all.

Finn Joins the Fianna
and Becomes Its Captain

AFTER he had proved himself a poet, Finn left Finnegas's place and set out to reclaim the leadership of the Fianna from Goll Mac Morna. He made his way to Tara, the great court of Conn of the Hundred Battles, who was then the High King of Ireland. The feast of Tara was in progress and all the provincial kings and chiefs were there for the ceremonial festival. For the six weeks that feast lasted, peace was maintained across the land. It was solemnly upheld at this time that no battle could be fought, no feud or quarrel pursued. Conn sat on his throne, his son Art beside him, and close by in a place of honour sat Goll Mac Morna because the leader of the Fianna had royal prestige. As the banquet was in full swing, Finn walked into the room, uninvited, and sat down. The king stared at the youth whom no one had ever seen before and then sent for his ceremonial horn. He placed the horn in the young man's hand and said, 'Whose son are you?'

'I am Finn, son of Cumhall, the warrior who used to be the commander-in-chief of the Fianna,' Finn replied. 'High King of Ireland, I have come to make friends with you and put myself at your service.'

'Lad, your father was a friend of mine and a trustworthy man. You are welcome. Come here! Join us!'

Then Finn swore his allegiance to Conn and was put next to Art, the king's son, in a place of honour. The feasting and entertainment continued for a while and then the king rose and, lifting aloft his polished drinking horn, waited for silence.

'Men of Ireland,' he said, 'tomorrow is the solemn day of Samhain when the doors of the Otherworld stand open and the Tuatha De Danaan come out and mix with mortals. Aillen Mac Miona, one of those Ever Young, will come to Tara as he has come for the last nine years and he will burn it down. He will lull us to sleep with his enchanted music and then, when we are asleep and powerless, he will send out a blast of fire from his throat and set Tara alight. If anyone here can preserve Tara from the man of the Sidhe, I will give that person his rightful heritage, however big or small it may be.'

No one spoke, for everyone there except Finn had heard that sweet, irresistible music and knew that no one could withstand its spell. Anyone who heard it, even those tormented with pain, fell into a deep sleep.

Then Finn rose to his feet and addressed the king. 'If I save Tara who will guarantee my heritage?' he asked.

'The kings of the provinces of Ireland will go surety for you as well as the druids and poets,' Conn answered.

When Finn heard this and knew that through these guarantees his heritage would be restored to him, he undertook to save Tara.

Now one of the chiefs present at the gathering was a man called Fiacha who had been a trusted friend of Finn's father when Cumhall led the Fianna and who was still secretly loyal to Clan Bascna. Fiacha went to Finn when no one was looking and offered to help him.

'If I should give you a certain spear which never misses its mark what reward would you give me?' he said to the youth.

'What reward are you looking for?' Finn asked.

'To receive a third of the profits gained by your right hand and to be one of your three most trusted advisers.'

'They're yours!' agreed Finn.

Fiacha brought the spear to Finn, handed it to him and whispered: 'The minute you hear the first note of Aillen's enchanted music, strip this casing from the head of the spear and put the weapon against your forehead. The power of this weapon will keep you awake.'

Finn took the spear and left the assembly to go outside the ramparts of Tara to begin his watch.

Before long he heard the first notes of the timpan and quickly he pulled the hood off the spear and held the spearhead flat against his forehead as the plaintive, hypnotic music filled Tara's halls and one by one those who heard it fell fast asleep. Aillen played on till he thought everyone was in a deep sleep, then he opened his mouth and sent out a great tongue of flame to engulf Tara. But Finn was still awake and he held up his crimson fringed coat in the path of the flame. The fire was directed downward by the cloak and it scorched a great crater into the earth. From then on that hill was called the Hill of the Fire, and the valley opposite it the Glen of the Cloak.

When Aillen realized that his powers had been overcome, he fled back to his rath on the summit of Slieve Fuad. Finn chased after him and as Aillen was entering the door of his underground dwelling Finn threw Fiacha's magic spear at him and impaled him with it. Then he cut off Aillen's head and brought it back with him to Tara. He fixed the head on a pole that everyone might see it when dawn broke.

Next morning the king led his household to the green at Tara where Finn was waiting for them. Finn pointed to the pole and said to Conn, 'Look, Conn, there is the head of the man who used to set fire to Tara. Here is his timpan and his flute. His music is over and Tara is safe!'

'Then you must be given your reward,' said the king and called Goll Mac Morna to his side. 'This youth is Cumhall's son, so it is his rightful heritage to be at the head of the Fianna,' he told him. '*He* should lead the Fianna instead of you. Will you agree to surrender your position and serve under him? Or will you leave Ireland? Those are your choices.'

'I give you my solemn word that I will serve Finn,' said Goll.

Then the Fianna champions rose to proclaim their new captain. This they did by striking their palms against his and Goll Mac Morna was the first man to strike the palm of Finn Mac Cumhaill, son of his old enemy.

Finn's Captaincy

With Finn Mac Cumhaill leading them, the Fianna of Ireland came into a heyday of such glory that stories were told about them for centuries afterwards. Their exploits were so famous and the tales of their adventures so fabulous that over the ages they grew larger than life in people's imagination and Finn himself is remembered as a giant.

While Finn was their captain he allowed only the noblest, the bravest, the swiftest, the strongest, the most honourable of men to join the Fianna. Under his command they stood ready to defend the state, support the king and protect the safety and property of the people.

From November to May the men of the Fianna were billeted on the country and given a fixed salary by the king. During this time they patrolled the coasts, looking out for invaders and pirates. They collected fines and put down riots and punished public enemies. In the summer months they received no pay but had to provide for themselves by living off the land. They fished and hunted and sold the skins of animals for income.

Any man who wanted to enlist in the élite militia was accepted only after he had agreed to certain conditions, had sworn to obey certain rules and had proved himself in ordeals of strength, courage and skill.

There were three conditions. First, a man was allowed to join the Fianna if his family accepted that there would be no compensation if he were wounded or killed. They had to promise that they would not avenge his death; if honour and justice required this, his comrades-in-arms would do it. In return the family would suffer no reprisals for any injury or death that a man of the Fianna might inflict on others. The second condition was that he must have studied the art of poetry so diligently that he could compose and appreciate poetry and be familiar with the old texts. And the third was that he should have perfect mastery of his weapons.

When these conditions had been fulfilled, the candidate took solemn vows. He swore on his honour that he would choose a wife, not for her dowry but for herself; that he would never hurt or dishonour any woman; that he would help the poor as best he could and that he would be courageous enough to fight, single-handed, as many as nine enemies at one go. Lastly he took an oath of allegiance to the commander of the Fianna and swore to remain faithful to him.

When he had pledged to do these things, his skill as a hunter and proficiency as a soldier were tested to the limit by his comrades-in-arms.

First of all they put him into a meadow, knee deep in rushes, with a shield and hazel rod in his hand. Nine experienced soldiers of the Fianna would stand a short distance away and they would all hurl their spears at him at the same time. He would have to ward off the hail of spears using the shield and branch. If a spear as much as scratched him he would not be admitted to the ranks of the Fianna.

Next they would put him through trials of agility, speed and endurance over difficult terrain. They would take him to a forest, with his hair plaited and coiled, give him a head start the breadth of tree trunk, and then all chase him at full speed. If he was overtaken or wounded he had failed the test. He had to weave through the dense wood, his comrades in pursuit, and if there was a hair out of place at the end of the chase he had failed the test. If a dry stick cracked under him while he ran, he had failed the test. If he could not spring over a branch higher than his forehead or duck under one lower than his shin he had failed the test, and if he had to stoop or slow down while the chase was on, in order to take a thorn out of his foot, he was not considered worthy to join the Fianna.

As well as being light-footed he had to be strong-armed. He had to hold his heavy weapons perfectly still for a long time and if his hand shook at all he was rejected. When a young man was capable of all these things, then and then only was he allowed to become one of Finn's people.

The Fianna were excellent huntsmen, light-footed and stealthy, agile and strong, accurate and swift. For six months of the year their survival depended on these skills and disciplines. They roamed the woods in small companies but they all observed the same rules and habits during the hunting period. They ate only one meal a day and that in the evening, and they observed a set routine in the cooking and eating of the meal. The hunt started at dawn. In the early afternoon a small party went ahead with the catch to a special place where there was plenty of wood and water. There they lit great fires. They collected the large, flat stones that had been brought to the cooking place and put them into the fire. While the stones were heating up, the huntsmen prepared the meat and dug a deep pit. When the stones were red hot, they lined the bottom of the pit with them and on this oven floor they would place the food they had caught. Large bundles of venison or wild boar were trussed tightly and wrapped in broad green sedge or bullrush leaves and laid on the hot stones. Over the meat joints they would place another layer of hot stones. More bundles of meat would be added and so on till the pit was full. The meat would stew gently and when it was tender the layers of stones were removed and the meal began. If they had caught a young, tender animal that morning they would put it on a spit instead and roast it over the flames.

All over Ireland and in parts of Scotland, farmers ploughing the land sometimes turn up earth that is scorched and black and they know that hundreds and hundreds of years ago in that place there was once one of the Fianna's ovens.

In the evening the rest of the Fianna company came to the cooking place for their evening meal, but before they could eat they first had to wash off the sweat and dust of the hunt. To do this they would go to another large pit filled with water. In this makeshift swimming pool they would wash and massage their limbs until the fatigue and strain of the day fell away and they were as fresh and active as they had been at daybreak. When they were fully refreshed they would dress again and begin to eat.

After the meal they set up camp for the night. They would build bothies made out of branches, rushes and stones, or put up skin tents. Then they would make their beds to a specified plan. They would lay first a base of brushwood and springy branches, on top of this a layer of dry moss and, right on top, fresh rushes were spread out. Until recent times, country people called these materials 'the three beds of the Fianna'.

The three great poets of the Fianna, Oisin, Caoilte and Finn celebrated the hills and valleys of Ireland and the life they led with their companions roaming the country. They praised the singing of the birds in summer and the belling of the stags in winter, the excitement of the chase and the stories told around the campfires, the companionship of their friends and the code of honour by which they all lived.

Years later when Oisin was an old, old man and when all the other Fianna were dead, he was asked by Saint Patrick what was the music that Finn and the Fianna loved best to hear. Remembering those days and the sunburnt companions who were long gone he told the holy man that the best music was the music of what happened.

The Birth of Finn's Hounds

ONE DAY Finn Mac Cumhaill and Conan sat on the Hill of Allen watching Bran and Sceolan, Finn's favourite hounds, criss-crossing the terrain, disappearing into thickets and out again staying close together always. It was Finn's custom to direct the chase from a hilltop and these two hounds were so close to their master they seemed to be able to read his mind. Finn loved them as if they were his children and when they came up to him to be stroked and petted they looked at him with eyes that seemed human.

Bran was a most distinctive animal. He was a huge staghound whose head was as high as Finn's shoulder. His legs were fawn-coloured and his belly white. His sides and back were black and were speckled brown over his hindquarters. His ears were a deep crimson. He accompanied Finn everywhere he went and if by chance Finn was hungry after a bad day's hunting Bran would go into the forest and bring him back something to eat. The cry of Sceolan, Finn's other favourite hound, was so sweet that it rang out above the baying of all the other hounds when they were in full cry.

'They say that these dogs are cousins of yours,' Conan said to Finn. 'How could such a strange thing come about?'

'I'll tell you the story,' said Finn.

'My mother, Muirne, came here once to pay me a visit and she brought her sister Tuiren with her. At that time Iollan, of the Ulster branch of the Fianna, was in love with Tuiren and asked my permission to marry her. I allowed him to marry my aunt on two conditions. The first was that he would send her back here if I ordered it and the second that he would enlist the aid of the Fianna chiefs as guarantors of his promise on that matter. Now I made the Ulsterman agree to these conditions for this Iollan had a lover already, a woman of the Sidhe, the daughter of Bodb. I was afraid that in her jealousy she might use her powers to destroy Tuiren. So before Tuiren left my protection, I called the Fianna chiefs together. Then I took Tuiren's hand and placed it on Oisin's hand. He in turn handed her over to Caoilte. Caoilte gave her to Diarmuid and so on till every Fianna chief had pledged her safety. Then Tuiren's hand was placed in the hand of the Ulsterman by Lugaid who said these words to him: "I give this woman to you on the condition that you will make it your solemn duty to restore her safely to Finn if he thinks fit to have her back." So Tuiren became Iollan's wife and went back with him to Ulster. Some time later, when Tuiren was expecting a child, Iollan's jealous sweetheart decided to take her revenge. She assumed the shape of one of my woman messengers and came to Tuiren with instructions from me to arrange a feast. Then she lured my aunt away from the house on the pretence of making secret arrangements for the feast. When they were some distance from the house, the woman of the Sidhe drew a dark druid's wand from under her cloak and struck Tuiren with it and changed her into a beautiful staghound, the most elegant and beautiful creature you could imagine. Then she brought the hound far away with her to the house of a chief called Fergus who lived in Galway. Now this chief was a byword for his lack of hospitality. He was the most unsociable being in Ireland and he particularly hated dogs. So much so that he never allowed a hound to come near any house that he was in. He was very surprised indeed, then, when Bodb's daughter, still disguised as my messenger, brought the staghound to him and said, "Finn Mac Cumhaill sends you his greetings and asks you to look after this hound till he arrives here in person. She is soon to give birth to a litter, so Finn wants you take particular care not to let her hunt too much. If she comes to any harm, Finn will not be pleased."

'"I'm very surprised to hear all this!" Fergus exclaimed. "Finn knows very well I'm an unsociable man and that I particularly dislike dogs. But I won't refuse Finn's request concerning the first hound he has ever sent me."

'So Fergus took the hound and the messenger went away. Now Fergus proved true to his nature. While he still had time he decided to test the worth of my hound. He brought her to the chase one day and she ran so fast, she left the other hounds standing. That day and every day for a month she hunted down every wild animal that she saw. By then she was too heavy with the litter she was carrying to run fast and so she wasn't brought out to hunt any more. But she was such a beautiful dog and such a good hunter that even Fergus grew to love her and from then on, hounds were welcome in his house. The staghound gave birth to two pups, Bran and Sceolan, the two you see there.'

'And how did you come to get them?' Conan asked.

'When I learned that my mother's sister was no longer living in Iollan's house, I demanded that she be brought back safely to me as had been agreed in the marriage terms. I insisted that the men of the Fianna honour the pledge they had made to guarantee her safety. Lugaid was the man who had handed her over to Iollan so on *him* fell the job of getting her back. Lugaid told me that he would either bring back Tuiren alive, or the head of Iollan in place of her. Iollan, the Ulster chief, asked for time to find Tuiren and pledged that he would surrender himself if he failed to find her. His request was granted and he hurried to the dwelling of the Sidhe where his De Danaan sweetheart lived. She agreed to tell him where Tuiren was if he would agree to take her instead of Tuiren as his wife and let her remain so for the rest of his life. Iollan agreed to do this. Then the woman went to Fergus's house and led the hound away. As soon as they were a little distance from the house, she restored Tuiren to her own natural shape and brought her to me here at Almu. She told me that Tuiren had been pregnant when she had turned her into a hound and that the pups that were born to her could be restored to human shape if I wished. I asked that they be given back to me and that they be left as they had been born. So they are indeed kindred of mine and I love them as if they were my children.'

Centuries have passed since Finn Mac Cumhaill told this story to Conan as they sat outside the fort of Almu and watched the hounds at play, but until recent times people coming home at night near the Hill of Allen had a strange story to tell. They told of seeing two staghounds break through the thickets and lope over the slopes in the moonlight, whining and barking, and they knew that Bran and Sceolan were searching for their master, eager again for the chase.

The Enchanted Deer:
the Birth of Oisin

ONE FINE DAY as the Fianna were returning home after a day's hunting, a beautiful deer started up in front of them and began to run as fast as the wind towards the fort of Almu. The doe ran with such speed that she outstripped most of the hunting party. The men and their dogs fell back exhausted and in the end only Finn and his two hounds, Bran and Sceolan were still in pursuit. As they swept along the side of a valley, the deer stopped suddenly in full flight and lay down on the smooth grass. Finn was surprised at this strange behaviour. Bran and Sceolan ran ahead of him and when Finn came close to the beautiful doe, he was even more amazed to see his two best hunting dogs frolicking around her. Instead of wounding and killing her they were licking her face and neck and patting her limbs.

Finn knew by this that he should not harm the animal so he called his dogs to heel and they set off for Almu. When he looked back he saw that the doe was on their heels following them home. When they reached the white fort, Finn, his hounds and their strange companion went in and the deer was given safe quarters for the night.

After the evening meal Finn retired to his room. As he lay down a lovely woman walked into his room. She was dressed in clothes of the finest material, richly ornamented. Finn stared at her in surprise and admiration and then the woman spoke.

'I am the fawn that you and your hounds spared this evening and brought back safely to Almu. I am called Sadb. A druid of the Tuatha De Danaan, the Dark Druid, changed me into a deer because I refused his love. For three years now I have endured the hardship and danger of a wild deer's life in a part of Ireland far, far from here. In the end one of the druid's servants took pity on me and told me that if I could get inside a Fianna fortress, the druid's

175

power over me would come to an end and I would become a woman again. All day have I run through the woods of Ireland without stopping until I came here, near to the Hill of Allen. I came into your territory, Finn, for I knew you were the leader of the Fianna. I outran your hunting party until Bran and Sceolan were the only pursuers on my track for I knew *they* wouldn't kill me. They recognized my true nature which was like their own.'

Finn fell so deeply in love with the beautiful woman that he would not leave her side. For months he was so enchanted by her that he abandoned all his former activities and was not seen at any hunt, fight or feast. Instead he stayed at the side of his beloved Sadb and he called her the Flower of Almu. But word came to Almu from Cormac Mac Art that the Lochlann invaders had sailed across the cold north sea and were in Dublin Bay. The Fianna were under oath to defend the country from invasion so, reluctant as he was to go, Finn had to leave Almu and beautiful Sadb.

For seven days Finn was absent driving back the Lochlann. The moment the battle was over he hurried back to Almu. As he ran over the plain towards his fort, his mind was full of Sadb. When Almu came into view, his eyes scoured the ramparts for his first glimpse of her. He knew she would be out to welcome him home as soon as news of his approach reached her but there was no sign of her. Instead of his wife, his servants came out to meet him. They cheered his safe return but their faces were sad.

'Where is my beautiful Sadb?' Finn called out anxiously. No one spoke for no one wanted to be the first to break the bad news. 'Where is my wife?' Finn asked them again, his face full of fear and they had to tell him.

'Don't blame us, Finn!' they implored. 'While you were fighting the fair-haired Lochlanns, yourself and Bran and Sceolan appeared here outside the fort. You put the Dord Fianna to your lips and its humming music filled Almu, soothing us all. Sadb, your beautiful, gentle wife, heard the music and she came running out of her room thinking you had returned. She flew down through the pass and out of the gates. We tried to stop her, for by then we knew that it was not you that was blowing the Dord Fianna, but someone who had assumed your shape. Sadb would not listen to us. She ignored both our entreaties and our commands. "I must go to welcome my husband back. I must go to meet my Finn!" she called out to us. "He saved me. He protected me. And I am carrying his child!" We begged her to stay here but she was so overjoyed at your safe return that none of us could stop her. She threw herself into the arms of the one who had taken on your shape. A second later she realized her mistake. She gave a wild shriek and drew back but the sorcerer struck her with a wand. Instantly a beautiful frightened doe stood in her place. She stood trembling on the plain for a moment looking back towards Almu. Then the druid's two hounds circled round her barking wildly and chased the terror-stricken deer out of the fort. Three or four times she made desperate attempts to spring back into the fort, but each time the hounds seized her by the throat and pulled her back. Oh, Finn!' they cried, seeing the grief and horror on his face, 'we swear to you we tried our best to save Sadb. Before you could count to twenty we had snatched our spears and swords and rushed out on to the plain to rescue her, but the plain was deserted. We could see nothing, no sign of a woman or deer, man or dog anywhere. But we could hear the beat of running feet drumming the hard plain and the howl of dogs. These noises filled the air all around us and confused us, for each of us heard the sound coming from a different direction.'

Finn threw his head back in anguish when he heard this and hammered his breast with his fists. He uttered not one word but went alone to his quarters and there he stayed all that day and all night and wasn't seen until dawn broke over the Liffey Plain.

For seven years after that, unless he was leading the Fianna against the Lochlann raids, he was scouring the country, exploring the remotest corners of the land in search of his beloved Sadb. For seven more years he mourned the beautiful woman who had made him so happy though their time together had been so short. All that time his face was sad and he was never seen to smile. Except in the heat of battle or the excitement of a chase, his spirits never lifted. When he went hunting he left his main pack of dogs behind and took with him only Bran, Sceolan and three other hounds he trusted. He wanted to be sure that Sadb would be left unharmed, if by good chance they ever found her.

At the end of fourteen years he and his Fianna companions were hunting on the side of Ben Bulben in Sligo when they heard a huge clamour from the pack of hounds who had gone ahead of them into a narrow pass. They rushed to the place and when they arrived there, they found Finn's five hounds forming a circle round a naked youth whose long hair reached almost to his feet. Finn's hounds were fighting furiously to hold back the rest of the pack as they tried to seize him. The youth stood calmly at the centre of the circle, unconcerned by the turbulent dog fight that surged around his feet. He stared curiously at the men of the Fianna as they hurried to rescue him. As soon as the other dogs had been called off, Bran and Sceolan went up to the wild boy and whined at him, licking his face and limbs and jumping up on him as if he, and not Finn, was their master. Finn and his companions went up to the handsome youth and touched his head gently and hugged him to show him he would not be harmed. They brought him with them to their hunting bothy and gave him food and drink. Then they gave him some clothes and cut his hair and he began to be easy in their company and to forget his sudden, wild ways. Finn, gazing at the youth, saw in his features a shadow of the lovely features of Sadb. He judged his age to be about fourteen, the number of years since Sadb had gone, and he felt confident that he was their child. When he returned to Almu the boy came with him and Finn loved him so much that he kept him at his side the day long. He talked to him and told him stories and the boy learned to speak. Bran and Sceolan loved their new companion so much that they spent all their time frolicking around him waiting to be petted. When the boy learned to talk he told Finn everything he could remember of his previous life.

He had been looked after by a gentle doe, he said, who had protected him and sheltered him and whom he loved like a mother. They lived in a wild lonely place, ranging together through valleys, over rocky slopes, drinking from the streams, hiding in the dark woods. During the summer he had fed on berries and fruit and in the winter provisions were left for him in a sheltered cave. A dark-looking man visited them from time to time. He would speak to the doe, sometimes gently and persuasively, sometimes in a loud, threatening voice, but however he addressed her the doe shrank away from him with terrified eyes, every limb trembling with fear. The man always left in a great rage. Though the deer and the child were free to roam this mountain park they couldn't leave it. It was surrounded by high peaks and sheer cliffs so that there was no escape.

One day the Dark Druid arrived and cornered the doe. First he spoke tenderly, coaxing her to come with him. Then he harangued her, threatening her in a loud harsh voice. He kept up this treatment for a long time but the doe still shrank away from him shivering with fear. At last the Dark Druid took a hazel wand and struck her with it. She was powerless then to do anything but follow him, but as she was led away, she kept looking back at the boy, bleating and calling out with heartbroken cries. The boy made desperate attempts to follow her but he, too, was enchanted. He sobbed with fear and grief but try as he might he could not move a limb. He heard the deer's cries grow fainter and more desperate and he was so overcome that he fainted and fell to the ground.

When he woke up, the hilly region where the doe and he had lived so happily had gone and though he searched for days for the high mountains and cliffs he could not find them. He wandered alone in the new terrain until the hounds of the Fianna had picked up his scent and Finn had taken him home.

When Finn heard this story he knew for certain that the youth was his son and the son of his beloved Sadb and he gave him the name Oisin which means 'little deer'.

The Pursuit of Diarmuid
and Grainne

IN BROAD ALMU IN LEINSTER, Finn Mac Cumhaill, leader of the
Fianna, rose early one morning and sat down on the grassy
green without a servant or companion with him. Two of the household saw him there and followed him out. They were Oisin, his son,
and Diorruing O'Bascna.

'What's the reason you're up so early, Finn?' Oisin asked.

'I have a good reason,' Finn replied. 'I've been without a wife
since Maignis died and a man without a suitable wife doesn't sleep
long or sweetly!'

'Why should it be like that,' exclaimed Oisin, 'when there is not a
woman in the whole of Ireland's green isle that we wouldn't bring
to you if you fixed your eye on her?'

Then Diorruing spoke. 'I know the very woman for you,' he said.

'Who is she?' enquired Finn.

'She is Grainne, daughter of Cormac Mac Art, granddaughter of
Conn of the Hundred Battles, the most beautiful woman in the
entire world in face, figure and fashion.'

'Diorruing, you know that I've been at odds with Cormac for a
long time now and I wouldn't give him the satisfaction of refusing
me my marriage request. I'd rather the two of you went to ask for
Grainne and then I wouldn't lose face if Cormac turned me down.'

So Oisin and Diorruing went to Tara.

When they arrived there, the king of Ireland was holding a feast
and a gathering of the clans, and the chiefs and the notable leaders
were all present. Oisin and Diorruing were welcomed with great
honour by Cormac. He adjourned the feast for the day, for he knew
that these two had come to him on an important mission. Oisin
took the king aside and told him that they had come, on Finn Mac
Cumhaill's behalf, to ask for his daughter's hand in marriage.

Cormac replied, 'There is not a prince, hero or champion in the whole country whose proposal my daughter has not rejected at one time or another and *I'm* the one that's held responsible! So I'll promise you nothing until you meet Grainne in person and hear her response for yourselves. Then I won't be blamed if the answer is no.' And Cormac led the two emissaries into Grainne's quarters and sat down beside her bed.

'Grainne,' he said, 'these two men here, were sent by Finn Mac Cumhaill. They've come to ask you to marry their commander. What is your answer going to be?'

'If you think Finn will make a suitable son-in-law for you, then he'll make a suitable husband for me!' his daughter replied, and Oisin and Diorruing were satisfied with her answer.

Grainne and her women entertained them both royally in her summer quarters so that they became exhilarated and merry and their laughter rang out across Tara. When it was time to go, Cormac arranged for them all to meet a fortnight later in Tara. Then Oisin and Diorruing returned to Almu and told Finn and the Fianna the good news from beginning to end.

The weeks soon passed as weeks will do, and it was time for Finn to meet Cormac. He brought to Almu seven battalions of the Fianna from all arts and parts and they went, in all their might, to Tara.

Cormac came out to the green to meet them, surrounded by his chiefs, and welcomed Finn and his Fianna and took them to the banqueting hall. The king sat down at the feast with his wife, Eithne, and his daughter, Grainne, on his left hand and Finn Mac Cumhaill on his right. The king's son, Cairbre, sat on the royal side, with Oisin, Finn's son, next to him. Everyone was seated according to birthright and rank. A druid called Daire sat next to Grainne and before long the two of them fell into conversation.

'What is the reason Finn Mac Cumhaill is here tonight?' Grainne asked the wise man.

'If *you* don't know the reason how do you expect *me* to know it!' Daire retorted.

'I would like you to tell me what you know,' Grainne said.

'In that case,' said the druid, 'I can tell you Finn came here tonight to ask you to be his wife.'

'I'm astonished that Finn is after me for *himself* rather than for his son, Oisin. I would consider *him* a better match than a man old enough to be my father.'

'Keep your voice low! If Finn heard you talking like that he wouldn't have anything to do with you, and then Oisin daren't touch you either, whether he wanted to or not.'

Grainne looked across the table at the men of the Fianna who sat at Finn's side.

'Tell me,' she said, 'who is the soldier sitting next to Oisin?'

'That's Goll Mac Morna, a ferocious fighter.'

'And who is that, next to Goll?'

'That's Oscar, Oisin's son and Finn's grandson.'

'And that athletic man next to Oscar?'

'That's Caoilte,' said Daire, 'the fastest runner in the Fianna.'

'And beside him?'

'Finn's nephew, Lugaid.'

'Tell me,' said Grainne, after a moment's pause, 'who is that freckled, sweet-talking fellow, the curly-headed lad who is standing at Oisin's left hand?'

'That handsome fellow with the flashing smile, is Diarmuid O' Duibhne, a charmer, who is the best lover any women could want.'

'And who is that at Diarmuid's shoulder?'

'That is a druid of the Bascna tribe, a knowledgeable man called Diorruing.'

'That's an interesting gathering indeed!' said Grainne.

Shortly after this, Grainne summoned her lady-in-waiting and told her to go to her summer house and bring back a golden jewelled goblet that she kept there. When the women returned with the goblet, Grainne filled it and handed it back to her. 'Take this, first of all, to Finn and invite him to take a drink from it. Tell him it was me who sent it.'

The handmaiden did as she was told, and Finn took a deep drink out of the goblet, and began to fall into a drugged sleep.

Cormac drank from the goblet and passed it to the queen. She sipped from it and passed it to her son. Cairbre had barely time to pass it on before he and his parents were all in a stupor. Soon the king's retinue and Finn Mac Cumhaill all lay fast asleep, drugged by the sleeping draught that Grainne had slipped into the wine. Then Grainne, who had been watching all this, rose from her own seat and went over and sat down between Oisin and Diarmuid O'Duibhne.

'I'm surprised at someone as old as Finn Mac Cumhaill wanting to marry me, when it would fit him better to make a match for me with someone my own age,' she said to Oisin.

'Don't say that, Grainne,' Oisin warned, 'for if Finn were to hear it, he wouldn't take you, and then neither could I!'

'Would you accept advances from me, Oisin?' Grainne asked.

'I would not!' Oisin cried. 'For I wouldn't come between Finn and his promised wife.'

Grainne turned round to Diarmuid.

'And what about you, Diarmuid O'Duibhne? Will you accept a proposal from me?' she asked.

'I will not!' Diarmuid replied. 'For I wouldn't take a woman who had been offered to Oisin, never mind one who had been promised to Finn!'

'Is that so?' said Grainne. 'Well, here and now, Diarmuid, I am putting a *geis* on you, to take me out of this place before Finn Mac Cumhaill and the king wake up! If you deny this solemn injunction, it will bring destruction and disgrace on your head.'

'Those are wicked bonds you have put on me!' Diarmuid cried out. 'Tell me why, out of all this high-born company, why you chose *me* to curse in this way. Any one of these princes, here, is as worthy of you as I am.'

'Oh, Diarmuid, it is not just by chance that I have laid the *geis* on you. Here's the reason. One day when my father was presiding over a festival on Tara's plain, Finn and some of the Fianna came by. A hurley match started between my brother Cairbre's team and the Fianna athletes. That day, Diarmuid, only you, the king and Finn were watching the game. The score was going against the Fianna team when you suddenly jumped up. You knocked down the player closest to you, seized his hurley stick and rushed into the game. In no time at all you had scored three goals against the Tara team. I was watching you through the stained-glass windows of my summerhouse, and as I watched I fell in love with you. From that day to this, I have never looked at another man and I never will!'

'It's a wonder you fell in love with me rather than Finn, for there is no man in Ireland who likes women better than he does!' Diarmuid exclaimed. 'And Grainne, do you know, it's Finn, now that he's here, who holds the key to the gates of Tara? So without him we cannot leave the place!'

'No,' said Grainne, 'that isn't so. There's an escape route through my summerhouse and we can leave through there.'

'I have another *geis* laid on me, and that is that I may never use an escape door to avoid my enemies,' Diarmuid told her.

'I've heard that you Fianna warriors can escape over the fortifications of any fort or house, using your spear staves, so *I'll* go out through the escape door and you follow me over the walls in that fashion,' said Grainne and left the hall.

Diarmuid turned to his friends. 'Oh, Oisin, what am I to do about the *geis* that Grainne has put on me?' he asked.

'You didn't deserve the *geis*,' said Oisin, 'but now that it has been laid on you, I advise you to follow Grainne. Just make sure to protect yourself against Finn's wily tricks!'

Diarmuid turned to Oscar. 'What do *you* think I should do about this *geis*?'

'You have no option but to follow Grainne, for a man is doomed if he breaks his *geis*.'

'And you, Caoilte, what would you advise?'

'Though I have a suitable wife already, I would give all the wealth I have to be loved by Grainne!' Caoilte replied.

'What advice have you for me?' Dairmuid said to Diorruing and the druid replied, 'Follow Grainne. You have no choice. But I pity you for she will be the cause of your death.'

'Then you all have the same advice for me,' Diarmuid said sadly.

'We have!' they all said together.

Diarmuid got up from his seat and with tears running down his face, he took farewell of his friends.

He went out of the hall and climbed to the top of the ramparts.

Then, using the shafts of his javelins, he vaulted like a bird high into the air over the fortifications and landed safely on the green plain beyond the fort. Grainne ran happily up to join him, but Diarmuid pleaded with her to change her mind.

'Grainne, I know in my heart that you are setting out on the wrong course. Turn back! Go back to your quarters straight away and Finn will never know you tried to escape. You would do much better to marry him. If you elope with me, he'll pursue us the length and breadth of Ireland and I don't know where we could go to hide from him. Go back into the fort, Grainne. Go back to Finn!'

'I will *never* go back!' Grainne cried. 'And I will never part from you till death parts us!'

'Well, then, Grainne, on we go together!' said Diarmuid.

About a mile out of the town Grainne told Diarmuid she was getting tired.

'You chose the right time to get tired,' he told her, 'for it means you can turn back home now, and no one will be any the wiser about your escape. But be sure of one thing, I am not going to carry you, or any other woman, now or ever!'

'You won't need to carry me! My father's horses are in a field, unguarded, and the chariots are close by. You can go back and yoke two horses to a chariot and come back here for me. I'll wait for you.'

Diarmuid did what he was told and they travelled in the chariot as far as Athlone. When they reached a ford on the River Shannon, Diarmuid said to Grainne, 'Having horses with us makes it all the easier for Finn to track us.'

'Then we'll leave the horses here and I will go with you on foot from now on,' she answered.

So Diarmuid unloosed the horses and left one of them on each bank of the river. Then Grainne and he travelled westwards for a mile, wading in the shallows of the river, so they would leave no tracks. They came ashore in the province of Connacht and travelled on till they reached the oak wood, called Derry Da Both. There Diarmuid made a clearing and in the centre of it he made a hut out of the saplings that he had cut down. He made seven entrances into the bothy and seven wattle doors. In the centre of the hut he laid down springy birch boughs, and on top placed fresh rushes, and made a bed for Grainne to lie on.

When Finn Mac Cumhaill rose in Tara the next morning and found that Diarmuid and Grainne had eloped, he burned with rage and jealousy. He hurried out on to the plain and, marshalling the Clan Nevin trackers, he ordered them to find the runaways. The trackers traced the couple as far as Athlone but lost their trail at the ford on the Shannon. Finn stormed and raged at the huntsmen and threatened to hang them all, on either side of the ford, if they didn't get on the trail of the fugitives again. So the Clan Nevin trackers followed the river a mile westwards and found the horses still grazing where Diarmuid had left them. Then the trackers picked up the trail that led into Connacht.

'I know now where Diarmuid and Grainne have gone! They've gone across the plain into the woods of Da Both!' Finn exclaimed.

When Oisin and Oscar and Diarmuid's other friends heard Finn say this, they were fearful for his safety.

'Finn knows this terrain so well that there's a good chance he might be right, and the pair of them *are* where he says,' Oisin said to the others. 'We must warn Diarmuid of the danger he's in. Oscar, go and find Bran, and send him to warn Diarmuid. That hound loves Diarmuid as much as he loves Finn!'

Oscar called Bran to him and told what he must do and the hound, with his human intelligence, understood. He stole to the back of the crowd so that Finn wouldn't see him leave, and then he followed Diarmuid's trail at full speed until he reached Derry Da Both. He found Diarmuid asleep in the clearing and he pushed his muzzle into his neck. Diarmuid woke up with a start and recognized Bran. He jumped up and went into the shelter where Grainne lay asleep and shook her awake. 'This is Bran, Mac Cumhaill's own hound. I know he has come here to warn me that Finn's on my trail!'

'Then take heed of the warning and fly!' Grainne beseeched him.

'I won't!' declared Diarmuid. 'Finn may as well catch me now as any other time, because he'll catch me in the end.'

When Grainne heard this she trembled all over with fear and Bran turned back to join the Fianna. When Oisin saw the dog back among them again, he said to Caoilte, 'I don't know if Bran got the chance, or the space, to reach Diarmuid. Our friend may still be in danger. We'd better send him another warning. Where is Feargoir, that henchman of yours whose voice carries over ten townlands? Tell him to let out a roar that Diarmuid will hear in Derry Da Both!'

Feargoir was found and he let out three piercing yells and Diarmuid heard them in his hideout. He wakened Grainne again. 'That's Feargoir's voice. He's a kinsman of Caoilte Mac Ronain and since Caoilte is in Finn's company at the moment, that means they're warning me that Finn's on my trail.'

'Take heed of that warning and fly!' Grainne pleaded again.

'I will not!' said Diarmuid again. 'We'll not leave these woods until Finn and his trackers overtake us.'

Meanwhile Finn pressed on in great haste and sent his trackers into the oak woods of Da Both. When they came back out of the woods, they told Finn that Diarmuid was in the woods with a woman whose tracks they didn't recognize.

'Bad luck to all those who are on Diarmuid's side!' Finn exclaimed angrily. 'But in spite of them, he'll not leave these woods until I have got full revenge for all the harm he has done to me.'

Oisin turned to him and said, 'You're out of your head with jealousy, Finn, if you imagine that Diarmuid would be foolish enough to loiter in Derry Da Both knowing that you're on his heels!'

'That trick won't work, Oisin! I know very well that Diarmuid is nearby. You sent my own dog to warn him that I was on his trail. And I heard Feargoir roaring as well. I knew he was calling out a warning to Diarmuid. But it's no use. O'Duibhne won't leave the woods until he has paid for every insult and humiliation he has inflicted on me!' And Finn ran after his trackers into the trees.

This time Oscar made a last attempt to deflect him.

'You're demented with jealousy, if you suppose for one minute that Diarmuid will stay here on the plain till you take the head of him!' he shouted, but Finn had already reached the clearing and seen the shelter that Diarmuid had made.

'Save your breath, Oscar,' he said, pointing to the hut. 'No one but Diarmuid could have made a bothy like this, snug and warm and with seven tight, narrow doors into it.' He raised his voice and shouted into the enclosure, 'Who's right, Diarmuid, Oscar or me?'

'You're right as usual, Finn!' Diarmuid shouted back. 'I *am* here and Grainne is with me!' And in full view of Finn and his men he put his arms round Grainne and kissed her three times.

When he saw this Finn was in such a rage that he felt weak. But he steadied himself and promised Diarmuid that he would pay for those kisses with his head. Then he called his soldiers to surround the shelter.

At that instant an icy wind encircled Diarmuid, and his guardian from the Tuatha De Danaan, Aengus Og, appeared and spoke to him. 'Why are you in this predicament, Diarmuid?' he asked.

'The king of Ireland's daughter, Grainne here, has fled with me from her father and from Finn Mac Cumhaill. She put a *geis* on me and I came with her against my will,' Diarmuid said.

'Both of you slip in under the border of my cloak and I will take you out of here without Finn and the Fianna realizing you've gone,' Aengus said.

'Take Grainne with you,' Diarmuid told him, 'but I won't go with you. If I survive I'll follow you, if I don't, send Grainne back to her father's house and let him deal with her well or ill.'

So Aengus Og put Grainne under the hem of his cloak and they both left unbeknownst to the Fianna and landed near Limerick. As soon as they had left the clearing, Diarmuid raised himself to his full height, straight as a pillar, and put on his armour. He took up his weapons and his sharp daggers and, going from door to door, he challenged the Fianna warriors outside. His friends, Oisin and Oscar and the Bascna clan were at the first door and they would have let him pass through unharmed, but Diarmuid refused their protection. The second door was guarded by Caoilte Mac Ronain and his followers and they offered to fight to the death to protect him, but Diarmuid refused to leave by that door. Conan, heading the Clan Morna stood outside the third door, and as they were old adversaries of Finn they too offered Diarmuid safe passage. He refused their offer and it was the same story at the next two doors. Diarmuid was determined to deal with Finn himself, and was unwilling to bring Finn's enmity on anyone else. Outside the sixth door Finn's loyal trackers stood at the ready. They challenged Diarmuid to come out and fight them and they swore they would hack him to death, but Diarmuid refused their challenge with contempt and moved on to the seventh door and this time Finn himself answered.

'This is Finn Mac Cumhaill, commander of the Fianna and head of Clan Bascna and with me are four hundred mercenaries. You are no friend of ours, Diarmuid O'Duibhne, and if you venture out through this gate you'll be hacked to pieces.'

'Then I give you my oath, I will leave by this door and no other,' Diarmuid shouted back.

Finn was enraged by Diarmuid's taunts and ordered his men, under pain of death, to stop him leaving. Diarmuid heard Finn's command and he vaulted from his javelin shafts high into the air, out and over the door, over the heads of his enemies, and he moved so swiftly that they didn't even know he had gone. He looked back at them triumphantly and taunted them with his escape, then he slung his shield over his broad, curved back and headed out of range of his pursuers. When he knew they were no longer on his trail he doubled back to follow the route that Aengus and Grainne had taken. He followed that trail without straying until he reached Limerick. He found Aengus and Grainne in a warm, brightly lit hut, roasting a side of wild boar over a big, crackling fire. Grainne's heart flew into her mouth with delight when Diarmuid walked in. He told her the whole adventure and when they had eaten their fill of the wild pig, they all went to sleep for the night.

Aengus rose at daybreak to go back to his underground fort near the Boyne but before he left he gave Diarmuid some advice on how to outwit the cunning Finn.

'Never enter a cave that has only one exit or climb a tree that has only one trunk, and never sail to an island with only one inlet.

Don't eat where you cook and don't sleep where you eat. And in the morning, don't rise from the same bed you settled in the night before.'

When Aengus had gone, Diarmuid and Grainne set out again on their long wanderings around Ireland, always on the move and always Finn behind them, relentlessly pursuing them.

First of all they travelled south-westwards, on the left bank of the Shannon, until they came to the River Laune and there Diarmuid caught seven salmon. He skewered them and cooked them on a spit, but he kept one salmon untouched. They crossed the stream to eat their meal, as Aengus had recommended, and before they moved onto find a camping spot for the night, Diarmuid left the salmon that had not been touched on the bank. He had left a piece of untouched venison at Derry Da Both in the same way, to show Finn that he had not taken Grainne to him as a lover. When Finn came on these signs, he knew what they meant and he trailed the fugitives with even greater urgency, in the hope that Grainne might still be his wife, since she was not yet Diarmuid's.

The next morning the couple met a young warrior who was well built and handsome, but his clothes were shabby and his weapons poor. He told them his name was Muadan and that he was seeking military service with a champion.

'What service are you offering?' Diarmuid asked the young man.

'I will look after your needs by day and guard you by night,' said Muadan.

'Take him up on his offer, Diarmuid,' Grainne urged. 'You can't always live without retainers.' So Diarmuid agreed to take on Muadan and a contract was made between them.

The three of them journeyed westwards until they reached the River Carra and Muadan offered to carry both Diarmuid and Grainne across the stream. In spite of Grainne's protests the servant took both of them on his back across the water. When it was near dark, they stopped in a cave at the edge of a bog to shelter for the night and Muadan prepared fragrant beds for Diarmuid and Grainne. Then he went to a grove close to the cave and cut a long straight rod from a rowan tree. He tied a strand of hair to it to make a line, and knotted a hook on to the end of it. Then he put a holly berry on the hook and with this fishing rod he cast into the stream. A fish took the first berry and Muadan unhooked it and cast again. A second fish took the second berry, and with a third berry, he caught a third fish. Then he stuck the rod into the earth, tucked the line and hook into his belt and went back to the cave and cooked the fish on a spit.

When the fish was ready Muadan said to Diarmuid, 'You divide the fish between us.'

'I would rather you divided it yourself,' Diarmuid replied.

Muadan asked Grainne to divide the fish, but she too declined. So Muadan took the fish and served it out.

'If Grainne had divided the fish, she would have given the largest one to Diarmuid, and if Diarmuid had divided them he would have given the largest one to Grainne. Since I'm the one who's doing it I'll give the largest one to Diarmuid, the second largest one to Grainne and I'll take the smallest fish myself.'

They ate their meal together and when it was over, Diarmuid and Grainne went back to their beds in the cave, and Muadan kept watch all night.

At daybreak Diarmuid woke Grainne and told her to keep guard so that Muadan could sleep and he could go out to check the lie of the land. He went to the highest headland and from the top of it he looked around him in all directions.

Before long he saw a great, sinister fleet of ships coming towards the strand that lay at the foot of the cliff. When the ships touched land, a crowd of warriors, nearly a thousand in number, came ashore. Diarmuid went down to meet them and find out why they had come.

Three of the strangers, the captains of the fleet, stepped up to Diarmuid and spoke to him.

'We're three royal chiefs from across the sea, in the pay of Finn Mac Cumhaill. Our names are Blackfooted, Fairfooted and Strongfooted and we are looking for a man that Finn has outlawed, a bandit and a traitor called Diarmuid O'Duibhne. When we find him we'll put an end to him. We have three venomous hounds with us to help us overcome this rascal, and when we loose them on his trail, they'll soon track him down. Fire can't burn these hounds, nor water drown them nor any weapon wound them. Between these hounds and the thousand fighters we have with us, we'll soon put an end to Diarmuid O'Duibhne. And who are you? Tell us your name. Have you heard any word of this bandit?'

'I saw him yesterday,' said Diarmuid to the chiefs. 'Now, *I'm* just an ordinary warrior wandering the world, fending for myself with my head and hands, but if you meet Diarmuid O'Duibhne it will be a different story. *He* is no ordinary man, I can tell you! Have you got wine on board the ships?'

'We have,' they answered.

'Bring out a wine barrel and I will do a trick for you,' Diarmuid said.

A tun of wine was brought out and Diarmuid took a long drink from it and so did the chiefs. Then Diarmuid carried the barrel to the top of the hill and jumped on it and sent it rolling down the hill at great speed, while he balanced on top of it. At the bottom of the hill, Diarmuid stopped the barrel, still keeping his balance, and brought it back up the hill and down again three times. All the time the strangers looked on.

'You haven't seen many tricks if you think *that's* a good one!' they jeered and one of them sprang up on the barrel. Diarmuid gave the tun a kick and the man fell off and the heavy barrel crushed the life out of him. Another man tried and suffered the same fate and another and another, until fifty of them lay dead on the mountain top. As evening drew in the rest of them returned to the ship and Diarmuid went back to Grainne and Muadan but he told them nothing of his adventures.

The next day as Muadan slept and Grainne kept guard, Diarmuid went out to meet the foreign mercenaries again.

'I have another trick for you,' he told them.

'We would rather have news of O'Duibhne,' they said.

'I saw a man who saw him yesterday,' Diarmuid replied.

Then he laid down his arms and armour and stripped down to his tunic. He stuck his spear, the one that Manannan Mac Lir had given to him, into the ground with the point up. He rose into the air as light as a bird and landed on the point of the spear. He balanced there a moment, and jumped off unharmed.

The strangers scoffed again and one of them jumped into the air as Diarmuid had done, but he landed heavily on the spearhead and the sharp point went through his body and killed him. Diarmuid set the spear straight again and another man took up the challenge. He too was pierced through the heart. Before they gave up and returned to the boat, fifty men had been killed by Manannan's spear.

The next morning Diarmuid challenged the strangers to another feat of skill. He set the sword that Aengus had given him between two forked sticks and then he walked the length of the razor-sharp blade three times. The first stranger to try the trick landed with his feet on either side of the sword and was cut in half lengthways. The second one fell across the blade and was cut in half breadthways. By evening a hundred of them were dead and one of the captains said to Diarmuid, 'Take away your sword! Too many men have been killed on it. Tell us, have you heard any word of the outlaw O'Duibhne?'

'I saw a man who saw him today, and I'll go and get news of him tonight,' Diarmuid said and off he went, back to Grainne and Muadan.

The next morning when Diarmuid awoke he put on his heaviest armour and took up his most powerful weapons. Then he woke Grainne and told her to keep watch and let Muadan sleep. When Grainne saw Diarmuid in full battle array and fired up for a fight, she trembled with fright. Diarmuid comforted her and reassured her that he had dressed for battle in case he met an enemy by chance. Then he went out again to meet Finn's foreign mercenaries.

'Have you any news of Diarmuid O'Duibhne?' they asked him.

'I saw him a while back,' said Diarmuid.

'Then lead us to him so that we can bring his head to Finn Mac Cumhaill!' they said.

'It would be an act of treachery on my part to do what you ask,' Diarmuid told him, 'for O'Duibhne's life is under my protection.'

'Is that true?' the chiefs exclaimed.

'It's true,' Diarmuid replied.

'Then we'll take *your* head to Finn instead of his!' they shouted and rushed at him. Diarmuid lifted Manannan's spear and Aengus's sword and raged through them, sending them flying the way a hawk scatters a flock of small birds, or a wolf tears through a herd of sheep. In the end only the leaders and a few followers escaped to the ship but Diarmuid was unharmed and he rejoined Grainne and Muadan.

The next morning he set out in battle gear again and this time the leaders themselves, Blackfooted, Fairfooted and Strongfooted, challenged him to combat. Diarmuid fought the three of them, overwhelmed all three, and forced them to the ground. He didn't kill them; instead he tied them up in tight, tight knots so they could hardly get a breath and he left them there on the ground. He returned to Grainne and Muadan unharmed and said nothing of his victory.

The next morning Diarmuid warned Grainne that there were enemies close by. Then, for the first time, he told her about his adventures of the previous days and about the hordes of enemies he had overcome in battle with feats of strength and force. He finished his story by telling her that the three chieftains from across the sea were lying trussed up on the cliff top.

'But they still have three poisonous hounds to set on me and no weapons can wound the evil things,' Diarmuid said.

'Why did you not behead those chiefs when you had a chance?' Grainne cried when she heard all this.

'Because this way they'll suffer longer!' Diarmuid said. 'Only Oisin, Oscar or Lugaid could set the chiefs free, because only they know how to untie those knots. Since they're my friends they won't do that. But still, Finn's bound to hear about all this and he will be cut to the heart when he discovers I've defeated his hired squadrons. We must leave this cave immediately before the hounds are set on our trail.'

So once more Diarmuid, Grainne and the faithful Muadan stole away, taking cover in the woods and wildernesses. When they reached the moor at Tralee, Grainne was weary and footsore and Muadan carried her on his back until they reached the foothills of lofty Slieve Luachra and there they rested. They washed their clothes and cleaned themselves after the long journey and Grainne borrowed Diarmuid's dagger to pare her nails.

The last few survivors of the fleet that Finn had dispatched to destroy Diarmuid, ventured out the following morning and found their masters trussed up and lying helpless on the ground, gasping for breath. They struggled to untie the bonds, but the more they worked at them, the tighter the knots grew until their leaders could hardly draw breath.

They went back to the ship and brought to shore the three venomous hounds and loosed them on the trail of Diarmuid. The hounds picked up the scent of the fugitives and with the mercenaries following traced them from one hideout to another. They caught up with the three on the slopes of Slieve Luachra just as they were washing off the dust of the journey.

Diarmuid saw the banners approaching, and when he picked out the green cloaks of the leading warriors he became full of rage and hatred for them. Quickly Grainne handed him back his dagger. Muadan hoisted Grainne on his back and the three of them ran a mile further along the mountainside. But soon they saw one of the deadly hounds loping after them, following their scent. Muadan told Diarmuid to take Grainne to safety and he would fight the hound. Then he took from beneath his belt a tiny pup and set the little creature on his open palm. As the poisonous hound sprang toward Muadan, its jaws gaping, the pup sprang from Muadan's hand straight down the hound's gullet and went like an arrow to its heart forcing it out through the animal's side. Then it lit back on to Muadan's outstretched hand leaving the huge hound dead on the ground. Muadan hurried after Diarmuid and Grainne and the three of them covered another mile along the slopes of Slieve Luachra. A second hound came after them and sprang to the attack. This time Diarmuid killed the animal with his magic spear. The third hound, the most savage of all, raced after the fugitives and overtook them just as Diarmuid had set Grainne down on a wide, high flagstone.

The hound sprang over Diarmuid's head to seize her, but Diarmuid caught it by the two hind legs as it flew over his head and swung it against the foot of the rock and knocked out its brains. Then, using all his skill, Diarmuid cast his spear at the green cloak of the leader and felled him, and with two more casts killed the other two leaders. When the men saw their chiefs fall they panicked, and they turned tail and ran back to the ship. But Diarmuid followed and scattered them; one survivor alone made it back to Finn with the news of their annihilation at Diarmuid's hands.

As Diarmuid had predicted, Finn was humiliated and enraged by the defeat of his foreign allies. He summoned the Fianna from all over Ireland and, when they were gathered, led them by the shortest, fastest route to the place where the fleet had landed. There they found the three captains lying on the ground, gasping like fish out of water.

'Loose the knots and set these three men free!' Finn ordered Oisin.

'I will not!' Oisin replied. 'For I've given Diarmuid my word that I will never set free anyone that he has bound.'

Oscar gave Finn the same answer and so did Lugaid and while they were arguing the chieftains died from lack of breath. Finn buried his allies with a heavy heart and raised a stone over the grave.

Just as he had buried the leaders, the sole survivor of their vast army came running up to Finn. His tongue was lolling, his eyes were rolling and he was dropping from terror and exhaustion. He told the Fianna chief of the carnage Diarmuid had wrought on his companions on the slopes of Slieve Luachra and of the death of the three hounds they had thought invincible.

'And where is Diarmuid?' Finn asked.

'That I don't know,' the man replied.

When he heard all this Finn was in despair for he knew that he had been outwitted and defeated by Diarmuid. He turned round and headed back northwards to Leinster, bringing his followers with him, and Diarmuid and Grainne continued their wanderings through the south and west of Ireland.

One morning Muadan told Diarmuid that the terms of the contract had been fulfilled and it was time for him to leave. Both Diarmuid and Grainne pleaded with him to stay but he wouldn't change his mind. He took his farewell of them and left their service directly. The couple were sad at the loss of such a loyal and devoted friend, but they had to keep moving and they travelled into Galway that day. On the way Grainne's strength and courage began to flag. Before this, Muadan had always carried her when she had been tired, but now he was gone and there was only Diarmuid left and he had declared at the outset that he wouldn't carry her or anyone else. When Grainne pondered this and reconciled herself to it, she recovered her strength and her spirits, and walked boldly on, happy to be alone at Diarmuid's side.

As they walked through a stream a little spurt of water splashed up on to Grainne's leg and she began to mock Diarmuid for his self-restraint and timidity in matters of courtship that was so different from his forcefulness and courage in battle. 'This trickle of water is more adventurous than you are when it comes to love,' she teased him, and at long last Diarmuid allowed his love for her to override his fear of Finn. When they stopped that night, he built a bothy out of saplings and made a bed out of birch boughs and fragrant rushes for both of them, and so, for the first time on their wanderings, Diarmuid O'Duibhne of the winning smile and Grainne, the king of Ireland's daughter, lay down together as man and wife.

Not long after Finn Mac Cumhaill had returned to Almu, following the defeat of the foreign mercenaries, he was sitting with the men of the Fianna around him, when they saw a band of fifty warriors coming towards them. At the head of the band were two tall, imposing men who were noticeable for their proud bearing and for their handsome faces. Finn asked his companions if anyone recognized them, but no one did.

'I don't know them either,' Finn said, 'but I have a feeling they are enemies of mine!'

The warriors came up to him and told him they were indeed enemies of his, champions of Clan Morna whose fathers had taken part in the killing of Finn's father at the battle of Cnuca.

'But our *own* fathers died as a result of Cumhall's death,' they said, 'and as we were still in our mothers' wombs at that time and had nothing to do with the whole thing, we would like to make peace with you and take our rightful place among the ranks of the Fianna.'

'You can take your places in the Fianna,' said Finn, 'when you have compensated me for my father's death.'

'We have no wealth that we can give you in compensation, no gold or silver, cattle or flocks to our name,' said the warriors.

Oisin pleaded with Finn to be generous with the three young men. 'Don't ask for blood-money, Finn. Their own fathers' deaths were atonement enough for Cumhall's death.'

'If I were to die, Oisin, it's easy to see *you'd* come to a convenient settlement!' Finn retorted. 'But no one will join the Finna without compensating me for Cumhall's death.'

'What compensation are you looking for?' young Art Mac Morna asked.

'All I want is the head of a warrior or a fistful of the berries from the rowan tree of Dubhros,' said Finn.

Oisin took the Morna chiefs aside and said to them, 'Go back home immediately and don't try to make peace with Finn ever again! Do you know whose head he wants you to bring to him? The head of Diarmuid O'Duibhne! That's what Finn's asking you for and if there were two thousand of you, you *still* couldn't overcome Diarmuid and take off his head!'

'Then what about the berries that he has asked us to get?' the Mac Mornas asked.

'That's an even harder task!' Oisin told them. 'The rowan tree of Dubhros is a magic tree. It grew out of a berry from a tree in the Land of Promise that the Tuatha De Danaan dropped as they passed by that place. Those berries have marvellous qualities. A person who eats three of them will be free from sickness and injury. He will feel as satisfied and exhilarated as if he had been drinking wine or ale, and even if he's a hundred years of age he'll feel like a thirty-year-old again. But the Tuatha De Danaan have sent a huge, monstrous young man from their own land to guard the magic berries. He is called Searbhann Lochlann and he is an ungainly, big-nosed, crooked-toothed, bleary-eyed, rough-bearded giant of the wicked Cam tribe. His magic is so powerful that fire cannot burn him, sword pierce him, or water drown him. He has only one eye and it is set in the middle of his brow. Round his body is a thick iron hoop and, chained to that hoop, a heavy iron club. He can be killed only by three strokes of his own club. At night he sleeps in the top of the tree and all day long he guards it. The district around him is wild and deserted and he has terrorized even Finn and his men to such a degree that they don't dare hunt in that region. And *those*, my friends, are the berries that Finn wants you to bring to him!'

But the two cousins paid no heed to Oisin's warning. They left their followers in Oisin's care and set out together in pursuit of Diarmuid and Grainne so as to take off Diarmuid's head as Finn had requested.

After two days of travelling westwards, they picked up the couple's trail and followed it to the hunting bothy where they were living. Diarmuid heard the brothers approaching and seized his weapons. He fastened the door and challenged the men outside to give their names.

'We are two cousins of the Morna clan. Art and Aed Mac Morna are our names.'

'What brings you here?' Diarmuid enquired.

'If you are Diarmuid O'Duibhne, we're here for your head!' they called back.

'That's who I am!' Diarmuid shouted.

'Well then, Diarmuid, Finn has given us a choice of blood payments for his father and the choice is this: your head or the berries of the rowan tree of Dubhros!'

'Neither of those things will be easy to get, I can tell you!' Diarmuid exclaimed. 'And I pity you even more if you have put yourself in Finn's power. I happen to know it was *he* who killed your fathers. Surely *that* should be payment enough from the Morna tribe.'

'And it should be enough from you that you stole Finn's woman without bad-mouthing him into the bargain!' Aed Mac Morna exclaimed.

'I'm not bad-mouthing Finn when I say what I say!' Diarmuid answered. 'I know from experience that, whichever of these things you bring back to Finn, it will not be enough. It will not buy you peace at the end of it all!'

Grainne had listened to all this and then she said to Diarmuid, 'What sort of berries are these that Finn wants so badly and that cannot be got for him?'

Diarmuid told her about the magic rowan tree of Dubhros and its marvellous properties, and about the terrible Searbhann Lochlann who guarded the tree.

'Finn is afraid to come here himself,' Diarmuid said to the cousins, 'but when he outlawed me and made an enemy of me I got permission from the giant to hunt in his territory on the strict condition that I would never touch the berries. So now, you bold Morna boys, make your choice. Fight with me for my head or fight the giant for the berries.'

'We'll fight *you*!' the cousins said and reached for their weapons. Before they had time to pick them up, Diarmuid had overcome them and had tied them both up.

'Well done, Diarmuid!' Grainne said as she looked at the two of them lying helpless in the clearing. 'But now I have a craving for those berries myself, and I need to taste them, especially now that I'm pregnant. Even if these two won't go to get them, I need to taste them or I'll die.'

'Don't ask me to break my pact with Searbhann Lochlann,' Diarmuid begged. 'He won't allow me to get the berries either.'

'Loose these ropes and set us free,' the two cousins said, 'and we'll help you to fight the giant.'

'You would be no help,' said Diarmuid, 'for just one glimpse of the giant would be enough to scare the two of you to death.

'Please set us free so that at least we can go with you and watch you fight the giant,' the cousins begged.

Diarmuid untied them and the three warriors set off for Dubhros. When they arrived there the giant was dozing under the rowan tree. Diarmuid woke him up with his foot and the giant stared at him.

'Have you come to break our agreement, O'Duibhne?' he asked.

'I don't want to break our pact,' Diarmuid said, 'but the daughter of King Cormac is expecting our child and she has a craving for these berries that you're guarding. I'm here to ask for a fistful of the berries for her.'

'If you were never to have any child but the one Grainne's carrying now, and if she were to die having it and the race of Cormac to die with her, I still wouldn't give you as much as one berry for her to taste!' the giant shouted.

'I'll tell you no lie!' Diarmuid shouted back. 'By fair means or foul I'll get those berries!'

When he heard this the giant leapt to his feet and taking his iron club he swung it at Diarmuid. Three times Diarmuid parried with his shield and three times the giant's strength was too much for him and he was knocked to the ground and injured in spite of his skill. After he had hurt his opponent Searbhann lowered his club for a moment and when the giant was off guard, Diarmuid threw down his weapons and sprang up at him with a fierce bound. He grabbed the club with both hands and, with all his strength, lifted the giant off his feet and swung him in a wide arc round his body by the chain that was attached to the club. Then he let go and the giant flew through the air and crashed to the ground. As he lay there winded, Diarmuid gave him three mighty blows on the head with the club and knocked out his brains. Then Diarmuid collapsed on the ground, battered and exhausted. When the two cousins saw the giant lying lifeless on the ground, they came out from their hiding-place and ran up to Diarmuid. He told them to bury Searbhann Lochlann under brushwood so that Grainne would not see what an ugly monster he had fought. When they had done that, the brothers were sent to bring Grainne to Diarmuid and she found him still lying under the rowan tree, worn out and bleeding from the fight.

'Grainne,' Diarmuid said, pointing to the tree, 'here are the berries you asked me to get you. Reach up and pull as many as you want.'

'I will not eat a single berry, Diarmuid, unless you pull it off the tree and hand it to me yourself,' Grainne said.

So Diarmuid rose and picked some berries and gave them to Grainne and the two cousins and took some himself. They all ate their fill and soon Diarmuid's wounds were healed. His battle weariness left him and the four of them were in excellent spirits.

Then Diarmuid picked a fistful of the berries and handed them to the two warriors. 'Sons of Morna, take these berries to Finn and tell him that it was *you* that killed the giant.'

The brothers took the precious berries and, thanking Diarmuid with all their heart, set off for Finn's fort at Almu. When they had gone, Diarmuid and Grainne climbed up the tree to the bed that the giant had made at the top and there they lay down. They ate the berries that were within reach and these berries were so sweet they made the berries below taste as bitter as sloes.

Aed and Art Mac Morna reached Almu and handed Finn the magic berries. 'Here are the berries from the rowan tree of Dubhros,' they said. 'We killed the giant and pulled these berries for you as a recompense for your father's death. We're asking you now to keep your word and peacefully restore to us our rightful place among the ranks of the Fianna.'

Finn took the bunch, examined it and saw that they were the berries he wanted. Then he brought them to his nose and sniffed them. 'I get the smell of Diarmuid's skin off these berries!' he exclaimed. 'It was Diarmuid who plucked them and Diarmuid who killed the giant, not the two of you! These berries are no good to me as compensation. You didn't get them, so you will not get your place among the Fianna. But now that I know where he is I'll go immediately to Dubhros, to the rowan tree, and see if I can catch Diarmuid there.'

Finn called together the standing army of the Fianna, seven battalions of them, and brought them with him to Dubhros. They followed Diarmuid's tracks to the rowan tree and, finding the tree unguarded, ate their fill of the enchanted berries.

The noonday heat was beating down and Finn lay in the shadow of the tree. 'I'll wait here till the heat is past for I know that Diarmuid is at the top of this tree,' he said.

'Envy has put your head astray, Finn, if you can believe that Diarmuid would stay at the top of this tree knowing that the man who wants to murder him is lying beneath it!' Oisin said.

Finn didn't answer. He called for a chessboard and challenged Oisin to a game. Oisin's supporters sat on one side of the board and Finn sat alone at the other. Finn played a skilful, crafty game until it came about that a single move would win the game. Then he said triumphantly to his son. 'Look at that, Oisin! The right move wins this game, but I defy either you or your henchmen to make it.'

Diarmuid, who had a bird's-eye view of the game through the branches of the tree, saw Oisin's predicament.

'It's a bad thing, Oisin, that you're in these straits without me to help you out,' he murmured.

'It's a worse thing, Diarmuid, to be sitting up here in the giant's bed surrounded by seven battalions intent on killing you than that Oisin misses a move!' Grainne exclaimed.

Diarmuid studied the board, then he picked a berry and aimed it at the chesspiece that ought to be moved. Oisin moved that piece and turned the game against Finn.

It was not long before Oisin was in the same situation again and once more Diarmuid threw a berry at the right chessman and saved the game. For the third time Finn turned the game against Oisin, and this time, as before, Diarmuid aimed a third berry at the crucial chesspiece and won the game for Oisin. The men watching gave a great roar, but Finn was angry.

'Oisin, it's no credit to you to have won the game, seeing you had the expert advice not only of these three helpers here at your side but of Diarmuid O'Duibhne up above you as well!'

'Jealousy has driven you mad, Finn, if you think that Diarmuid would stay in the top of the tree with you lying in wait for him at the bottom,' Oscar said to his grandfather.

Finn looked up through the branches of the tree and shouted,

'Which of us is right, O'Duibhne? Oscar or me?'

'You're always right, Finn!' Diarmuid shouted down. 'I *am* here in the giant's bed and Grainne is beside me!' And with that he stood up and pulled Grainne into his arms and kissed her three times in full view of Finn and all the Fianna.

'You gave more scandal to the Fianna the night you stole Grainne from me in Tara, and you one of my own bodyguards, than you do with that kiss!' Finn said contemptuously. 'But you'll give your head for it all the same.'

Then Finn ordered his mercenaries to join hands and form an unbroken ring round the tree. He warned them that they would all be killed if Diarmuid broke through their ranks and he promised great honour among the Fianna to anyone who would bring him Diarmuid's head. As one of the soldiers climbed up the tree to behead O'Duibhne, Aengus, in his tumulus at Brugh na Boinne, sensed the straits that his foster son was in and came to save him. He landed beside Diarmuid in an icy wind, invisible to the men below. As the soldier reached the top of the tree, Aengus put Diarmuid's shape on him and Diarmuid kicked him back down. He landed among his companions and they fell on him and cut off his head for they thought it was Diarmuid himself. As soon as he had been beheaded, his own shape returned and his comrades recognized him too late. Nine other men climbed up and met the same fate until Finn intervened and stopped any more from trying. Aengus wrapped his magic mantle around Grainne and spirited her away to his fort on the banks of the Boyne and Diarmuid promised to join them if he made his escape.

Then Diarmuid shouted down to Finn, 'I'll go down to you, Finn and face you, for you want my death in one place or another and I'll fight you all single-handed since you won't let me escape. I've no allies left in any case, for I made enemies of them through my loyalty to you. I was a fearless fighter for you, Finn, always fighting *your* cause, but now I'll fight to the death on my own behalf!' With that Diarmuid rose and stood up on the highest branch of the tree. From there he rose like a bird from the shafts of his javelins and sailed out over the heads of the men below. They realized, too late, that he had escaped. Finn raged but there was nothing he could do, for Diarmuid had outwitted him again. He went with his army back to Almu while Diarmuid made his way safely to Aengus and Grainne at the Boyne.

The next morning Aengus went to Finn in his fort at Almu and asked him to make peace with Diarmuid. Finn agreed. Then Aengus went on to Tara and asked Cormac Mac Art to forgive Diarmuid for having eloped with his daughter and Cormac agreed. Aengus returned to Brugh na Boinne and asked Diarmuid and Grainne to make peace with Cormac and Finn and they agreed. The terms Diarmuid demanded were these: that he be granted his father's territory, free of tax or tribute to Cormac ever after; that Finn and the huntsmen of the Fianna be forbidden from hunting there; and that Grainne be granted her own large territory in Keshcorran in Sligo, far away from her father and Finn. These terms were accepted and after sixteen years on the run, Diarmuid and Grainne settled peacefully in Keshcorran. They lived happily there in Rath Grainne and had four sons and one daughter. They prospered and grew rich, so rich that the people around said they were the wealthiest couple in the land.

They lived a happy and prosperous life in Keshcorran for a long time until one day Grainne called Diarmuid aside and said to him, 'It seems a pity, considering the importance and the excellence of this household, that the two best men, the most eminent in the country, Cormac Mac Art and Finn Mac Cumhaill, have not spent as much as one night here.'

'Why would they come here?' Diarmuid asked in surprise. 'They are our enemies!'

'I would like to give a feast in their honour and reconcile them to you,' said Grainne.

'I would approve of that,' Diarmuid said.

'Well then, tell your daughter to prepare a feast for them in her house too,' Grainne said. 'Who knows, she might find a fitting husband from it all.'

For a full year Grainne and her daughter were busy preparing for the two great feasts. At the end of the year, when the preparations were complete, they sent messengers to Cormac and Finn inviting them to the feasts and they both accepted the invitations and came with their followers to Rath Grainne. The festivities went on for a full year and were greatly enjoyed by everyone.

The night the feast ended, Diarmuid started up from his sleep in panic and woke Grainne. She caught him and held him tightly and asked him what had caused the alarm.

'I heard a hunting hound in full cry and it's strange to hear such a thing in the middle of the night,' Diarmuid said.

'May your guardians protect you well!' exclaimed Grainne. 'The Tuatha De Danaan are bewitching you, in spite of Aengus at the Boyne. Lie down and go back to sleep!'

But Diarmuid couldn't close an eye and soon he heard the hound's cry again. He made to get up and look for the animal, but Grainne held him back and at last he went back to sleep. As day broke, he was disturbed for the third time by the baying of the hound and this time Grainne was not able to detain him. With his sword in one hand and his favourite hound on a leash in the other, he set out to find the chase. He made his way swiftly to Ben Bulben for he heard the sound of a chase coming from that direction and there he found Finn Mac Cumhaill sitting alone on a hillock.

'Have you organized this chase, Finn?' Diarmuid asked him angrily.

'No,' replied Finn. 'A company of men and dogs took the field around midnight and they came across the Wild Boar of Ben Bulben and went after him. They're foolish to follow him for he has given them the slip often before. As well as that he has killed scores of men this morning already. Look! Here he comes! Run, Diarmuid! Run and escape while you can!' Finn jumped up from the tummock as a group of terrified hunters came rushing towards them, scattering in all directions to escape the wild boar's ferocious charge.

Diarmuid didn't move. 'I'll face the boar! He won't drive *me* away!' he cried.

'You can't do that, Diarmuid,' warned Finn. 'Remember, there is a *geis* on you never to hunt a pig. And this boar is enchanted. He is an enemy of yours who has been turned into a boar and it has been foretold that you and he will live for the same length of time and that you will bring about each other's death. So run, Diarmuid, run. Save yourself while you still have time!'

'This is the first I've heard of these prohibitions!' Diarmuid exclaimed. 'But I won't leave this place for fear of a pig. Leave Bran with me, Finn, to help my own hound face the boar.'

'No,' Finn replied, 'I won't leave Bran with you, for the Wild Boar of Ben Bulben has escaped from Bran many times before.'

With Bran at his heels, Finn ran as fast as he could out of the path of the charging animal, leaving Diarmuid all alone on the tummock. As Finn disappeared Diarmuid cried out bitterly, 'I know in my heart, Finn, that you arranged this hunt to bring about my death. But I can do nothing about it. If my time is up I can't escape my fate.'

The wild boar charged up the mountainside towards the hillock where Diarmuid stood waiting. Diarmuid let slip his hound but it turned tail and fled in terror. Diarmuid took his yellow spear and hurled it at the boar. It hit the creature fiercely, fair and square in the middle of his snout but it didn't as much as shave a whisker or break the skin. When Diarmuid saw this, his courage began to fail, but he took out his heavy sword and with both hands brought it down on the pig's rump. Not even a bristle bent but the sword was smashed in two. Then the wild boar charged at Diarmuid and tossed him head over heels on to his back, so that he lay face down, and back to front, along the pig's length. The enchanted boar raced down the slope of the hill, leaping and twisting, but was unable to throw Diarmuid off his back. He tore across the countryside until he reached the waterfall at the Red Stream and he jumped across the waterfall three times but still could not dislodge Diarmuid. Then he doubled back and, by the same path, headed back up Ben Bulben. At the summit of the mountain he flung Diarmuid from his back and as the man lay on the ground he gave a mighty spring on to him, and gored Diarmuid with his tusks and ripped the entrails out of his body. As the boar turned away, Diarmuid made a last valiant cast with the hilt of the broken sword, which was still in his hand. It hit the creature and dashed out its brains and it fell dead on the hillock not far from where Diarmuid lay. To this day that place on the mountain top is called Rath na h-Amhrann, the Rath of the Sword Hilt.

Very soon after Diarmuid's victorious cast, Finn and the Fianna came upon him lying dying where he had fallen, the Wild Boar of Ben Bulben stretched out close by. Finn looked down, without pity, at his fallen enemy and said, 'It pleases me to see you brought to this state, Diarmuid. It would please me even more if all the women of Ireland that you once charmed could see you too. Where are your famous good looks now, Diarmuid? Where is your athletic shape? All gone. You're ugly now, and deformed!'

'That may be so, Finn, but ravaged as I am, if you wanted to, you could still heal me,' Diarmuid told him.

'How could I heal you?'

'Easily. When you tasted the Salmon of Knowledge at the Boyne, you received special powers and this was one of them: if you gave a drink from the palms of your hands to an ailing person, that person would be restored from any sickness he was suffering from at the time.'

'You don't deserve that drink from me,' Finn said.

'That's not true! I well deserve it! I have protected you from your enemies time and again and I know if I'd been injured *then* and asked for a drink, you would have given it to me without question, so why not give it to me now?'

'Because you took Grainne away from me in Tara and humiliated me in front of all the men of Ireland,' said Finn. 'You don't deserve a drink from my hands.'

'I can't be blamed for that. Grainne put a *geis* on me to go with her, and I could not violate those bonds, not for anything in the world. I deserve your pity, Finn. I have proved my loyalty to you in the front line again and again. You would have given me a drink then if I'd needed it, so I implore you, give it to me now.'

Oscar could stand it no longer and he burst out, 'Finn, though I'm more closely related to you by blood than I am to Diarmuid O'Duibhne, I insist that you give him a drink. If any one else tormented Diarmuid the way you're doing now we would kill him instantly. So you'd better give him a drink at once.'

'There is no well on this mountain,' Finn said.

'There is. Only nine feet away from you is a well of the purest, freshest water in the world,' Diarmuid gasped.

Finn went to the well and cupped his hands and took the fill of his palms of water and walked slowly towards Diarmuid. When he had covered half the distance, he opened his hands a fraction and let the water run out through them. 'I can't bring the water to you,' he said to Diarmuid and the dying man groaned, 'You did that on purpose, Finn.'

Finn went back to the well and scooped up more water. As he walked towards Diarmuid, the memory of Grainne came into his head and again he opened his fingers and let the water pour away at his feet. When Diarmuid saw this he let out a moan of agony and Oscar roared at Finn, 'If you don't bring water to Diarmuid instantly I swear that *one* of us will not leave this place alive!'

This time Finn ran to the well, filled his hands with water and ran back with it to Diarmuid but it was too late. Just as he reached his dying enemy, Diarmuid drew his last breath.

When they saw that Diarmuid had died, all the Fianna of Ireland let out three great sorrowful shouts at the loss of their friend. Oscar went up to Finn and looked fiercely into his grandfather's face with rage and disgust in his eyes. 'It would be better if it was *you* who lay dead here,' he said. 'We have lost our best man today.'

Finn did not answer but turned away and called his troops to him. 'We have to leave this place immediately,' he urged. 'If Aengus of the Boyne catches us here beside Diarmuid's dead body, he'll blame us for his death, even though we didn't kill him.'

But Oscar could not be appeased. 'If I had guessed that you set up the chase on Ben Bulben to trap Diarmuid and have him killed, I would have killed you first!' he cried bitterly and made to attack Finn, but Oisin held him back.

Then Finn took Diarmuid's staghound by the leash and led the Fianna down the mountainside towards Rath Grainne. But Diarmuid's four friends, Oisin, Oscar, Caoilte, and Lugaid went back to the summit where Diarmuid lay and put their cloaks over his body. Then they went sadly down the mountain after Finn to Grainne's rath.

Grainne was out on the ramparts of her fort waiting for news of her husband when she saw Finn and his army coming towards her. When she saw Diarmuid's hound with him, she knew instantly that Diarmuid was dead. Grainne, who was heavy and ready to give birth, fainted and fell out over the ramparts and her three baby boys were born dead on the spot.

When she had revived and was able to speak, she asked Finn to leave Diarmuid's hound with her but he refused to do even that. Oisin turned the Fianna back from where Grainne lay, seized the leash from Finn's grasp and gave the staghound to her. Then he followed the rest of the Fianna away from Keshcorran.

When news of Diarmuid's death was confirmed, Grainne let out three piercing long-drawn-out cries of anguish and her keening was heard all over the compound. Her servants rushed out when they heard the wail and took her indoors and tried to comfort her. When she told them that Diarmuid had been tricked into fighting the Wild Boar of Ben Bulben and had been killed by it, her family and servants and Grainne herself raised three great passionate shouts of grief that reverberated through the firmament, through the clouds of heaven and into the upper air. Then Grainne sent three hundred of her household to Ben Bulben to recover Diarmuid's body and bring it home.

At the same time Aengus Og heard of Diarmuid's fate and with three hundred of the Tuatha De Danaan he appeared in a cold wind beside his body. As Grainne's warriors approached they recognized the people from the Otherworld and reversed their shields as a sign of peace, and Aengus recognized the followers of Diarmuid and Grainne. Then Grainne's people and Aengus's people raised their voices together in lament and sent up three great terrible shouts that reverberated through the vast spaces of the firmament, through the clouds of heaven and into the upper air, and rolled across the four provinces of Ireland.

When Grainne's followers told Aengus that they had come to

bring Diarmuid's body back to Rath Grainne, he told them they could not have it for he was going to take it back to his tumulus on the Boyne, where he would bring Diarmuid back to life for a while each day, and talk to him. Then the people of the Tuatha De Danaan put the body on a bier and took it back to Brugh na Boinne. When Grainne heard this, she knew she must accept it as she had no power over Aengus.

She sent word of Diarmuid's death to all her children who were living with foster parents and her family came to Keshcorran by the shortest routes they could take. Grainne welcomed her children with a feast and they sat round her in order of age and rank, and ate and drank their fill. When they were in good spirits from the wine and mead she had provided, Grainne called for silence and in a clear, carrying voice she addressed the assembly in these words:

'Children of Diarmuid O'Duibhne, your father was killed by Finn Mac Cumhaill in breach of a peace agreement they had made together, and you must avenge his death. Here are your inheritances: his armour and his weapons. Use them well! I will divide them among you but I will keep intact in Rath Grainne the precious goblets and vessels, and the other treasures of the household.' Then she raised her voice and intoned a war chant inciting her children against Finn. When her fierce, passionate tirade was over, Grainne told her children to leave Keshcorran and to learn from every possible source the practices of war and the disciplines of battle. The children of Diarmuid O'Duibhne left the rath and went to the four corners of the earth to train in the camps of champions, women warriors and experts in battle. They even went down to the Underworld to learn the secret arts that were practised there.

When Finn heard that Grainne's children and followers had gone to train for battle, he began to hate and fear them. He called up the seven battalions of the Fianna from all over Ireland and when they were mustered at Almu he told them how Grainne had sent her children to learn martial skills so that on their return they could take revenge on him for their father's death.

Oisin spoke out from the crowd in a loud voice and addressed his father: 'You, Finn Mac Cumhaill, and you alone, are responsible for Diarmuid's death. You made a contract with Cormac and him, and then you broke it. You have planted the oak; now you can bend it!'

Oscar and the other members of Clan Bascna sided with Oisin and Finn was left abandoned. He brooded over his predicament for a while and realized that, to survive, he must win Grainne over to his side. He slipped away secretly from Almu and travelled quickly westwards to Keshcorran and went immediately to Grainne's quarters. Grainne flew into a furious rage when she saw Finn and would not listen to a word he said. Her tongue was sharpened by hatred and she stormed at him and ordered him out of her sight. Finn didn't leave Rath Grainne in spite of Grainne's orders, but stayed there and persisted with his suit. Day after day he courted Grainne with sweet talk and tender cajolements until in the end he wore down her resistance, won her over and brought her round to his way of thinking. At long, long last she consented to be his wife.

The Fianna were still waiting in Almu when Grainne and Finn came towards them in harmony and peace. When they saw the pair approaching, the men of the Fianna let out such a derisive shout of mockery that Grainne hung her head in shame.

'Finn, from now on, you'd better mind Grainne well!' Oisin jeered.

When their seven years' training in war was up, Grainne's children came back to Rath Grainne to prepare for the battle against Finn. When they heard that their mother had slipped away with him, they could do nothing about it, but they were still determined to have revenge for their father's death. They marched to Leinster and advanced on the Hill of Allen and challenged Finn to battle. Finn sent out his first hundred soldiers and the O'Duibhne troops reduced them to three hacked heaps of heads, torsos and arms.

When Finn saw this massacre, he asked Grainne to intervene and make peace between her children and him, before all his men were killed. 'Promise them freedom for ever, and freedom for their descendants as well. Tell them they may take their father's place among the Fianna's ranks and I'll guarantee all of this and for all time,' he told Grainne.

Grainne went out alone to meet her children. She welcomed them to Almu and told them about Finn's offers and guarantees. She begged them to stop fighting and spilling blood and in the end she persuaded them to accept the peace terms Finn had offered. A banquet was prepared to celebrate the union between the two families and Diarmuid's children got their father's honoured place among the ranks of the Fianna. Grainne and Finn stayed together till they died, and in this way the pursuit of Diarmuid and Grainne ended.

Oisin in the Land of Youth

HUNDREDS OF YEARS after Finn and his companions had died, Saint Patrick came to Ireland bringing the Christian religion with him. He had heard many stories about the adventures of the Fianna and he was interested in these old heroes whom the people spoke about as if they were gods. Their story was written into the very landscape of Ireland; hills and woods resounded with their legends, rivers and valleys bore their names, dolmens marked their graves.

One day a feeble, blind old man was brought to Patrick. His body was weak and wasted but his spirit was strong. Patrick preached the new doctrines to him but the old warrior scorned the newcomers and their rituals and in defiant response sang the praises of the Fianna, their code of honour and their way of life. He said he was Oisin, the son of Finn himself. Patrick doubted the old man's word since Finn had been dead for longer than the span of any human life. So to convince the saint that his claim was true, Oisin, last of the Fianna, told this story.

After the battle of Gowra, the last battle the Fianna fought, Oisin, Finn and a handful of survivors went south to Lough Lene in Kerry, a favourite haunt of theirs in happier times. They were dispirited because they knew their day was over. They had all fought many battles in their time, but this last battle had brought them total defeat and bitter losses. Many of their companions had been killed at Gowra, among them the bravest warrior of the Fianna, Oisin's own son, Oscar. When Finn, the battle-hardened old veteran, had seen his favourite grandson lying dead on the field, he had turned his back to his troops and wept. Only once before had the Fianna seen their leader cry and that was at the death of his staghound Bran.

Around Lough Lene the woods were fresh and green and the

early mists of a May morning were beginning to lift when Finn and his followers set out with their dogs to hunt. The beauty of the countryside and the prospect of the chase revived their spirits a little as they followed the hounds through the woods. Suddenly a young hornless deer broke cover and bounded through the forest with the dogs in full cry at its heels. The Fianna followed them, rejuvenated by the familiar excitement of the chase.

They were stopped in their tracks by the sight of a lovely young woman galloping towards them on a supple, nimble white horse. She was so beautiful she seemed like a vision. She wore a crown and her hair hung in shining, golden loops down over her shoulders. Her long, lustrous cloak, glinting with gold-embroidered stars, hung down over the silk trappings of her horse. Her eyes were as clear and blue as the May sky above the forest and they sparkled like dew on the morning grass. Her skin glowed white and pink and her mouth seemed as sweet as honeyed wine. Her horse was saddled and shod with gold and there was a silver wreath around his head. No one had seen a better animal.

The woman reined in her horse and came up to where Finn stood, moon-struck and silent. 'I've travelled a great distance to find you,' she said, and Finn found his voice.

'Who are you and where have you come from?' he asked. 'Tell us your name and the name of your kingdom.'

'I am called Niamh of the Golden Hair and my father is the king of Tir na n-Og, the Land of Youth,' the girl replied.

'Then tell us, Princess Niamh, why have you left a country like that and crossed the sea to come to us? Has your husband forsaken you or has some other tragedy brought you here?'

'My husband didn't leave me,' she answered, 'for I've never had a husband. Many men in my own country wanted to marry me but I wouldn't look at any of them because I loved your son.'

Finn started in surprise. 'You love one of my sons? Which of my sons do you love, Niamh? And tell me why your mind settled on *him*?' he asked.

'Oisin is the champion I'm talking about,' replied Niamh. 'Reports of his handsome looks and sweet nature reached as far as the Land of Youth. So I decided to come and find him.'

Oisin had been silent all this time, dazzled by the beautiful girl and when he heard her name *him* as the man she loved he trembled from head to toe. But he recovered himself and went over to the princess and took her hand in his. 'You are welcome here, lovely Niamh,' he said softly to her. 'You are the most beautiful woman in the world and I would choose you above all others. I will gladly marry you!'

'Come away with me, Oisin!' Niamh whispered. 'Come back with me to the Land of Youth. It is the most beautiful country under the sun. You will never fall ill or grow old there. In my country you will never die. Trees grow tall there and trees bend low with fruit. The land flows with honey and wine, as much as you could ever want. In Tir na n-Og you will sit at feasts and games with plenty of music for you, plenty of wine. You will get gold and jewels, more than you could imagine. And a hundred swords, a hundred silk tunics, a hundred swift bay horses, a hundred keen hunting dogs. The king of the Ever Young will place a crown on your head, a crown that he has never given to anyone else, and it will protect you from every danger. You will get a hundred cows, a hundred calves, and a hundred sheep with golden wool. You will get a hundred of the most beautiful jewels you've ever seen and a hundred arrows. A hundred young women will sing to you and a hundred of the bravest, young warriors will obey your command. As well as all of this you will get beauty, strength and power. And me for your wife.'

'Oh, Niamh, I could never refuse you anything you ask and I will gladly go with you to the Land of Youth!' Oisin cried and he jumped up on the horse behind her. With Niamh cradled between his arms he took the reins in his hands and the horse started forwards.

'Go slowly, Oisin, till we reach the shore!' Niamh said.

When Finn saw his son being borne away from him, he let out three loud, sorrowful shouts. 'Oh, Oisin, Oisin, my son,' he cried out, 'why are you leaving me? I will never see you again. You're leaving me here heartbroken for I know we'll never meet again!'

Oisin stopped and embraced his father and said goodbye to all his friends. With tears streaming down his face he took a last look at them as they stood on the shore. He saw the defeat and sorrow on his father's face and the sadness of his friends. He remembered his days together with them all in the excitement of the hunt and the heat of battle. Then the white horse shook its mane, gave three shrill neighs and leapt forward, plunging into the sea. The waves opened before Niamh and Oisin and closed behind them as they passed.

As they travelled across the sea, wonderful sights appeared to them on every side. They passed cities, courts and castles, white-washed bawns and forts, painted summerhouses and stately palaces. A young fawn rushed past, a white dog with scarlet ears racing after it. A beautiful young woman on a bay horse galloped by on the crests of the waves, carrying a golden apple in her right hand. Behind her, mounted on a white horse, rode a young prince, handsome and richly dressed with a gold-bladed sword in his hand. Oisin looked in awe at this handsome couple but when he asked Niamh who they were, she replied that they were insignificant compared to the inhabitants of the Land of Youth.

Ahead of them and visible from afar, a shining palace came into view. Its delicate, marble façade shone in the sun.

'That's the most beautiful palace I have ever seen!' Oisin exclaimed. 'What country are we in now and who is the king?'

'This is the Land of Virtue and that is the palace of Fomor, a giant,' Niamh replied. 'The daughter of the king of the Land of Life is the queen. She was abducted from her own court by Fomor and he keeps her a prisoner here. She has put a *geis* on him that he may not marry her until a champion has challenged him to single combat. But a prisoner she remains for no one wants to fight the giant.'

'Niamh, the story you've told me is sad, even though your voice is music in my ears,' Oisin said. 'I'll go to the fortress and try to overcome the giant and set the queen free.'

They turned the horse towards the white palace and when they arrived there they were welcomed by a woman almost as beautiful as Niamh herself. She brought them to a room where they sat on golden chairs and ate and drank of the best. When the feast was over, the queen told the story of her captivity and as tears coursed down her cheeks she told them that until the giant was overcome she could never return home.

'Dry your eyes,' Oisin told her. 'I'll challenge the giant. I'm not afraid of him! Either I'll kill him or I'll fight till he kills me.'

At that moment Fomor approached the castle. He was huge and ugly and he carried a load of deerskins on his back and an iron bar in his hand. He saw Oisin and Niamh but did not acknowledge their presence. He looked into the face of his prisoner and straight away he knew that she had told her story to the visitors. With a loud, angry shout he challenged Oisin to fight. For three days and three nights they struggled and fought but, as powerful as Fomor was, Oisin overpowered him in the end and cut off his head. The two women gave three triumphant cheers when they saw the giant felled. When they saw that Oisin was badly injured and too exhausted to walk unaided, they took him gently between them and helped him back to the fortress. The queen put ointments and herbs on his wounds and in a very short time Oisin had recovered his health and spirits. They buried the giant and raised his flag over the grave and carved his name in ogham script in stone. Then they feasted till they were full and slept till dawn in the feather beds that were prepared for them.

The morning sun awoke them and Niamh told Oisin they must continue on their journey to Tir na n-Og. The queen of the Land of Virtue was sad to see them go, and indeed they were sad to leave her, but she was free now to return home, so they said goodbye to her and that was the last they saw of her. They mounted the white horse and he galloped away as boisterously as a March wind roaring across a mountain summit.

Suddenly the sky darkened, the wind rose and the sea was lit up by angry flashes of light. Niamh and Oisin rode steadily through the tempest, looking up at the pillars of clouds blotting out the sun until the wind dropped and the storm died down. Then, ahead of them, they saw the most delightful country, bathed in sunshine, spread out in all its splendour. Set amid the smooth rich plains was a majestic fortress that shone like a prism in the sun. Surrounding it were airy halls and summerhouses built with great artistry and inlaid with precious stones. As Niamh and Oisin approached the fortress a troop of a hundred of the most famous champions came out to meet them.

'This land is the most beautiful place I have ever seen!' Oisin exclaimed. 'Have we arrived at the Land of Youth?'

'Indeed we have. This is Tir na n-Og,' Niamh replied. 'I told you the truth when I told you how beautiful it was. Everything I promised you, you will receive.'

As Niamh spoke a hundred beautiful young women came to meet them, dressed in silk and heavy gold brocade, and they welcomed the couple to Tir na n-Og. A huge glittering crowd then approached with the king and queen at their head. When Oisin and Niamh met the royal party, the king took Oisin by the hand and welcomed him. Then he turned towards the crowd and said. 'This is Oisin, Finn's son, who is to be married to my beloved daughter, Niamh of the Golden Hair.' He turned to Oisin. 'You're welcome to this happy country, Oisin! Here you will have a long and happy life and you will never grow old. Everything you ever dreamt of is waiting for you here. I promise you that all I say is true for I am the king of Tir na n-Og. This is my queen and this my daughter Niamh, the Golden-haired, who crossed the sea to find you and bring you back here so that you could be together for ever.'

Oisin thanked the king and queen and a wedding feast was prepared for Oisin and Niamh. The festivities lasted for ten days and ten nights.

Niamh and Oisin lived happily in the Land of Youth and had three children. Niamh named the boys Finn and Oscar after Oisin's father and son. Oisin gave his daughter a name that suited her loving nature and her lovely face; he named her Plur na mBan, the Flower of Women.

Three hundred years went by, though to Oisin they seemed as short as three. He began to get homesick for Ireland and longed to see Finn and his friends, so he asked Niamh and her father to allow him to return home. The king consented but Niamh was perturbed by his request.

'I can't refuse you though I wish you had never asked, Oisin!' she said. 'I'm afraid that if you go you'll never return.'

Oisin tried to comfort his wife. 'Don't be distressed, Niamh!' he said. 'Our white horse knows the way. He'll bring me back safely!'

So Niamh consented, but she gave Oisin a most solemn warning.

'Listen to me well, Oisin,' she implored him, 'and remember what I'm saying. If you dismount from the horse you will not be able to return to this happy country. I tell you again, if your foot as much as touches the ground, you will be lost for ever to the Land of Youth.'

Then Niamh began to sob and wail in great distress. 'Oisin, for the third time I warn you: do not set foot on the soil of Ireland or you can never come back to me again! Everything is changed there. You will not see Finn or the Fianna, you will find only a crowd of monks and holy men.'

Oisin tried to console her but Niamh was inconsolable and pulled and clutched at her long hair in her distress. He said goodbye to his children and as he stood by the white horse Niamh came up to him and kissed him

'Oh, Oisin, here is a last kiss for you! You will never come back to me or to the Land of Youth.'

Oisin mounted his horse and turning his back on the Land of Youth, set out for Ireland. The horse took him away from Tir na n-Og as swiftly as it had brought Niamh and him there three hundred years before.

Oisin arrived in Ireland in high spirits, as strong and powerful a champion as he had ever been, and set out at once to find the Fianna. He travelled over the familiar terrain but saw no trace of any of his friends. Instead he saw a crowd of men and women approaching from the west. He drew in his horse and, at the sight of Oisin, the crowd stopped too. They addressed him courteously, but they kept on staring at him, astonished at his appearance and his great size. When Oisin told them he was looking for Finn Mac Cumhaill and asked of his whereabouts the people were even more surprised.

'We've heard of Finn and the Fianna,' they told him. 'The stories about him say that there never was anyone to match him in character, behaviour or build. There are so many stories that we could not even start to tell them to you!'

When Oisin heard this a tide of weariness and sadness washed over him and he realized that Finn and his companions were dead.

Straight away he set out for Almu, the headquarters of the Fianna in the plains of Leinster. But when he got there, there was no trace of the strong, shining white fort. There was only a bare hill overgrown with ragwort, chickweed and nettles. Oisin was heartbroken at the sight of that desolate place. He went from one of Finn's haunts to another but they were all deserted. He scoured the countryside but there was no trace of his companions anywhere.

As he passed through Wicklow, through Glenasmole, the Valley of the Thrushes, he saw three hundred or more people crowding the glen. When they saw Oisin approach on his horse one of them shouted out, 'Come over here and help us! You are much stronger than we are!' Oisin came closer and saw that the men were trying to lift up a vast marble flagstone. The weight of the stone was so great that the men underneath could not support it and were being crushed by the load. Some were down already. Again the leader shouted desperately to Oisin, 'Come quickly and help us to lift the slab or all these men will be crushed to death!' Oisin looked down in disbelief at the crowd of men beneath him who were so puny and weak that they were unable to lift the flagstone. He leaned out of the saddle and, taking the marble slab in his hands, he raised it with all his strength and flung it away and the men underneath it were freed. But the slab was so heavy and the exertion so great that the golden girth round the horse's belly snapped and Oisin was pulled out of the saddle. He had to jump to the ground to save himself and the horse bolted the instant its rider's feet touched the ground. Oisin stood upright for a moment, towering over the gathering. Then, as the horrified crowd watched, the tall young warrior, who had been stronger than all of them together, sank slowly to the ground. His powerful body withered and shrank, his skin sagged into wrinkles and folds and the sight left his clouded eyes. Hopeless and helpless, he lay at their feet, a bewildered blind old man.

THREE SAINTS
ONE GRAVE DO FILL

———

*The Patron Saints
of Ireland*

Saint Patrick

PATRICK came to Ireland for the first time when he was sixteen years old, brought from Roman Britain as a slave by the pirate forces of the Irish king, Niall of the Nine Hostages. He was sold to Miliucc, a Northern chief, whose lands extended from the shores of Lough Neagh to Slemish Mountain. For six years Patrick roamed the oak and hazel forests and climbed the slopes of Slemish, feeding and tending Miliucc's flocks. Ill-fed and ill-clad, exposed to snow and rain and a prey to the wolves and wild boars that roamed the forests, the slave boy was often frightened and always lonely. In his misery he turned to the religion of his childhood and prayed a hundred times each day and night.

One night as Patrick lay asleep, he heard a voice in a dream telling him that he would soon return to his own country. A few nights later the same voice said, 'Patrick, your ship is ready.'

Straight away he abandoned Miliucc's flocks and escaped from Ulster. He made the perilous journey across the country and at last arrived safely at a harbour on the south-east coast of Ireland, two hundred miles from Slemish. A poor man took pity on the fugitive, brought him to his hut, gave him food and shelter and guarded him while he slept.

When Patrick woke, there was indeed a ship ready to set sail. He asked permission to board the vessel, but the captain, recognizing a runaway slave, drove him away. Disconsolately he turned back towards the poor man's cabin and as he did so he began to pray. Before his prayer was finished he heard the sailors calling him back to the ship. The captain had changed his mind and Patrick boarded the vessel. In the hold he found a strange cargo: a pack of huge Irish wolfhounds, bound for the markets of Europe, where their marvellous size and fierce appearance made them valuable as guard dogs. Throughout the voyage Patrick gave thanks to God for his deliverance and talked to the sailors about his miraculous escape, but they were sceptical of both his story and his faith.

After three days the ship reached the coast of Gaul and the whole party disembarked. The country they found themselves in had recently been plundered and the travellers could find neither food nor shelter on their journey. Starving and angry, the sailors turned on Patrick. 'What have you to say now, Christian?' the captain jeered. 'You tell us the God *you* believe in is all-powerful. Well, pray to him now! Let him send us food or we'll all die of hunger in this wilderness.'

Patrick told them to put aside their own gods and believe in Christ and they would be saved. The sailors agreed to this and as Patrick began to pray, a herd of pigs appeared on the road ahead of them. The men were amazed at this miracle and when they had eaten their fill, they offered up prayers of thanks for their deliverance.

For many days the party travelled through the devastated countryside until at last they reached a town that had not been sacked. There Patrick parted from the sailors and set off alone, moving from monastery to monastery in Gaul and Italy, until he was able to make the journey back to Britain and his father's estate. When he arrived home his parents were overjoyed. They could hardly believe that their long-lost son had been restored to them. It was as if he had come back from the dead.

One night not long after his return, Patrick had a strange and vivid dream. 'And I saw in a vision in the night,' he tells us, 'a man named Victoricus coming from Ireland carrying countless letters. He gave me one of them and I started to read the letter entitled "The Voice of the Irish". While I was reading these words I heard the familiar accents of the people who lived in the wood of Focluti close to the western sea. They called out as if they had one voice: "We beseech you, holy youth, come and walk once more among us." I felt such great pain in my heart that I could read no more And so I awoke.'

Much as he dreaded returning to Ireland, Patrick was convinced that he had received a divine command and that he must obey it.

When he told his parents of his intentions, they were inconsolable and begged him to change his mind. They reminded him of the hardships he had endured as a slave and of their anguish at his capture and long exile. They offered him rewards and implored him not to leave them again. Though Patrick was tempted to stay with his family, his belief in the vision prevailed and he set out to Europe to become a cleric so that he could answer the voice of the Irish.

When Patrick came to Ireland for the second time, he came as a bishop. He was accompanied by a band of monks and he had come to banish the old gods and to convert the Irish to Christianity.

He landed first on Inis Padraig, an island off the Leinster coast, but then sailed further north and disembarked on the shores of Strangford Lough. As he came ashore, Patrick was confronted by a tall chieftain called Dichu who set his savage hound on him. Before the dog could harm the monk, the animal and its master became fixed as statues. Patrick took pity on them; he prayed that their paralysis would leave them and, immediately, movement was restored to both their limbs. Dichu was so grateful for his release and so impressed by Patrick's power that he became a Christian. He gave a large barn to the bishop as a place of worship and it became known as Patrick's Barn, Sabhal Phadraig. To this day that place near Strangford Lough is called Saul.

Patrick made his way south towards Tara, the headquarters of the High Kings of Ireland where Laoghaire, son of Niall of the Nine Hostages, now reigned. When he arrived in Leinster it was the eve of Easter but it was also the eve of Bealtaine, or May Day, a day that the Irish held sacred to the sun. All fires were extinguished on May Eve and it was decreed that no fire could be lit until the chief druid had lit the first fire in Tara in honour of the sun. Then, when the flames of the sacred fire rose at dawn, fire after fire would be kindled on hilltops all over Leinster.

On May Morning the High King and his household were assembled on the hill of Tara. As the first rays of the sun slanted over the horizon, the chief druid moved forward to light the

flower-strewn bonfire. But before he could set it alight the watchers
on the hills were astonished to see flames rising further east on the
hill of Slane. It was the paschal fire that Patrick had lit to celebrate
Easter.

Laoghaire stared, outraged, as the blaze on the neighbouring hill
grew stronger and stronger. 'Who has dared to light this fire?' he
demanded.

'We see the fire,' the druids answered, 'and though we don't
know who lit it, we know that unless it is put out immediately it
will *never* be put out. It will put out our sacred fires and the man
who lit it will have power over us all, over the High King himself.'

'Put out the fire and bring the man who lit it here to Tara,' the
king commanded and his messengers hurried towards Slane to
carry out his orders. They brought Patrick and his monks before
Laoghaire and when he saw the tonsured heads, cowled robes and
curved crozier he shivered with fear. He remembered that his druids
had prophesied the coming of men like these three years earlier:

> 'Adze heads will come over a furious sea
> Their robes hole-headed
> Their staves crook-headed
> Their altars in the east of the houses
> All will answer Amen.'

With his druids and warriors around him, Laoghaire pronounced
a sentence of death on Patrick, but the monk showed no fear.
Instead he reproached the king for worshipping the sun. 'The God I
believe in makes the sun above us rise each day for our benefit. But
this sun will never reign over us nor will its splendour last for ever.
Christ, whom I worship, is the true sun and He will never die and
He will give eternal life to those who do his will.'

Many of the king's household who were listening became Chris-
tians and though Laoghaire was not converted, he revoked the
death sentence.

With his handful of monks, Patrick travelled the length and
breadth of Ireland preaching the gospel as he went. Though he was
often in danger from hostile chiefs, he converted many men and

women to the new religion and Christianity spread across the country.

While Patrick was preaching in Munster, Aengus, the king of Cashel, became curious about the visitor and summoned him to his fort. Patrick preached the gospel and the king, believing in it, asked to be baptized. As Patrick blessed Aengus, the spike of his crozier went through the king's foot, but Aengus did not flinch. When the ceremony was over and Patrick saw the wound he had inflicted he was stricken with remorse.

'I didn't cry out or protest,' Aengus explained, 'for I thought the piercing was part of the ritual that I had to endure.'

Many years after he had first landed at Saul, Patrick felt his life drawing to a close. He made his way to Armagh, to the head-quarters of the church he had established, to await his end. While he was resting there, an angel appeared to him in a dream and said to him: 'Go back to the place were you started, back to the barn, back to Saul. It is *there*, and not here in Armagh that you will die, and, as you promised Dichu, you will rise from the dead.'

'I am a slave to the end if I cannot be buried where I wish,' Patrick said sadly.

'Don't be sad, Patrick,' the angel replied. 'Your primacy and power will always remain in Armagh.'

So the old man went to Saul where the abbess Brigid looked after him till he died. He was buried in Downpatrick and when Brigid died she was buried beside him. The third patron saint of Ireland, Columcille, is said to be buried in the same grave.

> Three saint one grave do fill:
> Patrick, Brigid and Columcille.

Saint Brigid

BRIGID was the daughter of a slave woman called Broicseach and Dubhtach, a chieftain who was Broicseach's master. Dubhtach's wife was jealous of the bondwoman and she ordered her husband to choose between the servant and herself. Now Dubhtach loved Broicseach and did not want to part with her but his wife insisted that he do so. It was with great sadness, then, that he went out with the servant to sell her to another master. On the way he passed the house of a druid, who, hearing the chariot wheels, came out to see which chief was passing by. He recognized Dubhtach and asked him who owned the slave who sat beside him in his chariot.

'She is mine,' Dubhtach answered. 'And she is bearing my child but my wife is forcing me to sell her.'

The druid looked at Broicseach for a moment and then made a prophecy about the child that she was carrying. 'Your wife's children will be servants to this servant's child, for the daughter who is in her womb will be marvellous and famous and she'll shine like a sun among the stars.'

When Dubhtach heard this he turned his chariot round and took Broicseach back home.

As the months went by, Dubhtach's wife got more and more jealous of the servant till, in the end, Dubhtach had no choice but to send her away. He sold Broicseach to a druid on the understanding that he had sold only the mother as a slave; he had not sold the unborn infant. She was his child and would be free born.

Broicseach worked as a dairy-maid in the druid's house and one day, just as she entered the house carrying a pail of milk, she gave birth to a daughter. She washed the infant with the milk from the pail and gave her the name Brigid, which means 'fiery arrow'.

Brigid grew up beautiful, wise and kind. She worked in the druid's household herding the sheep, feeding the fowl and looking after the beggars who came to the door. One day she heard one of Patrick's monks preaching, believed in the new religion and became a Christian. From that day on her kindness and love for the poor increased.

Though she was well treated in the druid's house, Brigid longed to see her father. So, taking her courage in her hands, she went to the druid to ask his permission to return home. He agreed, Dubhtach was sent for and Brigid was given back to her father, a free woman.

Dubhtach put his daughter in charge of running his household but Brigid was so charitable that she gave away to the poor anything that was available, whether it could be spared or not. Even stray animals were given a share of meat from the cooking pot. As time went on Dubhtach became resentful of his daughter's openhandedness, but in spite of his complaints Brigid would not change her ways. His wife, too, resented the beautiful girl and became as jealous of her as she had been of her mother. Between them they conspired to get rid of Brigid by hiring her out to a Leinster king.

As Brigid and her father got into the chariot to travel to the king's fort, Dubhtach, who was determined to break his daughter's pride, said to her, 'I would have you know you're not travelling in my chariot out of any honour due to you, but because I mean to sell you as a slave where you will grind flour in a millstone for your new master!'

At the king's fortress, Dubhtach left Brigid outside in the chariot. While he was away, a beggar with open sores came up to the chariot and asked for help. As she had nothing else to give the beggar, Brigid gave him Dubhtach's sword. Inside the fort the chieftain was offering to sell his daughter to the king.

'Why are you selling your own daughter?' the king asked in astonishment.

'She will not stop selling my property and giving away my wealth to outcasts and worthless beggars and I can stand it no longer!' Dubhtach told him angrily.

'Tell the girl to come in here,' ordered the king.

Dubhtach went out to the chariot to bring Brigid in and when he found she had given away his sword he was beside himself with rage. He marched her before the king and told him the story.

The king looked at Brigid and exclaimed, 'If you give away your *father*'s wealth, what will you do to *mine*?'

Brigid replied, 'I swear to God that even if I had your power, your land, your wealth, even if I owned the whole province of Leinster, I would give it all away to the Lord of the Elements!'

When the king heard this answer he said to Dubhtach, 'It is not for you or me to decide this woman's fate. Her merit is higher in God's sight than in men's!'

Then he set Brigid free and sent her back home and gave Dubhtach an ivory-hilted sword to replace the one that had been given away.

Because she was so beautiful, many men wanted to marry Brigid but she refused all their offers. It was her intention to found a convent and devote her life to doing good works and helping the poor. One man in particular was determined to have her for his wife and grew more and more enraged as Brigid steadfastly rejected his advances.

'That pure eye in your head is not much use to you if it doesn't look across a pillow at a husband!' he jeered.

Brigid was so angry and humiliated at this mockery that she pulled one of her eyes out of its socket until it lay on her cheek.

Seeing the disfigurement that his daughter was prepared to suffer to remain unmarried, Dubhtach promised her that he would never force her to marry against her will. When she had received these assurances, Brigid put her hand to her eye and it was healed at once.

The first convent that Brigid founded was in Kildare and she built a small church there beside a spreading oak tree. One day as she was praying in the church a pillar of flame appeared above her head and rose higher and higher until it reached the roof ridge of the building. A bishop called Mel saw the tongues of fire and knew it was a sign that Brigid had been specially chosen by God. He made her an abbess and conferred on her orders that were of the same rank as those of a bishop. Some of Mel's clerics objected to a woman being honoured in this way but the bishop told them that God, not he, had ordained it.

As her community grew, Brigid needed a bigger church and convent so she went to the king to ask him to give her a plot of land on which to build. The king promised her a piece of ground but, because he was reluctant to give away any of his land, he kept reneging on his promise. Brigid kept asking and the king kept stalling until Brigid lost her patience with him.

'Well, at least give me as much land as I can cover with my cloak,' she pleaded.

The king readily agreed to this and Brigid took off her cloak. Four of her nuns each took a corner of the garment, as if to lay it flat on the ground, but instead of doing so they turned round to the four points of the compass and began to run as fast as they could, holding on to the corners of the cloak as they ran. As the nuns pulled, the cloak grew longer and broader until it covered a full square mile. The king was very alarmed.

'Stop!' he shouted. 'Stop! What are you doing?'

'I'm taking the land you promised to give me,' Brigid retorted, 'and I'll take your whole province from you as a punishment for your meanness.'

'I'll give you the ground your cloak covers now if only your women will stop running!' the king cried.

Brigid called to her nuns to stop, the king kept his word and Brigid got the site for her church.

One rainy day Brigid ran into the convent for shelter. She took off her wet cloak and shook off the raindrops. Just at that moment the sun came out and the rays slanted through the window and fell across the room. Brigid spread her cloak over the sunbeams and they held it up as if were lying across the rafters. And there the cloak hung until it was dry.

*

Brigid wanted her community in Kildare to observe the Rule of Saint Peter and Saint Paul. Unable to go to Rome herself, she dispatched seven of her followers to go there for the Rule and bring it back to her. On their return to Ireland not one of them could remember a single word of what they'd learnt. So Brigid sent seven more messengers and, on the journey home, they too forgot the Rule. For the third time seven members of the community set out for Rome, but this time Brigid asked a blind boy to accompany them. The abbess trusted this boy to remember the Rule for he had never been known to forget anything he had ever heard.

Off the Isle of Man a storm blew up and Brigid's envoys had to cast anchor near the coast. When the storm died down they tried to lift the anchor but they could not move it at all for it was caught fast in the roof of a church that was under the waves. They cast lots to see who would clamber down the rope and free the anchor and the lot fell on the blind boy. So he slid down the rope, disappeared under the waves and freed the anchor from the ridge-tile of the church. His companions drew up the anchor and waited but the boy did not come up out of the waves. Sadly they decided to set sail without him and they reached Rome safely.

A year later they were returning home, and at the exact same spot another huge storm blew up. Again the sailors cast anchor. Suddenly, to their amazement, the blind boy appeared out of the water and shinned up the anchor rope to the ship. In his hand he was carrying a bell, and in his head the Rule of Saint Peter and Saint Paul which he had learnt by heart in the church below the waves.

When they reached Ireland the blind boy gave Brigid the Rule and she and her community observed it from then on. The bell was enshrined in a place of honour and was kept ever after as the bell of Saint Brigid's community.

Brigid entered the convent at eighteen and died in Armagh when she was eighty-eight. She was buried in Downpatrick beside Saint Patrick whom she had cared for when he was old and dying. All the days of her life everything that she touched increased, and anything she prayed for was granted. She was full of compassion and

234

patience and she was always ready to feed the hungry, comfort the stricken and befriend the outcast. She was renowned for her miracles and marvels. It was said of her that she was like a dove among birds, like a vine among trees, like the sun among stars.

After her death, people prayed to her for help in time of difficulty and danger. They called on her to calm storms and banish plagues. They believed her to be a prophet of Christ. They named her the Queen of the South, the Mary of the Gael.

Saint Columcille

COLUMCILLE was born in Donegal from a line of kings. Niall of the Nine Hostages was his great-grandfather on his paternal side and Cahir Mor, another High King, was an ancestor of his mother's. He could have been a king himself but he chose to become a monk.

Even as a child he was very devout and he was given the nickname Columcille, which means 'dove of the church', by the other children of the neighbourhood. Once a week they were allowed to play with their royal companion and they would wait impatiently for him to finish his prayers and join them at their games. 'Has the little dove come out of the church at last?' they shouted at him one day, and from then on he was called Columcille.

When he was a youth he went to a monastic school in Moville, run by a renowned abbot and missionary called Finnian. While he was there he learnt the discipline of a monk's life, and there, too, along with the skills of a scribe, he developed a lifelong passion for books. He moved from the monastic school at Moville to a bardic school run by a poet called Gemman and under this master's rigorous direction, he learnt to compose verse.

By the time Columcille was twenty-five he was already famous as a saint, a scribe and a poet. Everyone who knew him revered and loved him. He was strict with himself but lenient with others and though he was a prince he paid no heed to rank. He was tall and strong with curling hair and a handsome open face and his eyes were grey and humorous. His voice was sweet, but when he was addressing a crowd it carried for a full mile without the loss of a syllable, though those close by heard only a normal tone. It was said that he conversed with angels, and on several occasions the monks who lived with him saw him enveloped in an immense blaze of light, not just in darkness but in broad daylight.

*

While Columcille was staying in the great monastic school at Glasnevin, a plague swept across Ireland taking saints and sinners with it. Two of his closest friends, Mobhi, abbot of Glasnevin, and Ciaran of Clonmacnoise, died in the plague. Columcille headed north to escape the pestilence and at the River Moyola he prayed that it would not cross the stream. His prayer was answered and the northern part of the country was saved from the scourge.

On his return to his own territory Columcille was given a royal welcome and his cousin, the king of that region, gave him a piece of land on which to establish his own monastery. It was a little oval mound, about two hundred acres in size with the river curving round it on two sides. Along the slopes of the site a beautiful oakwood flourished and gave the place its name, Doire, the oakgrove, or Derry as it is known today. Columcille loved his oakgrove and would not allow it to be cleared even to build a church. His first church, therefore, was not facing due east as was the custom, because that would have entailed the felling of trees.

One fateful day Columcille went back to visit his first school in Moville, for he had heard that Finnian, his old teacher, had gone to Rome and brought back with him a precious book. It was a copy of Saint Jerome's translation of the Psalms, the first such book ever to have come to Ireland. Columcille went into transports of delight when he saw this treasure and asked Finnian for permission to copy the book for use in his own monastery in Derry. Finnian refused for he said the time was not yet right for the book to be copied. However, he gave Columcille his word that, when that time came, *he* would be the first scribe to copy the book. But Columcille could not wait. He took the book to his cell and there, night after night, secretly and speedily (for he was a swift and expert scribe) he made a faithful copy of Finnian's priceless book.

One night, as the community was reciting divine office, one of Finnian's monks noticed that Columcille had not taken his place in the chapel. He stole to the visitor's quarters to see the reason for this and as he approached the cell he saw light streaming out through every crack in the door. He put his eye to a chink to look inside the cell and he saw Columcille at his desk, busily writing. As he peered, Columcille's pet crane hopped up to the door, put its long, sharp beak out through the crack and pecked the monk in the eye. Shouting with pain the monk ran back into the chapel and told the abbot what had happened. Finnian rushed to Colmcille's cell and when he discovered that Columcille had disobeyed his orders and copied the book, he was furiously angry. He claimed the copy for himself and demanded that it be given to him. Columcille refused to hand it over. Finnian appealed to Diarmuid, the king, to arbitrate and the two abbots travelled to Tara to await the king's judgement.

The Convention of Tara was in progress when Finnian and Columcille arrived with their followers. They put their separate cases to the king and there, after consultation with his wise men, Diarmuid pronounced judgement: 'To every cow its calf and to every book its copy.' The copy, therefore, had to be handed over to Finnian.

Columcille was outraged at this decision and he was angry with the king for another reason as well. While he had been lodging at Tara awaiting the outcome of the dispute, a Connacht chief had killed a man. This was a violation of the solemn rules of the Convention which banned disputes of any kind while it was in progress. Knowing he would be put to death for the crime, the Connacht chief fled for protection to his allies, the Ulster chiefs. They in turn passed him on to their kinsman, Columcille, and the abbot gave the fugitive sanctuary. The king was determined to bring the offender to justice. He sent his servants into Columcille's quarters, dragged the man out and executed him. This violation of the sacred rules of sanctuary angered Columcille and his proud and passionate nature could not bear the double humiliation. He left Tara secretly and returned north to rally his own people to defend his honour.

When Diarmuid discovered this, he gathered *his* forces and the two armies met at Cooldrevna in Connacht. Columcille stayed at the back of his own battle lines, praying that Diarmuid's forces would be defeated. They were, but the battle was a bloody one and in the course of it three thousand men were killed.

When the heat of his anger had died down, Columcille was horrified at the destruction his pride had caused and was filled with remorse at his own hotheadedness. He went to visit the hermit Molaise, who lived on Devenish Island, to ask him how he could make reparation for the carnage. Molaise imposed a most severe penance on Columcille. He ordered him to leave Ireland for good and to save as many souls among the Picts in Scotland as had met an untimely end on the battlefield of Cooldrevna. So, with a heavy heart, Columcille boarded a boat to begin his exile. With a few followers he sailed up Lough Foyle, away from his beloved Derry, and landed on the island of Iona, off the Scottish coast. He founded a monastery there and from it he travelled through Scotland preaching Christianity. Everywhere he went crowds gathered to see the monk who could calm the seas, cast out devils and cure the sick. Before long he was as honoured and loved in Scotland as he had been in Ireland.

All his life Columcille had prophetic powers and could foretell events both great and small. One day as he was transcribing a book on Iona, he heard someone calling across the straits. He turned to his companion, Diarmuid, and said, 'The man who is shouting to be brought over here is an awkward fellow and he will knock over the inkhorn on my table!' Diarmuid posted himself at the door of the scriptorium to waylay the visitor but he was called away for a second and at that very moment the man arrived. He hurried into the room and in his haste to embrace Columcille he upset the inkwell with his cuff and spilled the ink.

Another time a young monk went to speak to Columcille and he found the abbot in a trance, a brilliant light coming off his face. The novice was too frightened to speak and he turned and ran away. Columcille clapped his hands gently and called him back and asked him what had scared him. When the young man confessed that he had been frightened by the abbot's appearance, Columcille soothed and comforted him and the young monk regained his composure and asked Columcille if he had seen a strange vision.

'I have seen a fearful disaster fall upon a Roman city,' came the reply. 'Fire and sulphur rained down on it and thousands of people are dead. Before the year is out you will hear my story confirmed by sailors coming from Gaul.'

A few months later on a visit to Kintyre, the young monk met the captain of a boat who brought the news of the destruction of the city just as Columcille had foretold.

In his eighty-eighth year Columcille knew that he would soon die. Though almost too old and tired to leave the monastery, he travelled to the western corner of Iona to take his last leave of the monks who worked there. When he had consoled his companions, he turned in his chariot to face the east and he blessed the whole island.

A few days later, as he rested on a stone outside the church, a white packhorse, carrying milk from the dairy, came up to him, laid its head on his breast and began to cry. It foamed at the mouth and shed tears like a human on the old man's lap. The attendant tried to pull the horse away but Columcille stopped him. 'Let the creature grieve. He knows through instinct what is hidden from your rational mind. He knows that he will never see me again.' Then the old abbot slowly made his way back to the monastery and went into his cell to finish the psalm he was copying.

'They that seek the Lord shall lack no thing that is good,' he wrote and then he put down his pen. 'I must stop writing. I've come to the end of the page. Let Baithen finish the work.'

At midnight the following night he made his way into the church ahead of the other monks and knelt alone in front of the altar. When his servant, Diarmuid, came close to the church door, he saw the interior filled with a brilliant light which faded as he entered and left him in the dark.

'Where are you Father?' he called out, his voice choked with tears. There was no reply and as the other monks came running in with lights in their hands, they saw Columcille lying at the foot of the altar close to death. Diarmuid raised the dying abbot's hand

and helped him to bless his community for the last time. The monks knelt around Columcille as he died and the expression on his face was so serene that he might have been in a deep and peaceful sleep.

Pronunciation
of Irish Names and Words

The following gives an approximate guide to the pronunciation of the Irish names and words that occur in the stories. Because there are both vowel and consonant sounds in the Irish language that do not exist in English it is very difficult to render the original sounds faithfully. What follows, therefore, is a simplified version of those sounds. Sometimes there is more than one way to pronounce the same word and I have given these alternatives where relevant. The stressed syllable is in italics, and some words are included for reason of accent rather than pronunciation. I have also added brief notes on the location of some of the places where this information is available.

Abcam	*av*-cam
Aed	ay (rhymes with day)
Aengus Og	*aen*-gus *og*
Aileach	*aisle*-yach
The Dagda's fort in Co. Donegal	
Aillen Mac Miona	*al*-yen mac *mee*-o-na
Aillil	*al*-yill
Ainle	*awn-leh*
Airmed	*air*-em-ed
Almu	*al*-moo
the Hill of Allen in Co. Kildare	
Amergin	*ah*-mer-gin/*av*-er-gin (hard g)
Aoife	*eef*-eh
Ardan	*aw*-ar-dhawn
Ath na Foraine	*ah*-na *for*-in-ya
Badb	bive/bahv
Baile's Strand	*bal*-yeh's strand
a stretch of coastline near Dundalk	
Baithen	*bawth*-en
Balor	*bah*-lor
Tory island, which lies about nine miles off the Donegal coast, is said to be the island where Balor imprisoned his daughter	
Banba	*ban*-ba
Banchuin	ban-*koo*-an

243

Bawn   bawn
   a fortified dwelling
Bealtaine   *bal*-tinna
   May Day
Ben Bulben   ben *bulb*-en
   in Co. Sligo
Black Sainglain   black *san*-glin
Blai   *bla*-ee
Birog   *birr*-ogue
Bodb Dearg   bov *jar*-ag
   Bodb Dearg's sidhe is on Slievenamon in Co. Tipperary
Borrach   *bor*-ach
Breg (Magh Breg in Irish)   mray (magh mray)
   in East Meath
Bresal   *bres*-al
Bricriu   *brick*-roo
Bri Leith   bree lay
   near Ardagh in Co. Longford
Broicseach   *broy*-shaugh
Brugh na Boinne   broo na *bone*-yeh
   the Boyne Valley in Co. Meath, New Grange
Cahir Mor   *ka*-hir more
Cairbre   *kar*-bir-eh
Calitin   *ka*-lit-in
Camal   *cam*-al
Caoilte Mac Ronain   *kweel*-teh mac *roe*-nawn
Carraignarone   carrig na-*rone*
Cathbad   *kath*-vhad/ *kaff*-a
Ceithlinn   *keth*-leen
Cian   *kee*-an
Ciaran   *kay*-rawn
Clan Bascna   clan *bask*-in-eh
Clan Morna   clan *mor*-na
Cnuca   k-*nuck*-a
   Castleknock in Co. Dublin
Colum   *koll*-um
Columcille   koll-um-*kill*
Conall Cearnach   *kon*-all *kar*-nah
Conan   *kone*-an
Condere   *kon*-dirra
Connla   *kon*-la
Conor Mac Nessa   *kon*-or mac *ness*-a

sometimes Conochobar (*kon*-kov-or) Mac Nessa

Cormac	*kor*-moc
Credne	*cred*-in-eh
Crimall	*kriv*-all
Crimthann	*crif*-han
Cruachan	*kroo*-ach-awn

Rathcroghan, Co. Roscommon, seat of the rulers of Connacht, associated in particular with Queen Medb

Crunnchu	krunn-koo
Cuchulainn	koo-*hull*-in
Culann	*kull*-in
Cumhall	kool/*cool*-val
Cu Roi	koo *ree*
Dagda (the)	*dag*-da

One of the most important leaders of the Tuatha de Danaan. His name means 'the good god'

Daire	*doy*-ra
Daman	*da*-mawn
Dechtire	*deck*-tir-a
Deirdre	*der*-dru [the u is barely sounded]
Demne	*dem*-na
Derravaragh	derra-*va*-ra

near Mullingar, Co. Westmeath

Dian Cecht	*dee*-an *keck*'t/*dee*-an haht
Diarmuid	*deer*-mid
Diarmuid O'Duibhne	*deer*-mid o *die*-neh
Diorruing O'Bascna	*dirr*-ing o *bask*-in-eh
Doire	*dirr*-ah
Derry	
Dubhros	*duv*-ros
Dubhtach	*duv*-tah/*duff*-ach
Dun Dealgan	doon *dal*-gan
Dundalk, Co. Louth	
Dun Rudraige	doon rory
Dundrum, near Newcastle, Co. Down	
Eiriu	*ay*-roo (ay rymes with day)
Eithlinn	*eth*-leen
Eithne	*eth*-nu (the u is barely sounded)
Emain Macha	*ev*-in *mach*-a
Navan Fort, just outside Armagh City	
Emer	*ay*-ver/*ay*-mer (ay rhymes with day)
Eochai Airem	(y)*och*-ee *ah*-rem

Eochai Mac Erc	*(y)och*-ee mac *erk*
Eogan	*oh*-en (Owen)
Erc	erk
Etain	ay-*thaw*-in / *aid*-een
Etar	*ay*-tar
Fachtna	*facht*-na
Falias	*fa*-lee-as
Fannall Mac Nechtain	*fan*-al mac *nek*-toyn
Feargoir	*far*-go-ir
Felimid	*fell*-im-eed
Ferdia	fer-*dee*-a

The fight at the ford between Ferdia and Cuchulainn took place at
Ardee, Co. Louth

Fergus Mac Roi	*fer*-gus mac roy
Fiacha	fee-*ach*-a
Fiacra	*fee*-ak-ra
Fial	*fee*-al
Fianna	*fee*-a-na
Fidelma	fi-*dell*-ma
Findias	*fin*-dee-as
Finn Mac Cumhaill	Finn Mac Cool (often spelt Fionn)
Finnabair	*fin*-a-var
Finnchoem	*fin*-koo-em
Finnegas	fin-*ay*-gas
Finnian	*finn*-ee-an
Fionnuala	fin-*noo*-la
Fir Bolg	fir bolg
Fodla	*foe*-la
Foill Mac Nectain	*foe*-ill mac *nek*-toyn
Folaman	*fol*-a-man
Fomor	*foe*-mor
Forgall	*for*-gall
Fomorians	fo-*more*-ee-ans
Fuamnach	*foo*-am-nak
Gae Bolga	gay boolga
Gamal	*gam*-al
geis	gesh (pl. geasa, pronounced *gas*-sa)
Gemman	*gem*-an (hard g)
Glas Gaibhleann	glas *gav*-e-lan

Port na Blagh and Dunkineely in Co. Donegal have particular
associations with Cian's wonderful cow, the Glas Gaibhleann

Glasnevin	glas *nev*in
in Dublin	

Goibniu	*gyb*-noo/*gwiv*-neh
Gorias	*gor*-ee-as
Gowra	*gow*-ra
Garristown in Co. Dublin	
Grainne	*graun*-ya
Grianan	*gree*-a-non
a summerhouse or sunny room	
Ibar	*ee*-bar
Ilbrach	*eel*-brach
Iollan	*ull*-an
Laeg Mac Riangabra	*loy*-g mac *ree*-an *gav*-ra
Lairgren	*lye*-er-gren
Laoghaire	*lair*-eh
Lendabar	*len*-da-var
Levercham	*lev*-er-ham
Lia Fail	*lee*-ah *faw*-il
Liss	liss
a rath or hill fort	
Lochan	*loch*-an
Lochlann	*loch*-lan
the Vikings	
Lough Lene	loch leen
in Co. Kerry	
Lugaid	*loo*-ee
Lugh	loo
Macha	*mak*-a
Magh Breg	Magh mray
in East Meath	
Maignis	moy-*nay*-ish
Manannan Mac Lir	*ma*-naw-*nan* mac *lir*
Medb	maeve
Miach	*mee*-uk
Midir	*mid*-ir/*mi*-yar
Milesian	mil-*ease*-yan
Miliucc	*mill*-uc
Mobhi	*mo*-vee
Molaise	mull-*ash*-a
Morrigu (the)	*morr*-ig-oo
Moville	mo-*ville*
in Co. Donegal	
Moyola	moy-*oh*-la

247

a river in Co. Derry

Moytura	moy-*toor*-a

Moytura lies on the northern shore of Lough Arrow in Co. Sligo

Muadan	*moo*-a-dan
Mugain	*moo*-gan
Muirne	*mur*-na
Muirthemne	mur-*hev*-na

in Co. Louth, lying along the coast between the River Boyne and Dundalk

Murias	*moor*-ee-as
Naoise	*neesh*-eh
Nechtan	*nek*-tawn
Niamh	*nee*-uv
Nuada	*noo*-a-ha
Ogham	*oh*-am

the runic writing of ancient Ireland

Ogma	*og*-ma
Oisin	ush-*een*
Plur na mBan	*ploor* na *mawn*
Rath na h-Amhrann	rath na *how*-ran
Ronan	*roe*-nan
Sabhal Phadraig	*saw*-il *faw*-rig
Sadb	*soy*-iv/sive

Sadb appears as Sabha in some versions of the story

Samhain	*sow*-in ('sow' as in female pig)

Hallowe'en

Samildanach	*saw*-vil-*dawn*-ach
Scathach	*scou*-ha/*skaw*-thach
Scemen	*skem*-in
Sceolan	*skeo*-lan
Searbhann Lochlann	*sarv*-an *loch*-lan
Sencha	*shen*-ha
Setanta	shay-*tant*-a
Sidhe	shee
Sidhe Fionnachaid	shee *finn*-eh-ee

on Slieve Fuad

Slemish	*slem*-ish

in Co. Antrim

Slieve Bloom	slieve *bloom*

in Co. Offaly

Slieve Fuad	slieve *foo*-ad

the highest point in the Fews mountains, known today as Carrigatuke Hill near Newtownhamilton, Co. Armagh

Pronunciation of Irish Names and Words

Slieve Luachra	slieve *loo*-achra
in Co. Kerry	
Srub Brain	srub *braw*-in

Some say Bran came to shore in West Kerry, others say near Moville in Co. Donegal

Sualdam Mac Roich	*soo*-al-dav mac *roy*
Tadg	*ta*-ig
Tailtin	*tile*-tin
Teltown, in Co. Meath	
Tain	toyn (a cattle raid)
Tain Bo Cuailgne	*toyn* bo *hoo*-ling-eh

the Cattle Raid of Cooley, the great saga of the Ulster Cycle

Tara	*ta*-ra

The name in Irish for Tara is Temair (pronounced 'towir' as in 'tower'). It was the ancient seat of the High Kings of Ireland and is situated in Co. Meath. The earthworks, fortifications and archaeological remains found on the site are associated with historical and mythological figures. Two of the raths are known as Medb's Rath and Grainne's Rath and there is a standing stone known as the Lia Fail, the stone of destiny. There is also an area called the Banqueting Hall which is said to be the place where Lugh offered his services to Nuada when he came to Tara

Tethba	*teth*-va / *teff*-a
Tir na n-Og	teer na n-ogue
Tracht Eisi	trackt *esh*-ee
Trenmor	*tren*-more
Tuachell Mac Nechtain	*too*-a-kill mac *nek*-toyn
Tuatha De Danaan	*too*-ha day *dan*-an
Tuiren	*tur*-in
Uathach	*ooa*-thack
Usnach	*oosh*-na

In compiling the above list I made particular use of the following publications:

Cross, Tom Peete and Slover, Clark, H., *Ancient Irish Tales*, London, 1937
Gregory, Augusta, *Cúchulain of Muirthemne*, London, 1902
—, *Gods and Fighting Men*, London, 1904
Joyce, P. W., *Irish Names of Places*, Dublin, n.d.
Kavanagh, Peter, *Irish Mythology: a dictionary*, New York, 1959
Kinsella, Thomas, *The Tain*. Oxford, 1970
Smyth, Daragh, *A Guide to Irish Mythology*, Dublin, 1988
—, and Kennedy, Gerry, *Places of Mythology in Ireland*, Co. Mayo, 1989

Bibliography

I have listed below the main source or sources that I used for each story. I have added a further list of books which I found particularly helpful. Some of these are academic studies and some are retellings and incidents and details from a few of them have been incorporated here and there in my text.

The Mythological Cycle

Tuatha De Danaan
   Gray, Elizabeth A., *Cathe maig Tuired, The Second battle of Mag Tuired*, Irish Texts Society, Dublin, 1982
   Gregory, Augusta, *Gods and Fighting Men*, London, 1904

Midir and Etain
   Cross, Tom Peete and Slover, Clark H., *Ancient Irish Tales*, London, 1937
   Gantz, Jeffrey, *Early Irish Myths and Sagas*, London, 1981
   Leahy, A. H., *Heroic Romances of Ireland*, London, 1905
   Müller, Eduard, from *Revue Celtique* III, Paris, 1876–8

The Children of Lir
   O' Curry, Eugene, 'The Three Most Sorrowful Tales of Erinn', from *Atlantis* IV, Dublin, 1858

Over Nine Waves: the Milesians Come to Ireland
   Mac Alister, R. A. S. and Mac Neill, Eoin, *Leabhar Gabhala: The Book of Conquests of Ireland* I, London, 1917
   Gregory, Augusta, *Gods and Fighting Men*

The Voyage of Bran
   Meyer, Kuno and Nutt, Alfred, *The Voyage of Bran, Son of Febal*, London, 1895

The Ulster Cycle

The Weakness of the Ulstermen
   Hull, Eleanor (ed.), *The Cúchullin Saga in Irish Literature*, London, 1898

Bibliography

The Birth of Cuchulainn
  as above

The Boyhood Deeds of Cuchulainn
  Dunn, Joseph, *The Ancient Irish Epic – Táin Bó Cualgne*, London, 1914
  Hull, Eleanor (ed.), *The Cúchulinn Saga*

Culann's Hound: Cuchulainn Gets His Name
  as above

Cuchulainn Takes up Arms
  as above

The Wooing of Emer
  Meyer, Kuno, from *The Cúchullin Saga*, ed. Eleanor Hull

Bricriu's Feast
  Cross, Tom Peete and Slover, Clark H., *Ancient Irish Tales*, London,
    1937

The death of Connla
  Cross, Tom Peete and Slover, Clark H., *Ancient Irish Tales*
  Brooke, Charlotte, *Reliques of Irish Poetry*, Dublin, 1816

Deirdre of the Sorrows
  O'Flanagan, Theophilus, 'Deirdri', *Transactions of the Gaelic Society of
    Dublin*, 1808

Cuchulainn and Ferdia's Fight at the Ford
  Dunn, Joseph, *The Ancient Irish Epic – Táin Bó Cualgne*

The Death of Cuchulainn
  O'Grady, Standish Hayes and Stokes, Whitley, from *The Cuchullin
    Saga*, ed. Eleanor Hull
  Hyde, Douglas, *A Literary History of Ireland*, London, 1901

The Finn Cycle

The Boyhood Deeds of Finn
  Hennessy, W. M., *Revue Celtique* II, Paris, 1873–5
  Kennedy, Patrick, *Legendary Fictions of the Irish Celts*, London, 1891
  O'Donovan, John, 'The Boyish Exploits of Finn Mac Cumhill' from
    Transactions of the Ossianic Society IV, Dublin, 1859
  O'Grady, Standish Hayes, *Silva Gadelica*, Dublin, 1892
  Mac Neill, Eoin, *Duanaire Finn* I, Irish Texts Society, London, 1908

Bibliography

Finn Joins the Fianna and Becomes Its Captain
Keating, Geoffrey, *The History of Ireland*, Irish Texts Society, London, 1908
O'Grady, Standish Hayes, *Silva Gadelica*
Kennedy, Patrick, *Legendary Fictions of the Irish Celts*, London, 1891

The Birth of Finn's Hounds
From *Transactions of the Ossianic Society* II, Dublin, 1856
Hennessy, W. M., *Revenue Celtique* II
Kennedy, Patrick, *The Fictions of our Forefathers*, Dublin, 1860

The Enchanted Deer: the Birth of Oisin
Kennedy, Patrick, *Legendary Fictions of the Irish Celts*, London, 1891

The Pursuit of Diarmuid and Grainne
O'Grady, Standish Hayes, 'The Pursuit of Diarmuid and Grainne', *Transactions of the Ossianic Society* III, Dublin, 1857
Ni Sheaghda, Nessa, *The Pursuit of Diarmuid and Grainne*, Irish Texts Society, XLVIII, Dublin, 1967

Oisin in the Land of Youth
O'Looney, B., *Transactions of the Ossianic Society* IV, Dublin, 1859
Joyce, P. W., *Old Celtic Romances*, London, 1914
Cross, Tom Peete and Slover, Clark H., *Ancient Irish Tales*, London, 1937

The Patron Saints of Ireland

Saint Patrick
Kennedy, Patrick, *Legendary Fictions of the Irish Celts*, London, 1891
Mac Neill, Eoin, *Life of Saint Patrick*,
Stokes, Whitley, *Lives of the Saints from the Book of Lismore*, Oxford, 1890

Saint Brigid
Hyde, Douglas, *A Literary History of Ireland*, London, 1901
Kennedy, Patrick, *Legendary Fictions of the Irish Celts*
Stokes, Whitley, *Lives of the Saints from the Book of Lismore*
– *The Calendar of Oengus*, Dublin, 1880

Saint Columcille
Hyde, Douglas, *A Literary History of Ireland*
Keating, Geoffrey, *The History of Ireland*, III, Irish Texts Society, London, 1908
Stokes, Whitley, *Lives of the Saints from the Book of Lismore*

Bibliography

— *The Calendar of Oengus*
McCarthy, Daniel, *Life of Saint Columba translated from Adamnan*,
    Dublin

Further reading

Campbell, J. J., *Legends of Ireland*, London, 1955
Coghlan, Ronan, *Pocket Dictionary of Irish Myth and Legend*, Belfast,
    1985
Curtain, Jeremiah, *Hero Tales of Ireland*, Dublin, 1894
Dillon, Myles, *The Cycle of the Kings*, London, 1947
— *Early Irish Literature*, Chicago, 1948
— *Irish Sagas*, Dublin, 1954
Ellis, P. Berresford, *A Dictionary of Irish Mythology*, London, 1987
Flower, Robin, *The Irish Tradition*, Oxford, 1947
Green, Miranda J., *A Dictionary of Celtic Myth and Legend*, London,
    1992
Gregory, Augustus, *The Blessed Trinity of Ireland*, London, 1985
Hull, Eleanor, *Cuchulain – the Hound of Ulster*, London, 1909
Hyde, Douglas, *The Three Sorrows of Storytelling*, London, 1895
Jackson, Kenneth Hurlstone, *A Celtic Miscellany*, London, 1951
Kavanagh, Peter, *Irish Mythology*, New York, 1959
Kinsella, Thomas, *The Tain*, Oxford, 1970
Kinsella, Thomas (ed.), *The New Oxford Book of Irish Verse*, Oxford,
    1986
Mac Cana, Proinsias, *Celtic Mythology*, London, 1970
Mac Neill, Eoin, *Duanaire Finn* I, London, 1908
Meyer, Kuno, *Death Tales of the Ulster Heroes*, Dublin, 1913
— and Nutt, Alfred, *The Voyage of Bran, Son of Febal*, London, 1895
Montague, John (ed.), *The Faber Book of Irish Verse*, London, 1974
Murphy, Gerard, *Duanaire Finn* II, London, 1933
Nutt, Alfred, *Ossian and Ossianic Literature*, London, 1899
— *Cúchulainn: The Irish Achilles*, London, 1900
O'Connor, Frank, *Kings, Lords and Commons: an anthology from the
    Irish*, New York, 1959
— *The Little Monasteries*, Dublin, 1963
O'Faolain, Eileen, *Irish Sagas and Folk Tales*, London, 1954
O'Grady, Standish Hayes, *Silva Gadelica*, 2 vols, Dublin, 1893
O'Grady, Standish James, *Fionn and his Companions*, Dublin, 1892
— *The Coming of Cuchulain*, London, 1894
— *The Triumph and passing of Cuchulain*, London, 1920
O'Hogain, Daithi, *Myth, Legend and Romance*, London, 1990

Bibliography

O'Rahilly, Cecile, *Táin Bó Cuailgne* (from the Book of Leinster), Dublin, 1967

– *Táin Bó Cuailgne* (from the Book of the Dun Cow), Dublin, 1978

O'Rahilly, Thomas F., *Early Irish History and Mythology*, Dublin, 1946

Rees, Alwyn and Brinley, *Celtic Heritage*, London, 1961

Rolleston, T. W., *Myths and Legends of the Celtic Race*, London, 1912

– *The High Deeds of Fionn*, London, 1910

Smyth, Daragh, *A Guide to Irish Mythology*, Dublin, 1988

Sjoestedt, M. L., *Gods and Heroes of the Celts*, Paris, 1949

Stephens, James, *Irish Fairy Tales*, London, 1924